RAT-LIKE CUNNING

A Memoir

of Fleet Street

by

Russell Miller

"The only qualities essential for real success in journalism are rat-like cunning, a plausible manner and a little literary ability"

(Usually attributed to my former colleague, Nicholas Tomalin, killed by a Syrian missile in 1973 while reporting on the Yom Kippur War, but actually coined by the late Murray Sayle.)

Also by Russell Miller

Bunny - The Real Story of Playboy (1984)
The House of Getty (1985)
Bare-Faced Messiah (1987
Nothing Less Than Victory (1993)
Ten Days In May (1995)
Magnum (1997)
Behind The Lines (2002)
Code-name Tricycle (2005)
The Adventures of Arthur Conan Doyle (2008)
My Story (2009)
Uncle Bill (2012)
Boom - The Life of Lord Trenchard (2016)

For Renate, my three daughters,
my son and my eight grandchildren

FOREWORD

I became a freelance by default. I had been hired by a dubious entrepreneur at a large salary to launch and edit a glossy lifestyle magazine which turned out to be no more than a figment of the entrepreneur's lively imagination. When I realised there was never going to be a magazine I walked out and found myself, at the age of 29, with no savings and no job, a pregnant wife and a young daughter to support, and a crippling mortgage. What else could I do but become a freelance - fast?

Once I discovered I could survive - that we could all survive - my single aim, my one ambition, was to work for the *Sunday Times Magazine*, the first and the best of the so-called "colour" magazines. It proved to be extraordinarily difficult. Most of the editorial staff of the ST Magazine were Oxbridge graduates and they were, perhaps understandably, completely disinterested in the offerings of an oik from Ilford who had left school at 16 - me. Every idea I put forward was ritually turned down.

In desperation I wrote an entire feature "on spec" - a profile of a colourful reformed hoodlum who was making huge sums of money converting barn-like pubs in the East End into discotheques, much to the horror of the locals. I remember he kept control with a mobile squad of bouncers in a radio-controlled van, ready to rush to the scene of any disturbance. I offered this feature, with photographs, to the *Sunday Times*

Magazine. It was rejected in a brief letter pointing out that they had already "done" the East End.

It was subsequently published in *The Observer Magazine* and I learned, many years later, that the editor at the *Sunday Times* who had rejected it held it up at the magazine's weekly conference as an example of the kind of feature they should be looking for!

Three years were to pass before I got a foot in the door at the *Sunday Times* and then it was only because I met one of the editors, Robert Lacey, at a party. He started giving me little research jobs, but I soon graduated to fully fledged feature writing and, eventually, a contract as a freelance contributor.

During the 30-plus years I worked for the *Sunday Times* I won five national press awards. When I look back today I realise they were the golden years of magazine journalism, with few of the budgetary restrictions that exist now. Editors were prepared to take risks and send writers on assignments around the world with no certainty that the story would work out. The reputation of the *Sunday Times* opened doors and publicists did not have the power they have today. When I was at the magazine we would never have agreed to give a celebrity copy approval as the price for an interview. You want to approve what we write? Forget it. We won't bother with the interview.

In my last 15 years at the *Sunday Times* I flew 648,510 miles on British Airways flights alone (I know this because I discovered by chance that every trip is recorded on the BA Executive Club website). Quite a few miles were added on the unforgettable occasion when I returned from interviewing Imelda Marcos in Manila on, I think, a Tuesday and found myself flying to Sydney the following day to cover the Prince of Wales' tour of Australia. It had not apparently occurred to anyone in London to stop me returning from the Philippines, which was two thirds of the way towards Sydney - and a lot less than half the cost of my Club Class ticket from London.

A friend whose daughter was recently appointed as a foreign correspondent for a national newspaper asked me, rather sadly, "I suppose when you were at the *Sunday Times* it was all five-star hotels and business travel?"

I shrugged and agreed, rather guiltily, that that was pretty much the case.

"Well, it's Air BnB and Easyjet now," she said bitterly.

CHAPTER 1: MURMANSK INCIDENT

It was pitch dark and snowing hard when my Aeroflot flight from St Petersburg landed at Murmansk on a December afternoon in 1999. Murmansk in the winter must rate as one of the most unalluring cities on earth. Two hundred miles north of the Arctic Circle, the sun disappears some time towards the end of November and does not rise above the horizon again until February. During Murmansk's long polar night average temperatures range between minus 20 and minus 30 degrees Centigrade, but it was the perpetual darkness, rather than the bone-chilling cold, that sapped my spirits. That and the certain knowledge that I was being watched by agents from the Russian FSB, the Federal Security Bureau.

I had been in St Petersburg to interview a very brave man - Aleksandr Nikitin, a former officer in the Russian navy, who had been charged with high treason after helping to compile a report alerting the world to the dangers posed by the rotting nuclear submarines of Russia's massive Northern Fleet, laid up in and around Murmansk. When the report, funded by the Bellona Foundation, an environmental group based in Oslo, was published it warned that the submarines' leaking reactors were tantamount to a "Chernobyl in slow motion" and that a major nuclear disaster would be unavoidable unless urgent action was taken.

Nikitin had served with the Northern Fleet and spent seven years in the Department of Nuclear Safety at the Ministry of

Defence before he retired, with the rank of full captain, in 1992. He was well aware of the problems in Murmansk, and when Bellona approached him for help, he did not hesitate. To him the project symbolised Russia's new spirit of democratic freedom after the break up of the Soviet Union in December 1991.

At first, Bellona researchers were surprised by the extent to which both the Russian navy and the authorities in Murmansk seemed willing to co-operate, but the ghost of Communism was soon stirring. The FSB, which had emerged as a replacement for the dreaded KGB, was supposed to be a more enlightened, reform-minded organisation, but since it was staffed almost entirely by ex-KGB officers, few Russians noticed much difference. To many FSB officers it was anathema that a foreign organisation like the Bellona Foundation should be allowed to inquire into a matter that might prove embarrassing to Russia, or produce a report that might be critical of the government.

On the night of October 15, 1995, FSB agents broke into the small office which the Bellona Foundation had set up in Murmansk. During a search lasting six hours the place was ransacked. All the research material relating to the Northern Fleet was carried away and confiscated, along with computers, cameras and office equipment. Bellona officials later protested that none of the material was even confidential, let alone secret, but their protests fell on resolutely deaf ears.

On the same night, six FSB officers turned up at the Nikitins' modest apartment on the outskirts of St Petersburg with a search warrant. Nikitin was take away for interrogation while his wife, Tatyana, and their 17-year-old daughter watched as every cupboard and drawer in their home was turned out in a hunt for incriminating evidence.

During the next few months, 60 Russian citizens who had been assisting with the Bellona report were detained and interrogated at length, some of them several times. The FSB was particularly interested in Nikitin because he had once, undeniably, had access to secret information. He did his best to prove to his interrogators that he had been scrupulous in ensuring his contribution to the report emanated solely from publicly available sources, but they remained unpersuaded.

Nikitin, increasingly convinced he was going to be made a scapegoat, applied for permission to emigrate to Canada with his wife and daughter. On February 5, 1996, they learned that permission had been granted, as did the FSB. At 7.30 the following morning, FSB agents banged on the door of their apartment and informed Nikitin that he was required to attend a further interrogation. Tatyana was told her husband would be back later that day; in fact he was arrested at the FSB headquarters, imprisoned and did not return home for more than 10 months, during which time he discovered he was to be charged with high treason, espionage and selling state secrets. The maximum penalty was death.

News of the arrest of Aleksandr Nikitin sparked an international protest supported by environmental and civil rights organisations around the world; Amnesty International named him as the first post-Soviet "prisoner of conscience." When the Bellona Foundation report was published it was promptly banned in Russia, earning it the dubious distinction of being the first publication to be proscribed since the fall of Communism.

Meanwhile Nikitin was living a nightmare that could have come straight from the pages of Kafka. He was banned from leaving the city of St Petersburg. He was under 24-hour surveillance, followed everywhere by men in black suits. His telephone was tapped. His friends and neighbours were warned not to speak to him and he was vilified in the media as a spy. He was constantly called back to the FSB headquarters for further interrogation and every time his case came to court the FSB secured another adjournment for further investigation. He discovered that public documents he had been using in his research had been retrospectively re-classified as secret, thus spuriously justifying the charge of treason.

Considering what he had been through, it was unsurprising that Nikitin looked tired and haunted when we met at Bellona's bleak office in a back street of St Petersburg, not far from where pathetic groups of homeless Russians huddled in the snow round burning braziers. A tall, gangling man with a bushy moustache and flecks of grey in his mop of black hair, he had, miraculously, retained his sense of humour. When I asked him, through an interpreter, if the room was bugged, he rolled his eyes, leaned back in his chair and spoke to the ceiling. "I hope you are listening carefully, sir," he said, naming the head of the St Petersburg FSB.

He said he had no worries when he began working for Bellona. "On the contrary, everyone, even high-placed military officials, seemed to be saying that they knew about Bellona and that it was doing very important, very necessary, work. I only started to worry when my friends still serving with the Northern Fleet called me and said the FSB had been round asking questions about me, what kind of person I am. Then, of course, my apartment was searched - they even went through my wife's underwear - and I knew we were in trouble.

"After I was released from prison, I couldn't believe the things that were happening to me. One day I was driving to my lawyer's office being followed by four carloads of FSB men. I parked and went in to see my lawyer, and when I got back I found glue in both locks of my car. None of the other cars had been touched. Other times I have found the tyres slashed.

"It's been a strain. It is not nice not to be able to live like a normal family. not to be free, to have an axe hanging over my head all the time. The most painful thing is that I can't see any end to it. Theoretically, it could go on forever, for the rest of my life. The people who want to see me convicted will never give up. Never."

[Nikitin was being overly pessimistic. In September 2000, more than five years after he was first arrested, he was acquitted of all charges by the Russian Supreme Court, the Presidium. He is still engaged in environmental and human rights issues on behalf of Bellona.]

* * * * *

Until I arrived in Murmansk I thought I had a pretty good chance of escaping the attention of the FSB. I had previously twice been refused a visa to visit Russia during the Soviet era and declared *persona non grata* because of something I had written years earlier criticising the government's treatment of Alexander Solzhenitsyn, so on this occasion I obtained a tourist visa and sailed through the immigration formalities at St Petersburg airport without difficulty. I was sure I had been spotted visiting the Bellona offices, but Bellona had many visitors - it was unlikely the FSB could have known who I was or what I was doing.

Everything changed when I arrived at Murmansk and found, to my dismay, a Bellona employee waiting for me holding up a board with my name written on it in large capital letters. I knew the FSB routinely kept watch on all Russian airports and it would not have required a Sherlock Holmes to discover that Russell Miller was a British journalist, or to figure out what I was doing in St Petersburg and Murmansk, or to discover that I had entered Russia illegally. When I tackled the Bellona guy about it, he just shrugged and told me not to worry.

Almost the first thing I did in Murmansk, after checking in to the shabby Hotel Arctic on the main square, was to buy a big fur hat, similar to those the locals wore, to ward off the biting cold. Opposite a massive statue of a Russian soldier in the Second World War was a sombre reminder that the area was the world's most dangerous nuclear dumping ground: a large illuminated sign showed the time, the temperature - and the current level of radiation. I learned that every morning Murmansk local radio station routinely broadcast the daily reading of radioactivity, along with the weather forecast.

Murmansk was an important supply port in the First World War and was used as a base by British French and American expeditionary forces in operations against the Bolsheviks in 1918. In the Second World War it was the main port for Anglo-American convoys carrying war supplies across the Arctic Ocean to the USSR. The harsh weather conditions and frozen terrain prevented the Germans from capturing the city, but it suffered extensive damage.

During the early years of the Cold War, the Soviet Union embarked on a major programme to build a navy that would match that of the Americans, but with the end of the Cold War Russia was left with a huge armada of nuclear submarines it neither needed nor could afford. Some 90 vessels were decommissioned and laid up in narrow fjords around Murmansk where, according to the Bellona Foundation, they were slowly deteriorating and constituted one of the world's greatest environmental threats.

I quickly ascertained that no outsider - certainly no foreigner - could visit the areas where the submarines were moored, or, indeed, get anywhere near them. All the roads into the naval shipyards were blocked by security posts manned 24 hours a day. Between 15,000 and 30,000 people lived in closed settlements round the five naval shipyards; even residents of Murmansk who wanted to visit friends or family in the settlements had to first obtain an invitation and then official permission.

Despite the security, it was common knowledge in Murmansk that a number of the submarine hulks were leaking, turning them into floating time bombs with ever shortening fuses. Almost all of them still had two nuclear reactors on board. If sea water entered the reactor there was a serous risk of an explosion and significant radioactive contamination, requiring the rapid evacuation of the immediate area.

Understandably, many people in the city were reluctant to talk to a foreign journalist, but Rear Admiral Nikolai Mormul, the former deputy commander of the Northern Fleet, was not among them and was cheerfully unbothered when I warned him that I was probably being followed by the FSB. The admiral lived alone in a flat on the eighth floor of one of the featureless tower blocks that dominated the skyline of Murmansk. Miraculously, the lift was working, but the depressing public areas stank of urine, boiled cabbage and wet dogs.

A sprightly 66-year-old, Mormul insisted on cracking open a bottle of fiery vodka immediately I arrived; we had finished most of it by the time I left. He was among those interrogated by the FSB after Nikitin's arrest and to his great credit remained unintimidated and unwilling to be silenced, either about his friend Nikitin, or about the condition of the Northern Fleet.

"It is tragic that so much time and energy is being wasted pursuing Nikitin," he told me, "and nothing is being done about the real problems. The other day I was told that a leak in a tank storing nuclear waste had only been discovered when a soldier on guard went outside to have a pee and realised there was other liquid running down the side of the tank. The tank was cracked and no one had noticed it up to that moment."

The admiral grinned and took another swig of vodka. "I don't think it is correct that nuclear safety should depend on soldiers wanting a pee. Do you?"

When it was time for me to leave Murmansk my plan was to fly to Oslo, where the Bellona Foundation was based, to meet with the team still agitating for Nikitin's freedom and for something to be done about the Northern Fleet. I had seen nothing of the FSB in Murmansk but I had no sooner joined the check-in queue at the airport than I was approached by two unsmiling goons in bulky military-style overcoats who looked like Monty Python caricatures of secret policemen. I would have laughed if I had not been so nervous.

They both reached into their inside pockets at the same time and flashed their FSB shields. "Roosell Miller?" one of them said. "Follow me, plis. Bring your bags."

"Where are we going?" I asked.

"Just follow me."

"Should I not check in first?"

"No. Follow me."

Watched curiously by everyone else in the queue, I was marched across the concourse, up an escalator to a mezzanine floor and a small bare overheated room furnished with a telephone, two tables and four chairs. The door was closed behind me. I was told to sit down. One man took my suitcase, unzipped the top and began unpacking my clothes, the other took my shoulder bag and up-ended the contents onto a table. My passport, travel documents, tape recorder, six or seven cassettes, notebooks, pencils, pens, receipts and Press identity cards tumbled out.

He picked up my passport and began turning the pages, examining the many entry and exit stamps with apparent interest. Then he flicked through one of my notebooks, frowning at my indecipherable scrawl mixed with scraps of shorthand. Then he switched on the tape recorder, heard a few words, switched it off again and removed the cassette.

Eventually he fixed me with a cold stare and said "You are journalist?"

There did not seem to be much point in denying it, so I nodded.

"Why are you in Murmansk?"

I had already decided how I would answer this inevitable question. "I'm on holiday," I said.

He turned to the other man, said something in Russian and they both laughed sarcastically, presumably at the absurd notion of anyone taking a holiday in Murmansk in the middle of the winter.

It was very warm in the room. I could feel a trickle of sweat emerging from under my fur hat.

"You were in St Petersburg?"

I nodded again.

"Why?"

"Holiday."

"No. You are journalist. Is not permitted for you to travel to Russia on tourist visa. You are not tourist."

He sighed, reached down to a briefcase under the table, produced what looked like an official file and then read out a list of everywhere I had been both in Murmansk and St Petersburg, including the Bellona office.

I said nothing. I had no idea what to say. He then had a long conversation in Russian with his colleague, who seemed not to be able to speak English. I looked at my watch. My flight was due to leave in 10 minutes. I tried to get the attention of my interrogator and pointed to my watch, but he ignored me.

I took out my handkerchief to wipe the sweat from my forehead.

When they had finished their conversation, the other man stood up and left the room. "I'm going to miss my flight," I said to my interrogator.

He shrugged. Fifteen minutes later the other man returned and another long conversation ensued. Although I obviously could not understand a word it seemed as if one was giving instructions to the other about what to do with me.

Finally my interrogator turned to me and said "It is not permitted for you to leave Russia…" I felt the blood rush to my head "… with product of illegal work."

It was some seconds before I understood what he was saying. "You mean I can go if you keep my notebooks?"

"And tape recordings."

"OK," I said immediately. I suppose as a matter of principle I should have protested about this outrageous abrogation of press freedom, but I was too scared and too anxious to leave. The prospect of spending Christmas in the Murmansk equivalent of the Lubyanka was not attractive.

In any case, the tapes they wanted were hidden in my hat. I am not normally paranoid, but before I checked out of the Hotel Arctic I decided, just to be on the safe side, that I would hide the tape cassettes of the interviews I had carried out in in Murmansk and St Petersburg. My hat had ear flaps which tied at the top, leaving a deep pocket all round the headband - a perfect hiding place.

They watched me without interest as I carefully set the notebooks and cassettes to one side on the desk, then stuffed everything back into my shoulder bag and repacked my suitcase.

"I can go?" I asked. My interrogator shrugged again as if he did not care either way. I took that as a yes and walked out. I assumed I had missed my flight to Oslo; my plan was to get a seat on the first flight out of Russia, no matter where it was going, but to my surprise I found an agitated Aeroflot employee standing outside the office. Aeroflot was notorious at that time for hiring the ugliest and most disagreeable staff; this one looked like a male all-in wrestler, although she was wearing a tight-fitting woman's uniform.

"Ticket and passport" she demanded.

"I've missed my flight," I explained. "I need to re-book."

"Ticket and passport!" she repeated. I handed her my ticket, which she examined as if she expected to find it was a crude forgery, then my passport, which got the same treatment. She handed them back along with a boarding pass. I saw it was for the Oslo flight, even though it was an hour past its scheduled departure time.

"Is it still here?" I asked, hardly able to believe it.

She pointed through the window. There, parked on the tarmac with all its lights blazing in the dark was a beautiful Aeroflot jet.

I was hustled rapidly through passport control and escorted to the aircraft. There was no time to check my suitcase so I lugged it up the steps and then down the aisle to a spare seat, enduring baleful scowls from my fellow passengers, who obviously realised I was the reason for the delay.

When we were safely airborne I took off my fur hat and surreptitiously felt for the cassettes I had hidden in it; they were still there. I spent the first part of the flight writing down what I could remember from my lost notebooks, then I began to wonder what the analysts at FSB headquarters in Murmansk would make of the confiscated tapes. I knew what was on at least three cassettes - lengthy interviews I had conducted, a month earlier in Utah, with Mormon fundamentalists talking about the joys of polygamy.

CHAPTER 2: "ARE YOU A MAN OR A WOMAN?"

I suppose you could say, and quite a few people did, that I was a little shit. (Actually, I wasn't little - I was 6 foot - but the qualification always seemed to accompany the pejorative in those days.)

The year is 1956. It is a Saturday. I am a bumptious 18-year-old indentured apprentice journalist employed by East London News Agency. I have recently passed my driving test which has liberated me from the office and I am out on the road in one of the agency's two decrepit cars - both of them ten-year-old Austin 8s. By luck I have the better of the two.

I have just called the office from a public telephone box in the hope of another assignment. This, decades before the advent of the mobile telephone, is easier said than done. Firstly I have to find a box with a working, unvandalised telephone (not easy) and secondly I have to adhere to a bizarre ritual to save the owner of the agency two pence. I put two pennies in the slot and dial the office number. A voice answers: "East London!" I do not press button A to connect, but bang the top of the metal box with a third coin. The voice says: "If that's Russell, bang twice." I bang twice. I am then given my instructions and told to bang once if I have understood. I bang once, put the telephone down and press button B to get my two pennies back. Throughout the whole exchange I have not uttered word.

On this occasion I have been told the police have just released the name and address of a milkman stabbed to death in a random attack in the street in Stepney the previous day. I am to interview the grieving widow and persuade her to let me borrow photographs of her late husband. With a bit of luck, I will be first on her doorstep, as I am already in the area. My instructions are to get hold of every photo, if that is possible, to deny them to the other reporters who will soon be arriving. In the vernacular of the trade they are known as "snatch pictures". (There was a story, possibly apocryphal, of a desperate reporter climbing through an open window and helping himself to a framed photograph on a mantel-shelf, only to discover it was the victim's brother.)

I do not, for one moment, pause to consider the feelings of the widow or whether it is an appropriate moment to pester her with questions. No, for me it is the thrill of the chase, an opportunity to beat "Fleet Street's finest" at their own game. I had been in considerable awe of Fleet Street reporters until I started meeting a few. I imagined, in my youthful naiveté, that they were true heroes, giants of our craft, relentless in the pursuit of a story. Instead I discovered that they were, by and large, idle buggers who spent most of their time in the pub, drinking and smoking and swapping information with their so-called rivals in order to avoid the wearisome business of doorstepping and news gathering.

Within a few minutes I am outside the block of council flats where she lives. I park the car (no parking meters yet), race up the concrete steps to the third floor and bang on her door. It is answered by a wretched-looking woman in her late thirties with red-rimmed eyes. Two small children, a boy and a girl, both whimpering, are hanging onto her skirt.

If she is surprised to find a tall, gangling, out of breath teenager on her doorstep she manages to conceal it. When I explain I am a reporter from East London News Agency I have to admit she looks faintly incredulous. I tell her how sorry I am to bother her at this time and ask if I can come in. She nods, steps aside to allow me over the threshold and shuts the door behind me. So far, so good.

She shows me into her small living room and asks me if I would like a cup of tea. I say yes if it would not be too much trouble. She disappears into the kitchen leaving me with the two children, who stare at me silently with big eyes. I ask them how old they are but they just shake their heads. I ask them their names but they shake their heads again.

By the time the widow returns with my tea I have a plan. I thank her for the tea and she attempts a wan smile and sits opposite me in a worn armchair. I tell her that unfortunately a lot more reporters will be arriving at any minute wanting to ask her questions, but she does not have to talk to them if she talks to me because I work for agency that supplies all the national newspapers. I am not sure she fully understands but when I slyly suggest that it might help if I dealt with them she seems pathetically grateful.

I start asking her questions about her late husband and she tells me what a wonderful man he was and how everyone liked him and how they first met and how no one ever expected something like this to happen and how she can't believe it and how the children can't really grasp what has happened and keep asking when their Daddy is coming home… Suddenly, she is weeping pitifully and the children are crawling on her lap and telling her not to cry which makes her cry even harder and then there is a knock at the door. Shall I answer it, I ask innocently, and she dabs her eyes with a handkerchief and nods.

I go to the door, open it a crack, and find two of "Fleet Street's finest" standing outside, a reporter and photographer. I say I am sorry but the family is too upset to talk and I close the door before they have a chance to utter a word. If they assumed I was a member of the family there was nothing I could do about it, was there?

I go back into the sitting room and continue asking questions of the widow and scribbling her answers in my notebook, wishing I had learned better shorthand and not given up the course after only six weeks. We are interrupted three more times and three more times I go to the door to say the family is too upset to talk, adding for good measure "we" wanted to be left alone to grieve in private.

On the fifth occasion I open the door a little too wide and before I can open my mouth a hand snakes through the gap, grabs my tie and attempts to pull me, violently, out of the flat. "You little shit," says an angry voice. "I know you. You're one of Harry fucking Mitchell's kids aren't you?" It is a reporter from the *Sunday Pictorial* whom I had met on another job a few weeks earlier. Harry Mitchell is the owner of the East London News Agency

"You little shit," he says again, pressing his face against mine. I can smell his beery breath. I am jammed in the gap between the door and the frame while he wraps my tie round his fist and pulls even harder.

"I'm sorry," I gasp, feeling the tie tighten round my neck. "She really doesn't want to talk."

"Then what the fuck are you doing in there?" he hisses.

It is a good question and I have no answer. I brace myself against the door and door frame and jerk back in a desperate attempt to get free. My tie slips from his grasp and I am able to slam the door shut. The letterbox opens immediately and I see a pair of squinting eyes glaring at me. "You'll be fucking sorry, you little shit," a muffled voice says from outside.

I return to the widow, red-faced and straightening my tie. It is time to raise the tricky subject of photographs. By then the widow is my friend. She is grateful to me for helping her out in handling the pesky representatives of the Fourth Estate banging on her door, so she is perhaps of a mind to be co-operative when I ask her if she has any photographs of her husband . Yes, she has lots, she says; in a family album. She shows me the album, tearfully explains who everyone is and where they were taken. Are there any other pictures anywhere else, I ask. No, she says, she pastes everything in the album.

Would it be possible to borrow the whole album, just for a short while, I ask. Obviously I will take great care of it and make sure it is returned to you. She is reluctant. I press her, she finally relents. You're sure I will get it back, she asks. Of course, I say.

I kill time for another half an hour. There are no further visitors. I know for certain where "Fleet Street's Finest" will be - in the saloon bar of the nearest pub, knocking back pints and discussing how they can shaft that little shit from East London News Agency.

I also know they will almost certainly be back to make another attempt to interview the widow so before I leave I suggest that she can get rid of any more reporters who call by simply referring them to East London News Agency. Just tell them they can get anything they want from East London News Agency and shut the door, I say to her, in the certain knowledge it will greatly increase the blood pressure of my friends in the pub.

Outside the coast is miraculously clear. Gripping the precious photo album under my arm, I bound down the stairs two steps at a time and get to my car before anyone sees me. I am so excited I can barely breathe. I drive a safe distance, then look for a telephone box to call the office.

To my surprise Harry himself answers the telephone. (The first time this happened I was so discombobulated that I pressed button A by mistake and got a bollocking for wasting two pence.) This time I have to lose my two pennies because I need to speak to him. I tell him I have got an "exclusive" (what a wonderful word that was then) interview with the widow and all the family pictures. I explain how I have fended off other reporters and he murmurs vague approval. I give him the details of my interview over the telephone and he instructs me where to take the photo album.

Next day my interview with the widow is included in the reports of the milkman's murder in all the Sunday papers along with a selection of pictures from the family album. I read every word avidly. "STABBED MILKIE WAS THE LOVE OF MY LIFE, SAYS WIDOW" ran one headline. She didn't actually say that, but so what? She certainly isn't going to dispute it.

No credit is attributed to me or to East London News Agency, but that does not matter. I have no idea how much Harry Mitchell has earned from my efforts but it is probably a sizeable sum, certainly a lot more than the £1 10s (150p) I get paid every week. Sometimes I work ten or twelve hours a day, sometimes more, but I don't care.

I love every minute.

* * * * *

I left my grammar school in Ilford five weeks after my 16th birthday with three O-Levels and no idea what I was going to do with my life other than find a job. It was the year rationing finally ended, the first Wimpy bar opened in Lyons Corner House and I was in love with Doris Day, whose hit single "Secret Love" occupied the No 1 spot in the charts for eight weeks, despite boasting some of the most banal lyrics ever penned: "So I told a friendly star, the way that dreamers often do…"

There had been no question of my staying on into the sixth form, or of going to university, partly because I was hardly an academic high-flyer and partly because, in a working class family like mine, staying on at school beyond the age of 16 was considered to be a ridiculous and utterly pointless indulgence.

Both sides of my family came from the East End of London. One of my grandfathers was a labourer on the railway; the other worked in a builder's merchant. The next generation dragged itself into the lower reaches of the middle class; my Dad had a white collar job as a clerk and moved with my mother and older sister to the so-called respectability of the suburbs, to Ilford, where I was born in 1938, 15 months before the outbreak of the Second World War. My parents were like gypsies, constantly on the move in the faint hope, never realised, of improving their circumstances. We lived, variously, in Oxford, Plymouth, Leigh-on-Sea and Bournemouth, always eventually returning to Ilford. I lost count of how many schools I attended. We moved from Bournemouth a few months before I was due to sit my O-Level exams; I discovered, to my dismay, that my new school in Ilford had a completely different curriculum to that in Bournemouth.

My first attempt to find work was a disaster. I answered an advertisement for someone to teach tennis to young people at a swank hotel in the south of France. I don't know why I thought I would ever get the job, since I had never played tennis and I could not speak French. It was true that I had an O-Level in French but that only meant I could conjugate a few verbs; I don't think my French teacher imagined any of his students would ever be called upon to actually converse in the language.

I had never been abroad and the thought of working somewhere as glamorous as the south of France was like a dream. OK, so I couldn't play tennis, but that didn't mean I couldn't teach it, did it? A few days after submitting my application I was invited to an interview at a house somewhere in South Kensington. As far as I can remember I was not required to confirm that I could play tennis or speak French on the application form, I suppose because it was assumed that no one without those skills would be stupid enough to apply. With the wonderful insouciance of youth on my side I turned up on time and full of enthusiasm.

I only had to wait a few minutes before I was ushered into a large room where a genial chap in a blazer and striped tie sitting behind a desk indicated with a smile and a wave that I should take a seat in front of it. I settled myself down and then, to my horror, he began speaking some gobbledegook which I could only suppose was French. He talked for some minutes before he became aware, presumably from my gormless expression, that I was perhaps not fully cognisant with what he was saying.

Switching to English he asked, with a hint of impatience, "You do speak French, do you?"

I nodded and confirmed I had an O-Level in French, whereupon he started talking to me in French again, with the same result.

Eventually, clearly exasperated, he said in English "Look, exactly how much French do you know?" He pointed to the window. "What's a window in French?"

I searched my memory with increasing desperation. I was sure I knew the French for window but I just could not recall it.

"I don't think there is much point in continuing, do you?" he asked, not unkindly, after a minute or two.

I agreed. As I was walking out I suddenly got it - *fenêtre*! I paused for a second, tempted to turn round and announce, triumphantly, my single French word and perhaps ask if I'd got the job, but thought better of it.

A few weeks later I had work of sorts, training to be a commercial traveller… in ladies' millinery. It came about through a family connection. While my family was firmly rooted in the working class, the two glamorous daughters of my father's elder sister had both made good marriages - Joan to a garage proprietor and Phyllis, known in the family as Billlie, to Alan Hyatt, a director of the millinery company Wortley, Hyatt and Griffiths. Wortley and Griffiths had disappeared into the mists of time and the company was owned by Alan, who travelled in the north of England and his brother, Victor, who ran the London showroom in Berners Street. Ladies' millinery in those days was a thriving trade - almost all women wore hats.

My parents thought it was a great idea that I should join what they could almost call, with not too much stretching of the imagination, "the family firm." I was less enthusiastic but faced with no other offers I reluctantly joined the company as a trainee salesman. The plan was that I would spend two weeks on the road with Alan, two weeks in the factory in Luton where the hats were made and two weeks in the London showroom where I got off on the wrong foot by addressing Alan's brother as "Vic", which was the name by which he was known in the family. He took me to one side and said that while he did not particularly mind being called "Vic" when no one was around - actually I got the strong impression that he minded quite a lot - in front of customers or the other staff I was to address him, like they did, as "Mr Victor". Later I would always be reminded of this incident when watching "Are You Being Served?" on television.

After six weeks I had had more than enough of the millinery trade, particularly as another job offer presented itself, out of the blue. My cousin Joan, Billie's sister, owned a children's clothes shop in Gants Hill; among her customers was

Anne Mitchell, the wife of the owner of East London News Agency. When she mentioned to Joan that her husband was always looking for likely lads to become apprentices Joan thought I might be interested and passed the information to me. Two weeks later, after a perfunctory interview with Harry, conducted in the dining room of his house, I signed indentures to become an apprentice journalist for three years at a salary of £1 10s a week.

East London News Agency occupied a small, scruffy room above the garage of a detached suburban house in The Drive, Ilford. An iron staircase led up to the room from the back, but there was also an internal door connecting it directly to the house, although the staff were never allowed to use it. Inside were three trestle tables, three old Remington typewriters and three telephones, one of them an old-fashioned candlestick type with headphones attached. There was a lavatory available for the use of the staff on the ground floor of the house, approached through an outside door, and inside was a notice which read "WILL THE PERSON WHO LEAVES THIS TOILET IN SUCH A DISGUSTING CONDITION PLEASE EITHER USE A PUBLIC CONVENIENCE OR THE CLEANING BRUSH PROVIDED."

The staff comprised an office manager by the name of Don Meldrum (who spoke with an astonishingly plummy accent on the telephone, but nowhere else), two or three senior reporters, who rarely stayed more than a few months, and three or four apprentices committed by their indentures to remain with the agency for three years. The office was manned on shifts, from seven o'clock in the morning to eleven o'clock at night, sometimes much later. All the staff, me included, smoked ferociously.

Harry Mitchell, the owner, rarely entered the office and ran the place from his sitting room, where he could usually be found lounging on a sofa in an open-necked shirt watching television - serious daytime programming was just getting under way thanks to the imminent arrival of independent television. Harry was a tall, heavily-built man with fleshy jowls usually sporting a three-day stubble, bulging eyes, thick lips, great hairy arms and a loud, deep voice. His favoured farewell at the conclusion of a telephone call was to boom: "All right old son, goodbye, keep your bowels open." His wife, Anne, was Scottish, small, thin and poisonous. They had two young daughters, an exceptionally pretty girl with a limp who was often unwell and was adored and cherished by her parents like a precious princess, and her younger sister, who was plump and plain and treated with such callous indifference that we apprentices sometime discussed reporting the Mitchells to the NSPCC, although of course we never did.

Harry had warned me at my interview that I would spend the first few months doing little else but "pushing copy". I had absolutely no idea what he was talking about and was too nervous to ask. What was this "copy" I was going to have to "push"? Why did it need pushing? Where? All my questions remained unspoken - I just nodded enthusiastically and indicated that I would be perfectly happy to do whatever I had to do.

Actually my first job, when I reported for duty at seven o'clock on a Monday morning with my stomach full of butterflies, was to sit on a little stool in the pantry in Mrs Mitchell's kitchen listening through headphones to a short-wave radio tuned to the police network. It was, of course, entirely illegal and whenever any of Harry's police contacts came calling, the radio was quickly switched off and the pantry door was firmly shut with me inside, in the dark. All I had to do was sit there with a notebook and pencil and listen out for anything that might make a story - a road accident, burglary, assault, robbery, disturbance of the peace… The reception was dreadful and intermittent and so I often failed to note down all the details, but anything that seemed promising was sent upstairs for one of the reporters to follow up.

After three days of sitting in the pantry, Harry decided I was ready for my first assignment. There had been a break-in at a house in Wanstead and I had somehow managed to note, through the crackling static on the radio, the correct name and address of the woman reporting the incident to the police. Harry told me to go up to the office, look up her telephone number and ring her to get more details. He gave me a list of questions to ask.

I was nervous. As I climbed the iron stairs up to the office I was almost hoping that I would not find her number and then I would not have to make the call. But there she was, clearly listed. I took deep breath and dialled the number. The conversation, as far as I can recall it, did not go well and ended up with me answering more questions than I could ask.

I had barely got out that I was calling from East London News Agency when the woman snapped: "What on earth is that? Some kind of newsagent?"

"No, no," I hastened to explain. "I'm a reporter."

"A reporter?"

"Yes, I'm sorry to trouble you, but I would like to ask you some questions about your burglary."

I could hear a sharp intake of breath at the other end. "How on earth do you know about that?" she demanded. "The police haven't even arrived yet. I only called them about 20 minutes ago. What's going on?"

I was still fumbling for an answer when she delivered a killer blow: "What are you anyway, a man or a woman?"

"I'm a man!" I squeaked indignantly, in my as yet unbroken voice.

"Well young *man*," she said, with an emphasis on the "man" as if she did not quite believe me. "I have absolutely no intention of answering any of your questions. Goodbye."

With that she put the phone down. I clomped back down the iron stairs to report my failure to Harry he immediately asked me why I had not called her back. I was aghast. She put the phone down on me, I said. A good reporter never takes no for an answer, he grunted, so I was sent back with instructions to tell her she had a much better chance of getting her stolen goods returned if the crime was publicised. Is that true, I asked. No, he replied, but tell her anyway.

I climbed back up the stairs with my heart in my mouth. Given a choice I would rather have chewed hot coals than ring that woman again, but I did as I was told and dialled her number. When she picked up I began "I am very sorry to trouble you again…" but she immediately cut me short.

"How *dare* you ring again," she shrieked. "Get off the line immediately and do not ring again or I shall report you to the police. Do you understand?" I nodded gloomily, although she obviously could not see me, and the line went dead.

I returned to my lonely vigil in the pantry convinced that my career was effectively at an end. But two days later I had better luck. A call came in on the radio to report that a lorry had run into an egg stall in an open market in Roman Road, Bow. Harry knew the market. There's a pub there, he said, the Earl of Granville, give them a ring and ask them if they have seen anything. This time he did not give me a list of questions.

I called the Earl of Granville and immediately struck gold. "Blimey, mate," said a cheerful Cockney voice on the other end, "you're quick off the mark. It only happened a few minutes ago. I'll tell you what, it's a bloody mess. There's broken eggs all over the shop. My missus told me to go out and scrape up a few so we could put omelettes on the lunch menu. Only joking. What do you want to know…"

Later that day a four-line paragraph appeared on an inside page in the final edition of the *Evening News* under the headline "Market Crash". "A stall holder in the open market in Roman Road, Bow, was lucky to escape serious injury today when a lorry skidded on the wet cobbles and ploughed into his stall, which was selling fresh eggs. No one was hurt but hundreds of eggs were smashed and traffic was disrupted while attempts were made to clean up the area."

It was my story. My first story. Of course it had no by-line, but I was as proud of it as if it was the front page lead.

The following week I learned what "pushing copy" was all about. East London News Agency provided "copy" (news reports) to the three London evening newspapers and all the national dailies. Before fax machines came into widespread use, the quickest way of delivering a story to a newspaper from outside the office was by telephone and all papers employed copy-takers, some of whom added a whiff of spurious glamour to their humdrum lives by describing themselves, absurdly, as "telephone reporters". These worthies, almost all men, spent their working days in headphones typing, on three sheets of paper interlaced with carbon, stories telephoned in by individual contributors around the country and organisations like East London News Agency.

Fleet Street copy-takers had a well-deserved reputation for extreme vulgarity and impatience if a story ran on too long ("Is there much more of this shit?" was a frequent irritable query; they seemed to take it as a personal affront if the story was so long they were required to insert fresh sheets of paper into their typewriters). Any reference to a woman in a story would inevitably invite some lubricious comment. I never met one, but I got to know them over the telephone. They obviously guessed from my voice that I was young and liked to yank my chain.

"Oh no!" a copy-taker on the *Daily Express* exclaimed one day while I was dictating a story. "You'll never guess what's happened."

"What?" I asked, walking right into it.

"Someone's just dropped a turd into my cup of tea. Do you think I should drink it now?"

Many of the stories we filed were no more than snippets and fillers, but Harry had excellent police contacts - whom he routinely bribed, quite shamelessly - which meant one of our reporters was very often first to arrive on the scene of a big crime story. East London News Agency also had a good reputation with Fleet Street news editors; if a story on our patch did not merit sending a staff reporter, the agency would usually be asked to tackle it. These were considered to be "ordered" stories and were greatly prized and given priority because (I discovered some time later) the agency would be paid even if the story fell apart or was not published for some other reason. We also scoured all the local newspapers for stories that might be followed up (journalism is a craft that feeds voraciously on itself) along with covering Thames Magistrates Court and coroners' inquests.

Virtually everything filed by East London News Agency was written by Harry Mitchell or, in his rare absence, Don Meldrum. Neither could write but of the two, Harry was marginally worse. The function of the reporters was simply to provide Harry with enough information for him to write the story. He would usually grill them (either on the telephone or face to face), while lounging on the sofa in his sitting room. Then he would prop a portable typewriter onto his lap, wind in a piece of scrap paper (often an old envelope, painstakingly unsealed, to turn it into a rectangular sheet; did I mention Harry was as tightfisted as Scrooge?) into the carriage roller and start stabbing at the keys with his podgy fingers. His attention was frequently distracted by the television in the corner, which was always switched on. He produced long, rambling sentences (often they were not sentences at all in the grammatical sense) which gathered up fact after fact in apparently random order. He made no attempt at structure or composition, rarely bothered with punctuation and never read through what he had written. As a result it quite frequently made no sense.

Up in the office whoever was available (usually me, because I was always available if I was not in the pantry) would start ringing round the three evening and seven daily newspapers to dictate the story, phonetically, to a copy-taker, using a kind of verbal shorthand to cover punctuation. ("Point, unquote, par" meant full stop, end of the quotation and start a new paragraph.)

In this way I became intimately familiar with Harry's tiresome verbiage, his interminable, maundering sentences often lacking a verb and frequent repetitions. All the copy-takers knew that Harry was the originator of the agency's output, never missed an opportunity to mock ("Is this sentence ever going to have a fucking verb?") and complained so frequently that I took to discreetly editing his copy as I was telephoning it over - breaking up sentences, adding punctuation, deleting repetition and changing a word here and there. I did it all in my head and the copy-takers, who liked to consider themselves as experts in matters of grammar, began to notice. "Fuck me," one said one day with feigned surprise, "what's happened to Harry? This stuff is almost intelligible."

Encouraged by the reaction of the copy-takers I progressed from cautious editing to re-arranging or re-writing entire paragraphs in my head. I had no need to worry that my editing would be exposed on publication because nothing was ever published as Harry had written it. But I began to notice that copy I had edited was sometimes published more or less intact.

What I was doing was, I readily admit, exceptionally precocious, not to say arrogant; my only excuse was that I was 16 years old and did not know any better.

It was not long before I got my inevitable comeuppance. Harry must have been passing the door that led from the office into the house and for some reason stopped to listen as I was dictating a story extensively re-written by me. Perhaps he heard a word he would never have used, I don't know. Anyway he must have realised that his golden prose had been tweaked and he burst into the office like a mad bull, spittle flying from his lips as he shouted at me. What the hell did I think I was doing? Had I forgotten I was just a bloody apprentice? Why did I think I had the right to change his copy? I had a bloody nerve, an apprentice five minutes in the job, thinking he knew better than someone who had been a journalist all his life. When he had finished shouting I was left in no doubt that if I ever tried such a thing again I would be out on my ear. I should have felt chastened, and I did, for a while.

I spent the next two weeks in the pantry as a punishment and suffered the cold opprobrium of Mrs Mitchell, who made it quite clear by her heavy sighs that I was now constantly in her way. Before, she had seemed to tolerate my presence, but now I was obviously a nuisance, blocking her way every time she wanted to retrieve something from the shelves above my head. Thereafter I restricted my editing to quietly improving the punctuation. Well, it was not so much *improving* the punctuation as inserting it; Harry could never be bothered with such niceties.

He had promised me at the start that as soon as I had obtained a full driving licence I would be sent out of the office on assignments. I longed for the day and applied for a provisional licence at the earliest opportunity so that it arrived on my 17th birthday. The problem was that I had no money to pay for driving lessons and neither did my parents. I was already leeching off them by living at home without making a contribution to the household budget; my 30 shillings weekly salary barely kept me in fags. I asked Don Meldrum if he thought there was any chance of Harry giving me a loan for driving lessons and he could hardly stop laughing.

Salvation arrived in the unlikely form of Les Stansfield, a cocky, rotund little Yorkshireman extraordinarily pleased with himself, who lodged with my Auntie Ivy and Uncle Horrie in their terraced house not far from my parents in Ilford. If Les wasn't my Aunt's lover, certainly everyone in the family thought he was. My uncle didn't seem to mind - his primary interest in life was his role as the diligent scorer for a local cricket club. Les had a job in the City and a car - a Hillman Husky - in which he drove to Redbridge underground station every weekday morning. Perhaps to ingratiate himself with my Aunt, he offered to give me a couple of driving lessons.

I knew that to have any hope of passing the driving test I needed more practice and I kept thinking about Les's Hillman Husky just sitting there, unused, in the car park at Redbridge underground station every day. It seemed such a waste. On the last of my lessons with Les I "absent mindedly" put the ignition key in my pocket and went home with it. By the time he telephoned to ask me if I had got it I had had a copy made.

Harry had generously given me time off (in my lunch hour!) for driving lessons and whenever a "lesson" came round I cycled down to Redbridge underground station, located Les's Husky in the car park and took it out for a spin. It was, of course, an incredibly stupid thing to do, but it was also a measure of my desperation to get a driving licence. Had I had an accident I would have been in big trouble. I was at the wheel of what I was sure the police would consider to be a stolen car, I had no insurance and no license. I tried not to think about it. Fortunately nothing went wrong, but I often had a problem returning the car - sometimes the slot from which I had taken it was no longer available and so I was obliged to park it as close as I could and hope that Les would not notice, when he got home, that it was in a different place from where he had left it. Nothing was ever said.

The result of these illicit excursions was that I passed my driving test at the first attempt and was thereafter occasionally allowed to take out one of the agency cars on assignment (usually if there was no one else available). When I was out on the road I never wanted to come in; I would drive slowly back to the office and check in two or three times (knocking on a public telephone box) in the hope of another job. I was completely unbothered by how many hours in the day I worked. I loved being out there, talking to people, ferreting out the facts, sitting in the front seat of the car scribbling my story in a notebook if there was time or putting it together in my head if there was not. Once I worked from seven in the morning until two o'clock the next morning, on the road the whole time, going from job to job, and I would have happily continued had there been more stories for me to cover.

The last assignment that day was a bit tricky. The news editor of the *Daily Express* had evidently promised a neighbour that he would get a reporter to look into a local campaign for a pedestrian crossing. He did not want to waste a staff reporter's time, so he asked Harry if East London would do it as a favour, even though it was out of our area. Harry agreed and promptly forgot all about it until I checked in at around midnight when he suddenly remembered and decided to send me. "Just go through the motions," he said. "They'll be satisfied that a reporter has taken the trouble to visit them."

"At this time of night?" I asked him.

"Oh yeah," he replied. "It'll be fine. All Ron [the editor] wants is to show his neighbours that's tried to help them."

It took me a long time to find the street, in Wandsworth, and even longer, in the dark, to find the house, which I eventually located by striking matches so I could identify the door numbers. The house was, of course, in complete darkness when I knocked at the door. At first there was no response, so I knocked again, harder. A light went on in an upstairs window and I could hear footsteps thumping down the stairs. Before the door was opened an angry voice shouted from within: "Who is it and what do you want?"

"I'm from the *Daily Express*," I said. (We were allowed to represent ourselves as staff reporters on "ordered" stories.) "I've come to talk to you about the zebra crossing petition." The door was wrenched open and I was confronted by a man in his early 40s wearing a dressing gown over striped flannel pyjamas, livid with rage. "You've come to talk to me about the zebra crossing *at one o'clock in the fucking morning*?" He looked as if he wanted to wring my neck and perhaps might have done if his wife had not made an appearance at the top of the stairs. "Who is it?" she called down. "Can you believe it,?" her husband shouted back to her, "it's some bloody reporter wants to know about the zebra crossing."

"Invite him in then," she said, coming down the stairs and buttoning her dressing gown, as if it was a perfectly reasonable time to call. Her husband eventually calmed down and the two of them explained about the accident black spot just up the road and the campaign they had been running to get a zebra crossing. I couldn't honestly see how it would ever make even a paragraph in the *Daily Express* or any other national paper, but I did not tell them that and left after half an hour, full of apologies for disturbing them.

Knocking on doors in the middle of the night did not trouble me in the least. More than a year had passed since I made that first timid call to the lady who had demanded to know whether I was a man or a woman and I had not only acquired a lot more confidence but I was also ferociously ambitious. I was tireless in the pursuit of every story, no matter how trivial, and I would follow up every lead, no matter how unpromising. I would ask anyone anything, no matter how embarrassing. I not only would not take no for an answer, I wanted the answer to be yes, come in, what do you want to know? If person A would not talk to me I would go straight to person B, and if person B would not talk to me I would go to person C. If it was necessary, I would work my way through the whole alphabet and then start over again.

My youth and obvious inexperience were sometimes a help. On more than one occasion I persuaded a reluctant interviewee to talk by hinting that I was on probation and that my editor had given me one last chance and that if I did not get the interview I would almost certainly be fired. I would probably have said I had a wife and three kids to support if I did not look as if I should still be in short trousers.

Whenever I was involved in a big story that led to the arrival of a contingent from Fleet Street it was a matter of personal pride to me that I, a kid and a newcomer, would keep my end up, get some new angle and try to beat the big guys at their own game. The boozy camaraderie of Fleet Street reporters left the field wide open for someone like me - while they were buying each other drinks on expenses and swapping jokes in smoke-filled saloon bars, I would be beavering away on the story, knocking on doors, shouting through letterboxes if necessary, following up leads.

In November 1956, I was standing in the freezing cold in a field outside the Ford plant in Dagenham on the fringes of a mass meeting at which union leaders were calling for another strike. (Ford Dagenham was particularly susceptible to industrial action; I had lost count of the number of mass meetings I had attended and the number of strikes that resulted.) When a massive show of hands approved another walk-out, I plodded across the field to the agency's car, drove to where I knew there was a working public telephone and filed my story. "A mass meeting of 2,000 workers outside the gates of the Ford Factory in Dagenham this afternoon overwhelmingly approved immediate industrial action in pursuit of a pay claim which union leaders asserted had been unnecessarily delayed by the management…"

Some of my colleagues just filed information, plain facts, back to the office and left it to Harry or Don Meldrum to turn them into copy, but I always tried to file a properly composed story, although it was inevitably re-written by Harry, and sometimes, but not always, by Don.

Half way back to the office I checked in, as usual. There was a tip-off from one of Harry's police contacts: a three-year-old boy, Boyd Fearon, had been reported missing from his home in Romford. I was told to head over there straight away. I looked up the address in my A-Z and set off without much expectation that it would become a major story; I would not have been surprised if the boy had been found by the time I arrived. But he had not and the parents were obviously distraught. They had been told by the police to co-operate with reporters as maximum publicity could help find their son, so they welcomed me inside and tearfully explained what had happened, how Boyd was playing in the front garden one minute and the next he was gone. He had never done anything like this before; he was such a good boy. When other reporters started arriving I went to talk to the neighbours. One of them said that yes, she knew Boyd, he was a sweet little chap, very small for his age; she used to call him Tiddler.

By nine o'clock that night, most of Fleet Street had arrived and was encamped in the nearby King's Head. I was at Romford police station trying to get more details of the search so far. Tracker dogs had been deployed in the dark but no trace of the boy had been found. At 11 o'clock, when it was very unlikely there would be any further developments that night, Harry sent me home and told me to return to Romford at first light, when the search was to resume.

Next morning I saw that almost all the dailies were referring to Boyd as Boyd "Tiddler" Fearon and one huge headline read "WHERE'S TIDDLER?" Harry had stretched my quote from the neighbour and turned it into a family nickname for the missing child. The parents were rightly mystified. "Why are all the papers calling him Tiddler?" Mrs Fearon asked me plaintively when I arrived at their house. "We never called him Tiddler." I thought it would be too complicated to explain so I told her not to worry; she had enough on her plate.

At a press conference later that day Romford police raised the startling possibility that Boyd might have been kidnapped. There were reports that a child answering his description had been seen with a woman of "gipsy appearance", along with a girl four or five years of age, later on the day he disappeared. All the gypsy "camps" around London were to be searched. Abducted by gipsies! This was now a major, major story. Two outside broadcasting television trucks appeared, one parked outside the Fearons' home, another outside the police station. I had never seen such things; did not even know they existed.

On Saturday twelve hundred volunteers, led by 70 police officers with dogs, answered a call to help the search in pouring rain. In vain had the overwrought parents tried to disavow their child's so-called nickname - most newspapers continued to call him "Tiddler".

That afternoon I sat in the agency car outside the Fearons' terraced house racking my brains to try and dream up a new angle. The whole area seemed to be crawling with reporters and photographers; everyone who had anything remotely interesting to say, and plenty who had not, had been interviewed. A television crew was inside the house filming the parents making an emotional appeal to anyone who had any information about the disappearance of their son to get in touch

When I eventually had an idea I had to wait until I could get a moment alone with Mrs Fearon. I found her in the tiny back garden smoking a cigarette, shivering in the cold and staring blankly into space. I asked her, stupidly, if she was all right and she looked at me as if I was mad. I could have kicked myself: this was not the way to enlist her support in my plan.

"I've been thinking," I said, "if Boyd has been kidnapped, do you think it would be worth making an appeal directly to whoever has got him?"

"How would I do that?" she asked listlessly.

"Well you could perhaps write an open letter and we could get it into the papers tomorrow morning."

She did not immediately reply, but took a last pull on her cigarette, then dropped it onto the ground and stubbed it out with a twist of her foot.

"They're going to let him go because of a letter from me?" she asked, her voice heavy with sarcasm.

"Well," I insisted, "it couldn't do any harm, could it?"

She thought about it some more. "I suppose not," she sighed. "How would we do it?"

I did not want to tell her I had already written a letter in my notebook. "I'll draft something," I said, "for you to look at it. If you're happy with it you can sign it and I'll do the rest. OK?"

She nodded wearily and lit another cigarette. Half an hour later I was back with a "draft":

"Dear Mr Kidnapper,

"Please, please, I beg you from the bottom of my heart to let my baby go and make our family whole again. If you are a parent yourself you will know that his place is by my side. I am sure he is frightened and worried wherever he is. Please return him to us so we can live again…"

The letter continued in this beseeching vein for several more paragraphs. Mrs Fearon read it through listlessly, then took the pen I offered and signed at the bottom of the page.

Within ten minutes I was in a telephone box dictating my story to Don Meldrum: "Mrs Dorothy Fearon, mother of the missing three-year-old Boyd Fearon, last night sat down and wrote a moving open letter to her son's kidnappers, appealing for them to release him…"

I then included the full text of the letter. "Great stuff," Meldrum said when I had finished. "Where's the letter now?"

"In my pocket."

"Perfect. Make sure it stays there."

I sat in the car for a while, glowing from Meldrum's rare praise. Earlier that day, at a police press conference, I had spotted the guy from the *Sunday Pictorial* who had tried to drag me out of the milkman's flat in Stepney a few months previously. I stayed well out of his way, but I could not stop thinking about what might happen when he called into his office and was asked if he knew that Boyd's mother had written an open letter to the kidnappers. He would obviously say no and then he'd probably be told that the letter had been circulated round Fleet Street by East London News Agency and he would realise it was the work of the same loathsome little shit - me - who had previously upstaged him. I laughed out loud.

Next day Mrs Fearon's tear-jerking letter to her son's kidnappers was published in full on the front page of the *Sunday Dispatch* and was mentioned in a number of other papers.

It made not a scrap of difference to the story's tragic outcome. Boyd Fearon had not been kidnapped: three days later his body was found face down in a ditch less than 500 yards from his home. He had drowned in a few inches of water. No one could explain how the search had failed to find him more than a week earlier.

Not long after that my career at East London News Agency - and my indentures - came to an abrupt and unhappy end, entirely because of my own stupidity and over-weening arrogance.

My cousin Roger, the only son of my Auntie Ivy and Uncle Horrie, had acquired a car - a brand new Ford Prefect. Where the money had come from I had no idea. He was planning to take the car on a short touring holiday in Europe with his friend Pete and asked me at the last minute if I would like to join them. I had never been abroad - no one in my family had - and it seemed like a wonderful opportunity, so I asked Harry if I could have the time off. The answer was no. It was too short notice, he said, for him to re-arrange the holiday roster.

I was upset and angry and still badly wanted to go. I knew I was doing well at East London News Agency. (Harry had recently given me a ten-shilling bonus - an unprecedented act of generosity on his part - after I had worked a 90-hour week.) I tried to think what might happen if I simply defied Harry and took the time off anyway. I calculated - cretinous, cocksure idiot that I was - that I was too good a reporter to be sacked.

So I went on holiday with my cousin and his friend, blithely disregarding Harry's refusal to give me the time off. We crossed the Channel from Harwich to the Hook and did a little tour of Germany. I had a good time. I don't think, such was my insouciance, that I worried for a moment about what might happen when I got back; I don't honestly recall giving it a thought.

Two weeks later I showed up back at work. I was just climbing the iron stairs up to the office when Mrs Mitchell spotted me, opened the kitchen door and called out "You're in big trouble. Harry wants to see you in the dining room straight away." I got the strong impression she was pleased.

I thought I would be in for a monumental bollocking, which I obviously deserved, but I was completely unprepared for what happened next. I was kept waiting in the dining room for 15 minutes before Harry appeared. He did not even seem to be angry. "I don't know if you thought you could get away with taking a holiday when you felt like it," he boomed, "but if you did you were very much mistaken. Your indentures are cancelled as of now…."

I think he went on to say something about my joining the Navy and perhaps I could then come back, but I was no longer paying attention. I just stood there, staring at him uncomprehendingly as it dawned on me that I was being fired.

Then I burst into tears.

CHAPTER 3: "YOU'RE A NATURAL, SON."

Once again, the family stepped in to help me out of my predicament. Poor cuckolded Uncle Horrie, whose immaculate pencil entries in the scorebook of the local cricket club were a legend, knew the sports editor of a local paper, the *Ilford Recorder*, and learned there was a vacancy for a junior reporter. Two weeks after being sacked by East London News Agency I got the job...

"Recorder House" was a nondescript two storey redbrick building with its own car park at the end of the High Road, opposite the Municipal Baths and next door to a pub called, strangely, the Cauliflower. Ilford, a drab Essex suburb with a population of less than 200,000, boasted two flourishing weekly newspapers (imagine!) - the *Recorder* and the *Ilford Pictorial*. There was considerable rivalry between the two: the *Recorder* staff looked down on the "Pic" as being cheap and flashy; the "Pic" boys dismissed the *Recorder* as dull and boring. Both views were credible.

The *Recorder* was not too stuffy to allow a little frivolity into its pages. One afternoon I stumbled by chance on a fashion show being held at a local department store and wrote a fanciful piece about it on the pretence of being a male reporter assigned to cover a women's event and the mock shame and humiliation that ensued. I did not really expect it to be published, but the editor liked it. He decided to send the paper's single girl reporter to cover a football match - a girl reporting on football, whatever next! - and run the two pieces together.

After occasionally jousting with "Fleet Street's Finest" while at East London News Agency, local newspaper journalism, with its endless round of flower shows, fetes, police calls and council meetings, inevitably seemed rather tame, but I soon knuckled down. And there were compensations. Firstly, I was earning much more - £5 a week. Secondly, I was given free rein to write up my assignments pretty much however I wanted without the certain knowledge that they would be re-written by the barely literate Harry Mitchell. Thirdly, I had a much more structured life, a more or less regular working week with my own desk, and companionship - most of the other reporters were not much older than I was.

The reporters' room on the first floor of "Recorder House" was enjoyably anarchic, a bit like a particularly disruptive and unruly class at a failing comprehensive school. On press nights everyone stayed late and the managing director often conducted guided tours round the building for local community groups to see their newspaper being printed. He would have been wise to avoid the reporters' room but he never did and we always put on a show in the faint hope it would look like the nerve centre of a particularly frenetic news organisation. As soon as the door opened everyone started rushing madly around, waving pieces of paper, shouting into telephones, pretending there were big stories breaking all over the place and behaving like extras in a scene from *The Front Page*. The managing director would stand behind his awestruck visitors, rolling his eyes and shaking his head before ushering them out.

After the paper had been "put to bed" a few of us would often stay behind to play cards, sometimes all night. Three-card brag was our game of choice for stakes which were pathetically small because none of us had any money. We would get beers and cigarettes from the Cauliflower next door to keep us going and guarantee we had thick heads and sore throats by dawn.

Thursdays, publication day, was pretty much our day of rest. People drifted in late, stayed longer in the pub at lunchtime and plotted mischief. We particularly enjoyed torturing the switchboard operator, a disagreeable middle-aged woman named Mary who sat at a board at the back of the reception desk on the ground floor. Picking up a telephone anywhere in the building would illuminate a light alongside a socket on the switchboard and she was then required to plug in a line. It was Mary's greatest pleasure to make the reporters wait for as long as possible; rattling the telephone cradle impatiently would only lengthen the delay and produce a tart comment like "I've only got one pair of hands you know."

We devised an excellent way of getting our own back. Clocks throughout Recorder House were synchronised, so we mustered as many people as possible around the building and at a certain agreed time, to the second, we would all pick up a telephone and start jiggling the cradle furiously. This had the magical effect of suddenly lighting up the entire switchboard like a manic fairground attraction, allegedly, on one occasion, causing Mary to fall off her stool, to our great delight. After she registered a formal complaint to the personnel department we were obliged to desist, but there was no truce - she continued to be stubbornly uncooperative and we continued to dream up new ways of tormenting her.

Thursdays was also the day when the dark room in the photographic department, having a lockable door, was often put to distinctly non-photographic uses. Jenny, the paper's token girl reporter, was an Australian very far from pretty but exceptionally generous when it came to dispensing her faintly dubious charms. She apparently needed very little persuasion, on a quiet Thursday lunchtime, to retire to the dark room and drop her drawers for the benefit of her testosterone-fuelled colleagues. On one occasion she was said to be in such demand that a small queue formed up outside the door. A few years later, after I had left the *Recorder*, I heard that she had eloped with a middle-aged hack from the "Pic" who was so lovelorn that he had left his wife and three children for her.

I knew from my time at East London News Agency how to sell stories to the national newspapers and I knew how the agency routinely pillaged local newspapers for stories it could follow up. Some of the *Recorder* reporters occasionally filed stories to the nationals - they called it "lineage" because they were paid by the number of lines printed - but most did not bother. It seemed to me that we were missing an opportunity and so I suggested we should organise a "lineage pool", working together to file stories to the nationals. The private benefit for me was that Harry Mitchell would henceforth be denied from making any money from Recorder stories because we would already have filed them before they appeared in the paper.

It was not long before the "Recorder Lineage Pool" was well established, filing copy on a regular basis and generating a modest monthly income in which we all shared. It enabled me to save up enough money to buy my first car - a decrepit, rusting and very elderly Renault that was built like a tank. I don't remember the model but I do remember that it was started by pressing a foot pedal which, if I was lucky, would stir the engine into reluctant life.

On the evening of Thursday, 30 January 1958. I was alone in the office working late. It was a cold, dark night, exceptionally foggy and I was reluctant to go home. When I looked out of the window the fog was so thick that I could not see the Municipal Baths on the other side of the road. Just as I was putting on my overcoat, a telephone rang in the reporters' room. My first inclination was just to let it ring, but then I decided to pick it up. Before I could say a word, an excited voice croaked "There's been a bad train crash just outside Dagenham East station. You better get down there." To this day I do not know who made that call.

I quickly got confirmation from the local fire brigade that there had, indeed, been a serious accident. There were few details available at that time. All I managed to find out was that a train packed with commuters had ploughed into the back of another train, also packed with commuters. An unknown number of people had been killed and there were, I was told, "many" casualties.

I ran out of the building and jumped into my car, praying it would start. It did. I knew where I had to go, but the swirling fog and my feeble headlights made the journey a nightmare. Eventually I fell in behind a fire engine with its lights flashing and siren blaring, which I figured must be on its way to the crash. The sight when I arrived, eerily illuminated by arc lights, was one of pure horror. Many carriages had been derailed but two had jack-knifed: the force of the collision had caused them to rear up so that they were suspended above the track in an inverted V. I could see through the smashed windows that both jack-knifed carriages were literally stuffed with a tangle of bodies. How many were dead and how many were alive it was impossible to tell. I wondered for one ghastly moment if they were all dead, but then an arm would move, or a leg, and I became aware of a terrible low keening from somewhere deep within the carnage - the worst sound I had ever heard in my young life.

Months later, an inquiry established what had happened. The late-running 18:20 Fenchurch Street to Shoeburyness train had halted at a signal outside Dagenham East station. The

18:35 Fenchurch Street to Thorpe Bay, also late running, missed a signal in the dense fog and plunged into the rear of the stationary train. Both were carrying around 500 passengers each. Ten people died and 89 were injured.

Within a few minutes of arriving at the scene I realised I was the first reporter there. It was a big story and I knew the Fleet Street pack would be showing up at any minute and so I did my best to make life difficult for them. The occupants of a row of bungalows bordering the line had gathered, aghast, in their back gardens, ignoring the cold and damp, to watch the emergency services trying to deal with the disaster.

I approached one couple and asked if they had a telephone. They said they did not, but their neighbour, two doors down, did. I hurried along the fence and found them. I explained that I was a reporter and asked them if they would consider selling me access to their telephone for the evening for £5 - all the money I had I my pocket. They were faintly mystified but agreed without hesitation - £5 was quite a lot of money in those days. They allowed me to climb the fence, then took me into the house to show me where the telephone was. I was welcome, they said, to come and go as I pleased; they would leave the back door unlocked. I warned them that other reporters would soon be arriving and might perhaps offer them more than I could; I hoped they would stick with me. "Don't worry, son," the man said. "A deal's a deal. Anyway the old guy at the end of the terrace also has a phone."

That was not good news. I wondered how I could tie up that line. After climbing back over the fence, I groped along to the end of the terrace. The "old guy" was, like the others, standing in his garden and was very surprised when I loomed up out of the fog. I said I had a message from the head of the rescue services. He was too busy to come himself and had asked me to deliver it: they needed to keep a nearby telephone line open for emergencies. Could he make sure his line was available for the rest of the evening to any uniformed personnel? He nodded, keen to help. Just to make sure he got the idea, I added that it was likely some reporters would be asking to use his phone and under no circumstances should he agree because they would tie up the line for ages and deny it to the emergency services. He nodded again. He never asked who I was.

By the time I had got all this organised, more *Recorder* reporters had arrived. We spread out to interview survivors and to pester the fire and ambulance services for quotes. By nine o'clock I had filed a comprehensive story on the crash to all the national newspapers before any of them had heard a word from their own reporters. (The Recorder Lineage Pool made more that night than it had in the previous two months.) Both the telephone owners, bless them, absolutely refused entreaties and bribes from Fleet Street's finest to allow them to use their telephones. I heard later that there were fisticuffs between frustrated reporters outside the nearest working public telephone, half a mile away from the scene of the crash.

When I got back to Recorder House, around midnight, I was surprised to find lights blazing in the editorial offices. It transpired that the train crash story was considered to be so important that a special edition of the paper was be produced the following day. The editor asked me if I would co-ordinate all the coverage and I spent the rest of the night at my desk working on it.

Local newspapers at that time tended to attract oddballs and eccentrics and there was a middle-aged Irish couple, the Dooleys, working for the *Recorder*. They had been journalists all their lives, had done everything, been everywhere, and had worked for some very prestigious newspapers around the world. How they ended up at the *Recorder* I had no idea.

As I was putting on my overcoat to go home, Pat Dooley shambled across the reporters' room, patted me on the back and said, in his thick Irish accent, "You're a natural, son. You'll go far."

CHAPTER 4: MILITARY MANOEUVRES

All the while I was an indentured apprentice at East London News Agency, National Service, which loomed over every male teenager in those days, was deferred (apprentices were allowed to finish their indentures before being called up). But once I had been sacked, the wheels of military bureaucracy began to turn and in the late spring of 1958 I was ordered to report for a medical in London, prior to being called up to serve Her Majesty.

I had heard of all kinds of ways of getting out of National Service, most involving "rat-like cunning". One was to pay someone who would certainly fail the medical to stand in for you - there were no serious identity checks. A friend who was riddled with tuberculosis took so many medicals for others - he charged £50 a go - that he began to worry he would be recognised.

I never seriously considered trying to avoid National Service; in fact I was rather intrigued to discover what it would be like. Invited to choose in which arm I wished to serve, I put the Royal Navy first, followed by the Royal Air Force, with the Army last. Naturally, I was allocated to the Army. I clung to a faint hope that my precocious skills as a journalist might somehow be put to some use, but it was not to be. Because I could type and write shorthand, after a style, I was assigned to the Royal Army Service Corps, which provided the military with clerks. It was not, to put it mildly, an enticing prospect.

In August, 1958, I reported for duty at Buller Barracks, Aldershot, as 23577873 Private Miller, R, RASC. (People say you never forget your military number and you never do.) The first two weeks of basic training passed in a blur: we were kitted out with ill-fitting uniforms, shouted at all the time, marched (shambolically) from place to place and taught arcane military arts like how to box blankets and how to produce a mirror-like shine on the toecaps of our boots - a skill I totally failed to master.

New recruits were fair game for those who had completed their basic training and there was a tradition of playing sadistic tricks on every intake of newcomers. You became so accustomed to following orders without question, no matter how nonsensical, that when someone showed up in our barrack room at four o'clock in the morning and began banging our bed frames and bellowing at us to parade outside in boots, pyjamas and berets, we all jumped to it and took no notice of who was issuing the orders.

We stood outside on parade in the freezing cold before dawn for almost an hour before we began to wonder if we might be the victims of a practical joke; even so, no one wanted to make the first move. Only when we saw grinning faces and rude gestures in the windows of the barrack block opposite did we realise what had happened. Most of us returned to our beds, but a few terrified souls remained outside until our drill instructor, Corporal Flint, turned up and asked them what the fuck they thought they were doing.

It took me no time at all to work out that the best way of getting through National Service would be to get a commission. Officers were better paid, better fed, lived in better accommodation and had servants to handle tedious chores like boxing blankets, polishing boots and ironing uniforms. And no one shouted at them.

The only problem was that my educational qualifications for a commission were inadequate. I possessed three O-Levels, whereas the minimum requirement, as I recall, was five, or perhaps even six. It called for more "rat-like cunning", along with a dash of elemental logic. If I admitted to having only three O-levels I would not even be considered. If I lied about my qualifications and was found out, I would be turned down. But if I lied and was *not* found out, I was in with a chance. What did I have to lose by lying? Nothing.

Working on the likely hypothesis that no one would bother to check, I awarded myself an additional three O-levels in solid subjects like Maths, History and Geography, all of which in reality I had signally failed. A few weeks later I was informed that my application was being put forward for consideration. When Corporal Flint heard about it he seemed rather less than impressed. "If you become an officer, Miller," he snarled. "I'm going to bleedin' shoot myself."

The next step was an interview. Now interviews I knew about. I had spent close on four years wheedling information out of people by being manipulative while being apparently personable, charming and interested, even if in truth I possessed those characteristics in rather small measure, if at all. When I was asked at an interview board why I wanted a commission I was ready with all the right answers. If I was honest, I should have said I wanted an easy life and my own batman, but instead I burbled on about honour and responsibility and making a contribution and getting the very best out of what the Army could offer me and realising what a wonderful opportunity it would be.

I sailed through and became what was known as a "POC" - a potential officer cadet. The POC course lasted about eight weeks and was geared to preparing candidates for the dreaded "Wosbee" - the War Office Selection Board. I don't remember much about it, but I do remember one of the most tedious duties was being a night watchman. All POCs were required to take turns patrolling the barracks alone on two-hour stints throughout the night armed, if you please, with a hefty pickaxe handle. Presumably we were intended to bludgeon intruders, burglars or enemy spies, not that we ever saw anyone.

There was no strict patrol route. We just wandered aimlessly around in the dark, swinging our pickaxe handles and hoping for the time to pass quickly so we could get back to bed. This seemed to me to be the most pointless occupation possible and after I had done it a couple of times I realised that no one was checking up on us. Next time I was on duty I turned up with an alarm clock hidden under my greatcoat. Ten minutes into my stint I was fast asleep, curled up in the back of a friend's car, with the alarm set to wake me five minutes before I was due to hand over to the next poor sod. I would certainly have been kicked out of the POC course if I had been discovered, but I never was.

The War Office Selection Board occupied a bleak camp of single-storey huts miles from anywhere in the middle of rural Shropshire. The Wosbee was the most critical step on the path to a commission. It lasted three days, at the end of which all candidates were paraded and handed a slip of mimeographed paper with a tick against one of three options: (1) recommended for a commission; (2) deferred, with the chance of applying again; (3) rejected. If you got a tick against option 3, that was it - you were never going to get a commission.

I arrived for my Wosbee with 30 other hopefuls in the middle of winter, transported from the nearest railway station in the back of a three-ton truck. As soon as we had jumped down from the truck with our kitbags we were herded into a lecture hall where a young and enthusiastic colonel explained what lay ahead. Addressing us as "gentlemen" (a first; Corporal Flint preferred "useless shithead wankers"), he warned us that we would be tested to the full in the coming three days and that we would be under intense scrutiny the whole time. Everything we did and said would be noted. He and his colleagues were looking for exceptional qualities of leadership, courage and determination. Only the best would get through, etcetera, etcetera. It was all strongly reminiscent of a scene in a second-rate war movie made at Elstree Studios.

Our programme was packed with lectures and tests, interviews, group discussions and exercises, all the time under the watchful eyes of men with clipboards. Each candidate had to deliver a 15-minute lecture to all the other candidates (and, of course, the clipboard men) on a subject we were given in advance. My heart sank when I got mine: "The growth of Tito-ism in Yugoslavia." But when I began research I quickly discovered that Tito was a fascinating and colourful character and his rise to power was a story so compelling I was surprised it had not been turned into a Hollywood movie.

And that was how I began my lecture, which I put together as if I was writing it for a newspaper. I cannot remember how many times I had been told, as a young journalist, that you needed to grab your reader's attention with the first line. I grabbed my audience by telling them that what they were about to hear was the stuff of Hollywood. At least no one went to sleep, which happened in some of the other candidate's lectures.

We were warned that the examiners would be constantly trying to trip us up with little psychological tricks. When I was marched in to face yet another interview board the first thing that was said to me was "Sit down, Miller." I looked around. There were no chairs, so I sat on the floor. The point was to do *something*; those who floundered around not knowing what to do were marked down. I learned later that one of my fellow candidates, similarly invited to sit down, sat on one of the examiner's laps, although I am not sure how well that went down.

The part of Wosbee that I most dreaded was the assault course. All the ex-public school boys - the great majority - seemed to be able to romp over all the obstacles effortlessly. I was hopeless, utterly hopeless. I just about managed to clamber up a net wearing a full pack, slither through barbed wire tunnels, cross a stream on a rope bridge and jump from tree stump to tree stump. But could I haul myself over a seven foot brick wall? No, I could not. And as for the "window", forget it.

The "window" was a square opening made of scaffolding, perhaps three feet wide, through which you had to jump without touching the sides. I watched in despair as all these public-school buggers dived through, performing an elegant somersault as they landed. I knew there was no possibility of my emulating them, so when my turn came I just ran full pelt at it and hurled myself through, ending up sprawled faced down in the mud on the other side, much to the amusement of those who had preceded me. Miraculously, I did not break any bones; all that was hurt was my dignity.

The final, and pivotal, element of Wosbee was the team challenge. By this time I had deduced what I believed to be a fundamental truth about the whole exercise. It did not matter greatly if you failed or succeeded. What mattered was that you *looked* as if you knew what you were doing and at all times gave the air of being in command of every situation. A little rat-like cunning also helped.

Nowhere was this more true than with the team challenge, when each of us was required to take charge of a team of six men (other candidates) and complete a task using only the rudimentary tools we had been given. Mine was to get an oil drum across a "river" marked out on the grass, ten feet wide, using a couple of planks of wood, some rope and three or four scaffold poles. I did not have the first idea how to do it but - and this is the point - I pretended I did.

I had seen other candidates go to pieces in the team challenge, standing there scratching their heads, staring hopelessly at the equipment and - big mistake - asking for ideas from other team members. I was not going down that road, so I gathered my team together and, brimming with confidence I certainly did not possess, told them: "Right this is what we have to do and this is how we are going to do it." I was soon barking orders and everyone was running around and by some miracle we managed to get the oil drum lifted into the air and half way across the "river" before it fell in.

It did not matter. What mattered were the notes that the examiners, who I could see from the corner of my eye, were scribbling on their clipboards.

Early next morning we were drawn up on parade to be handed our results - a slip of paper on which so much depended. I opened mine gingerly and saw a tick against Item 1 - recommended for officer training. Half the candidates had got through, a couple had been deferred and the remainder rejected - among them, to my great delight, two of those who had taken such pleasure at my ignominious landing in the mud at the "window".

After three days' leave I was ordered to report to Mons Officer Cadet School in Aldershot to begin a three-month course which, barring mishap, would culminate in a commission. We were settling into our barrack room on our first night when the door burst open without warning and a young officer came in followed by a retinue of other soldiers -

we could not tell whether they were officers or NCOs - wearing white coats and carrying clipboards.

"Stand by your beds" he bellowed. We all jumped to, not knowing what to expect. "Medical inspection!" he announced. "drop your trousers."

For the next 15 minutes we all stood to attention with our trousers and underpants round our ankles while the "officer" prodded our genitals with his stick, making derogatory remarks - usually about the size of our penises - which were diligently noted down by his clipboard associates. He singled out one poor devil for particular ridicule when he noticed that one of his testicles was larger than the other.

"Did you tell Wosbee about this?" he demanded.

"N-no, sir," the cadet stammered.

"Hmm, we'll have to see about this. We can't have officers with one ball bigger than the other, can we?"

The cadet, squirming, did not reply.

"CAN WE?"

"I don't know, sir," the wretched, thoroughly embarrassed, cadet whispered.

Next morning, on parade, we realised that the "officer" and his sidekicks were all cadets, just like us. We'd been victims of an initiation ritual that the course about to graduate traditionally inflicted on the course newly arrived. (We did the same, to our shame, when our turn came.)

Mons was a kind of half way house between the ranks and the commissioned. We were not yet officers, certainly not, but we were addressed as "Sir" by all the NCO instructors, although it was made quite clear to us that we remained a low form of military life. One nervous cadet who made the mistake of called a Sergeant Major "Sir" was put right in typically forthright fashion. "No sir," the Sergeant Major spluttered, his face contorted in fury and inches from that of the luckless cadet. "Not you sir me sir, me sir you sir."

We were marked out as officer cadets, in uniform, by white tabs on the lapels of our tunics and a white disc behind the badge on our berets. But we were similarly marked out in "civvies", since we all wore stiff beige riding mackintoshes and trilbies with curly brims. I am pretty sure I looked ridiculous in this outfit. It was probably OK in Aldershot, but in Ilford…

Alongside continued and intensive military training, we were also given lessons on social graces and how to behave as officers and gentlemen; how, for example, to reply to a formal invitation in the third person: "Second Lieutenant Miller thanks Colonel and Mrs Snooty for their kind invitation to cocktails and is delighted…" We were exhorted not to use the canes we would all carry as officers to slash at flower heads (a temptation, when the time came, I could almost never resist).

I cannot claim to have been very good at anything during my training as an officer cadet, with perhaps one exception - balloon debates. These were held every week. The premise was that six people were in the basket of a balloon that was losing height and each of them had to present an argument to the audience as to why they should not be thrown out to reduce the weight. The audience voted on each round and the winner was the last man in the basket. I possessed what was known in my family as "the gift of the gab" and I had no fear of speaking in public. Using my newly acquired story-telling skills as a journalist I found I was able to construct cogent, if convoluted, reasons why I should remain in the basket. I often won.

Night "exercises" featured prominently in our programme and one was unforgettable. We were due to be dropped off in pairs at various remote spots on Salisbury Plain equipped with a map, compass and torch to find our way across country to a rendezvous point by midnight. Unfortunately, the Royal

Armoured Corps chose the same moonless night and the same area for training tank crews with the result that we were frequently terrified by grinding, clanking roars all around us and tanks suddenly emerging in the gloom. It was very difficult to judge in which direction they were moving and had any of us been run over it was unlikely the tank crew would have known anything about it. No thanks to the organisers, everyone made it back safely to the rendezvous.

On 13 May, 1959, I was commissioned as a Second Lieutenant in the Royal Army Service Corps. We were all given a week's leave after the commissioning parade and I went home to Ilford, where I was still living with my parents in their small terraced house. I had always asked everyone in the family to let me know if they saw or heard anything that might make a story but when, two days later, my mother telephoned me at my girl friend's house to say she thought there was a big fire in the centre of town I ignored it - not because I was now in the Army, but because I was more interested in canoodling with my girl friend while her parents were out.

When it came time for me to leave, at about ten o'clock, I was astonished to discover, as I stepped outside, that the night sky to the south was brightly illuminated in a reddish glow. Christ, I thought, that was some fire. I jumped on a bus and tried to get to the town centre, but all the roads leading to the High Street were blocked, so I ran the last mile (I was very fit, after training for seven months in the Army.) I could hear and feel the heat of the fire before I could see it. As I turned the final corner I was met by an amazing sight. Harrison Gibson, a six-storey furniture store in the centre of the High Street, was ablaze from top to bottom.

Instantly forgetting that I was not, at that moment, an employed journalist, I set to work seeking out the fire chief, talking to exhausted fire fighters during their tea breaks and interviewing onlookers. Hundreds of people had flocked to see what was happening, nearby residents were warned to evacuate their homes, electricity was cut off over a wide area and the trolley bus service was suspended. I had not been there more than half an hour when Moultons, another big department store in the High Street, separated from Harrison Gibson by a row of smaller shops, suddenly burst into flames. The fire had licked across the rooftops and set light to an elevator on the top floor. Cables holding the elevator melted and it plunged like a fireball through the store almost literally exploding when it hit the ground. People ducked and screamed as windows shattered with reports like gunfire.

I stayed there all night until the twin fires had been brought under control. By dawn there was virtually nothing left of either store except blackened timbers and twisted girders. The High Street, never very pretty, looked as if two teeth had been knocked out of it.

When there was nothing left to see I walked along to Recorder House and offered to help put together the story. As far as I can recall, no one seemed particularly surprised to see me; it was as if I had never been away. Once I had explained I was on leave I was assimilated back into the team and spent several hours banging the keys of a typewriter with two sooty fingers, acutely aware that my clothes and hair stank of smoke.

A few days later I was crossing the Channel on the boat-train from Harwich, bound for Bielefeld in Germany, where I was to play my part in the Cold War, protecting the free world from Communism in the lowly - and entirely insignificant - role of a platoon commander in the 1st British Corps, the primary fighting force of the British Army of the Rhine at a time when Nikita Khrushchev, the belligerent Soviet leader, was demanding a solution to the "malignant tumour" of West

Berlin. No solution was found and within two years the monstrous Berlin Wall would start to be constructed.

We had previously been asked to state our preferences for a posting. My first choice was the Far East, my second the Middle East and my third Cyprus. Obviously, I was sent to Germany. It was only my second trip abroad after the fateful holiday with my cousin, Roger, that led to my precipitate departure from East London News Agency. I was met at Bielefeld Station by an army car and driver and taken straight to the officers' mess in a bleak garrison on the edge of town.

I was too late for dinner but was welcomed cordially by the other young officers and invited to join a ferocious drinking game about which I can remember little except that I ended up more drunk than I had ever been in my life. (I learned later this was the whole point of the game - to get newly arrived and newly commissioned officers insensible.)

So it was that I met my new commanding officer, Major John Regan, the following morning with a thunderous headache and the real fear that I would throw up all over his desk at any minute. Regan was the CO of 91 Car Company RASC, which provided personal transport for the senior officers of the 1st British Corps. He wasted no time welcoming me - I don't think he liked National Service officers very much - and curtly explained that I would be assuming command of B Platoon, which comprised 35 Champs, their drivers and ancillary personnel. The Champ was a British version of the American jeep, made by Austin with a Rolls Royce engine; they were mainly used when the Corps was in the field, on exercises, which was pretty much all the time.

Regan informed me that I would not be living in the garrison mess, where I had got so drunk the previous night, but at the Headquarters mess, where I would be in closer contacts with my platoon's "clients". I did not realise until later just what good news that was.

After my interview with Regan it was time for me to meet my "men" - most of them boys about the same age as me, also doing National Service. B Platoon had two NCOs - Sergeant "Smudger" Smith and Sergeant Ernie Walsh, both long-serving career soldiers. I knew that their support was vital and so I sat down with them in my "office" - actually no more than a cubicle in the corner of a garage - and was brutally frank. "You know," I said, "that I am a National Service officer and you probably think that I am wet behind the ears and possibly a bit of a prick." At this, Sergeant Walsh could not restrain a smirk. "You may be right," I continued. "But the fact is that I know nothing about how to run this platoon and you do. I will be relying totally on your experience. I'll give the orders but you are going to have to tell me what to do."

Their demeanour, which had been respectful but resigned, if a little bit surly, brightened considerably when they realised that I wasn't going to start throwing my weight around and that in effect they would be running the show.

After that I delivered a similarly conciliatory speech to the rest of the platoon, who were drawn up on parade by Sergeant Smith to meet me. I told them I was a National Serviceman, just like most of them, and that I would make their lives as easy as I could if they made mine easy by getting on with their jobs and not causing any trouble. Later that day my driver/batman, a wonderfully dour Scot by the name of McWhinnie, let me know that the blokes were relieved not to have been saddled with what he termed as "some jumped-oop twat." I was greatly flattered.

Officers - even the most junior officers - were assigned a batman (i.e. a personal servant) in the British army on the notion that they should be relieved of all chores in order to be able to concentrate on their duties and the welfare of their men. In reality it was a relic from a bygone age and for an oik from Ilford, like me, it was truly another world. But I knew by then that the easiest way to be accepted by my fellow officers - most of whom were career soldiers - was to pretend to be like them and take the army seriously. I could never admit I wanted a commission because I wanted an easy life, never admit that I had blagged my way through officer cadet school and never, never confess that I had lied about my educational qualifications. I was a fraud, I knew that, but I intended to keep that fact to myself.

During the course of my first day in Bielefeld McWhinnie moved my kit from the RASC garrison to the Headquarters mess - a handsome cream-painted stucco villa with a tennis court in the garden situated in a posh residential area, a five minute walk from the Headquarters, which had formerly served as a recreation centre for Luftwaffe officers. I had a large, comfortable room with an ensuite bathroom in an annexe built in the garden to provide extra accommodation. It had floor to ceiling windows opening onto little Juliet balconies and overlooking a street of civilian houses running alongside the mess. It was by far the most congenial bedroom I had ever had in my whole life; I could scarcely believe my luck.

I soon discovered that life in the Army as an officer after five o'clock was thoroughly amiable. Dinner was always preceded by numerous drinks in the bar. In the huge dining room we sat at a long polished table adorned with regimental silverware and candelabras and were served by waiters in crisp white jackets. I can't remember what the food was like - I had little interest in food at that time and my Mum, bless her, was no cook - but I suspect it was pretty mundane.

Wednesday was "mess night" when everyone was required to wear either a dinner jacket or "mess kit". I did not own a dinner jacket and mess kit in my case was a black bum-freezer jacket with white lapels, a white waistcoat and shirt, black bow tie, tight black trousers with white stripes down the side known as overalls, riding boots and spurs! (I don't think I had ever sat on a horse, let alone ridden one, in my entire life but as I was a fraud anyway, what did it matter?)

After dinner, decanters of port and Madeira were passed around the table and a toast was ritually drunk to the Queen. Thereafter, the evening usually degenerated into a rowdy, drunken, free-for-all; boisterous mess games not infrequently ended with blood being shed and furniture and fittings being smashed. The mess servants took all this in their stride and viewed clearing up the mayhem after a particularly riotous mess night as just another of their duties.

Heavy drinking was endemic partly because it was so cheap. There was no duty or tax on alcohol for the British services in Germany: spirits were two pence a tot and beer was three pence a pint. (This was in old money, before decimalisation.) It was hardly surprising that there was a laconic joke that if the Russians wanted to mount an attack they would certainly wait until after nine o'clock at night because most of the British Army of the Rhine was plastered by then.

A unique feature of the Headquarters mess was Mike's Bar, named after General Mike West, the commander of the 1st British Corps. West, a veteran of the Second World War and the Korean War, was a highly unconventional officer who loved parties, dancing and jazz and who would later number Mick Jagger and Bob Dylan among his friends. A big, handsome man, who was never happier than when he was surrounded by adoring females, he gave his enthusiastic blessing to the establishment of Mike's Bar, which was like a night club with its own entrance at one end of the mess. It was open every weekday evening from seven o'clock until late and all day every weekend. Officers were encouraged to bring their wives and girl friends and there was live music and dancing most evenings.

Unusually, German civilians were welcome, so long as they were guests of a member of the mess. Although 15 years had passed since the end of the war in Europe, the BAOR was still officially discouraged from fraternising with Germans. Mike West completely ignored this edict and was more than happy to fraternise with the locals, particularly if they happened to be girls.

It came in very useful when I found myself a German girl friend. My room in the garden annexe faced a row of German houses and there was a very pretty girl living in the house directly opposite to whom I would sometimes wave when she left for work in the morning. At first she ignored me, but then she took to giving me a shy wave back and a faint smile. One day I put up a sign in my window asking her, in English, if she would like to come to a party that Saturday night. (There was always a party on Saturday nights in Mike's Bar.) She crossed the street to read it, then nodded. That was how I met Marlies Bucher.

Marlies was a sweet 19-year-old student, bright, great fun and spoke flawless English. To my shame, I barely learned a word of German during my 18 months in the country, despite being encouraged by the Army to take free lessons. I enjoyed my free time far too much to bother with learning a language.

Anxious to impress her during our first date I casually mentioned I was the duty officer the following day and suggested she might perhaps watch out for me when I left the mess. It did not go well. The duty officer was required to get togged up in Number 1 dress uniform, which in my case was a dark blue tunic with a fearsomely uncomfortable high collar, overalls, boots and spurs. He also had to carry a sword.

When I emerged from the annexe in duty officer mode, mightily pleased with myself, I looked across at Marlies' house and saw her in an upstairs window. I gave her a cheery wave and she waved back and at that point my spurs somehow locked together and I only just managed to avoid falling flat on my face. McWhinnie was waiting with my Champ and I clambered into the passenger seat but when I went to slam the door it sprang back with considerable force - my sword was still sticking out through the door opening.

I looked back and saw Marlies was still watching, but her shoulders were shaking and she had one hand over her mouth. I don't think she was crying. Later I tried to convince her I had put on a show to make her laugh, but I don't think she believed me.

In the duty officer's room a rather well-drawn cartoon was pinned to the wall showing the gun of a huge Russian tank poking through the window while the duty officer excitedly brandished his sword at it. As a metaphor it worked rather well - I considered carrying a sword as duty officer was about as pointless as patrolling a barracks at night armed with a pick axe handle. In reality, the main responsibility of the duty officer was to deal with drunks. One night I was informed that a visiting RASC driver had been arrested for being drunk and was in the guardroom. When I arrived I discovered, to my amazement, that it was Corporal Flint, my drill instructor when I was in basic training, who had sworn to shoot himself if I ever became an officer. For some reason he pretended he did not recognise me, even when I identified myself. I let him know he was lucky I was duty officer; normally he would have been put on a charge and either fined or demoted. I just told him to get out and sober up as quickly as he could.

When I got to know Marlies better I took enormous risks to spend time alone with her in the mess. A curved staircase led up from the dance floor in Mike's Bar to a snooker room on the first floor. Beyond the snooker room were three unoccupied bedrooms, but the snooker room had glazed double doors opening onto the corridor that led to the bedrooms. It was quite easy to sneak up the staircase with Marlies unobserved, but if the snooker room was being used we had to wait on one side of the doors until no one was looking and then flit across and hope for the best. None of the bedrooms had locks and so, once safely inside, I had to push a wardrobe across the door to ensure privacy.

I am not sure what would have happened to me had Marlies and I been discovered, but it would not have been good. Smuggling a girl into a bedroom in an officers' mess was undoubtedly considered pretty disgraceful behaviour. General Mike West might have thought it a hoot, but John Regan, my humourless commanding officer, would have assuredly been outraged. However, we were never found out.

As the Cold War would soon be drawing to an end and the threat of a Soviet invasion was diminishing, the British Army of the Rhine had little to do but play at soldiers. This meant we were constantly on exercise, rumbling out into the German countryside in great convoys, setting up camps, fighting imaginary battles, organising field logistics - tents, supplies, food, ammunition, etcetera - then rumbling back again. Those concerned with their comfort - me included - usually tried to find accommodation in farmhouses rather than sleep in a tent. German farmers were usually willing, in exchange for a few *Deutschmarks*, to let out rooms and even cook for us. I spent my 21st birthday - 17 June, 1959 - in a farmhouse somewhere in the wilds of Schleswig Holstein. The family learned it was my birthday and very sweetly laid on a special dinner for me.

All this war-gaming was taken very seriously, but at the same time there was much about the Army that I found absurd, even childish. The other platoon in my company provided staff cars for officers in the Corps Headquarters above the rank of major, varying in size according to rank. Lieutenant-Colonels were allocated VW Beetles, which of course had only two doors. Rather than sit alongside the driver in the front, which any sensible person would do, many of them chose to claw their way into the back seat, apparently to enjoy the full chauffeur-driven experience. Watching an overweight Lieutenant Colonel struggling to get in and out of the back of a VW Beetle was surreal.

And then there was the case of the Brigadier who coveted my Champ and who should have known better. McWhinnie did not have much to do looking after me and so he spent his spare time titivating my Champ. It was something he enjoyed doing - he stripped it down to bare metal, re-sprayed it and polished it from end to end. It was, without doubt, the smartest Champ in the platoon and it obviously caught the eye of some unnamed Brigadier because he told Regan that he wanted it for himself. When Regan called me into his office and ordered me to hand over my Champ, I said nothing, but I wanted to ask when the Brigadier was going to grow up. To be honest, it did not matter much to me, but McWhinnie was furious and set about making the new vehicle he was given even smarter than the one he had been forced to give up.

Most of my contemporaries hated doing National Service, but I did not. It got me away from home, I grew up a lot, I enjoyed the perks of being an officer and after five o'clock the army was a lot of fun. There were moments in Germany when I even considered making a career in the army, but they were only moments and sanity prevailed. However, I do not believe that National Service ever did anyone any harm: most of us joined as boys and left as men, better for the experience.

CHAPTER 5: BANGING ON THE DOOR OF FLEET STREET

I was demobbed in August 1960, a few months before National Service finally came to an end, and returned to my old job at the *Ilford Recorder*, still yearning to make the big time in Fleet Street. Reporting jobs on national newspapers were never advertised - there were too many hopefuls banging on the door - and the usual way in was through a "friend of a friend" providing an introduction to someone who might know someone who might be looking for someone to take on the odd shift... It was in this way I met Ron Mogg, the news editor of the *Sunday Dispatch*, who I think took a shine to me and offered me a Saturday shift, starting towards the end of October. If I was any good, he said, he might be able to get me on the staff.

On the day before I was due to start my first shift, the Bishop of Woolwich, Dr John Robinson, had made a sensational appearance at the Old Bailey to give evidence for the defence in what would become known as the "Lady Chatterly Case". Penguin Books was being prosecuted under the newly introduced Obscene Publications Act for publishing an unexpurgated edition of *Lady Chatterley's Lover,* by D.H.Lawrence, which had been banned in Britain for more than 30 years.

The trial became a major public event and the cause of some public merriment when prosecuting counsel Melvyn

Griffith-Jones, in his opening address, asked the jury "Is it a book that you would have lying around in your own house? Is it a book that you would even wish your wife or your servants to read?"

In order to escape a guilty verdict, Penguin needed to prove that the book was a work of literary merit and had lined up a formidable array of writers and intellectuals as expert witnesses willing to testify for the defence, among them the Bishop of Woolwich, who generated headlines - and a minor barrage of hate mail - when he stepped into the witness box and declared his view that *Lady Chatterley's Lover* was a book which "every Christian should read."

I was early - and nervous - reporting for my first shift in Fleet Street on October 29. The *Sunday Dispatch* editorial offices were in Bouverie Street and were completely deserted when I arrived at 9.30. I did not know whether I should sit at a desk - or whether I even had a desk - and so I stood outside the glass cubicle where I knew Ron Mogg worked and waited for something to happen. Two or three older men - who I assumed were reporters - wandered in some time after 10 o'clock. They completely ignored me, settled at their desks, lit cigarettes and started reading through the morning newspapers.

Ron bustled in at 10.30 and, to my dismay, seemed surprised to see me. I wondered, for a moment, if I had got the wrong day, but then the penny dropped. "Sorry, son," he said, "I forgot you were starting today. Give me a few minutes and I'll find you something to do."

A "few minutes" turned out to be an hour, during which time I found somewhere to sit and pretended to be busy, like the other reporters, going through the dailies. I jumped up when I heard Ron calling my name and threaded through the desks to his office and hesitated until he beckoned me to go in. He introduced me to a large, florid-faced man slumped in a chair opposite his desk. "Harry's one of our best reporters," he explained. "As it's your first day I'm going to send you out with him so you can get to know the ropes. You've been following the Lady Chatterley case haven't you?"

I nodded.

"OK. What we need for tomorrow's paper is a good interview with the Bishop of Woolwich. No one expected a fucking bishop to speak up for some fucking pornographic novel, even if it was written by D.H. fucking Lawrence, so our readers will want to know what the fuck is going on. Harry here will do the interview, but you can sit in on it and see how we work. OK?"

I nodded again. I was disappointed that he did not trust me enough to do the job alone, but I did not let on. It was, after all, only my first day. Harry and I collected our coats, picked up an office car from the pool in the basement garage and set off for the Bishop's official residence in Manor Way, Blackheath. I drove, at Harry's request.

When we arrived, it was not difficult to find the right house because there was already a pack of reporters and photographers camped outside. It seemed every other Sunday newspaper had had the same idea and wanted an interview with the good Bishop but he, probably wisely, had decided to say no more on the subject of Lady Chatterley, or her lover: he was neither answering his telephone, nor responding to reporters ringing his door bell.

Harry took charge by telling me to join the pack waiting outside. "The bugger's sure to have to come out at some point," he said, "you can nab him then. You don't need me. I'll wait for you down there."

He pointed to a pub at the end of the road. To add insult to injury he invited a number of his mates to join him, telling them that they could rely on me to share whatever quotes I might get if the Bishop emerged.

So I was left standing outside in the cold, while Harry and his cronies enjoyed a convivial drinking session in the warmth of the saloon bar in the Old Tiger's Head.

If the Bishop had any engagements that day he must have cancelled them because he never left the house. I waited and waited, occasionally calling the news desk from a public telephone ostensibly to let them know what was happening but actually in the hope that we would be called off. One by one the other reporters were slowly withdrawn. In the end there was no one left but me - and Harry, of course, still in the pub.

I called the desk again to tell them that everyone had left and ask if I could now return to the office. I could hear some discussion in the background and then Ron himself came on the line. "Go back one last time, Russell," he said, "and shout through his letterbox. Tell him we'll give him fifty quid for an exclusive interview."

I gulped. "OK, Ron," I said meekly. In retrospect it seems odd that the precocious chutzpah I possessed working alone at East London News Agency trying to beat Fleet Street deserted me once I was actually in Fleet Street. I was appalled at what I was being asked to do.

The telephone box was about 300 yards from the Bishop's house and as I slowly and reluctantly made my way back I realised I could not do it - I could not kneel on a Bishop's doorstep, bellow through his letter box and offer him "fifty quid". In any case, he had made it quite obvious he had no interest in talking to the media. I waited 20 minutes then called the office again and lied. I told them I had done what I had been asked but the Bishop would still not come out. I was dreading that they would think up some new outrage, but to my relief they told me to come back; the last edition was about to be put to bed and even if the Bishop changed his mind there would hardly be enough time to get the story in.

By then it was about ten o'clock in the evening. I went to the pub to tell Harry we had been called off and discovered, perhaps not surprisingly after a day's drinking, that he was so pissed he could barely stand or speak. Slurring his words, he managed to tell me he lived not far away and asked if I possibly could drop him off at home on the way back to the office. I felt I had no alternative but to agree, so I helped him into the car and off we went. He gave me some very vague directions and then promptly fell asleep. Every time I woke him to see if we had arrived he would peer groggily through the windscreen and say something like "Jush up there, next left" then doze off again.

After driving around for nearly an hour I lost patience. I stopped the car in a residential street, woke him up and said "Here you are, you're home. Out you get." "Thanks, old boy," he said, "you're a real sport." He got out of the car rather shakily, slammed the door and I drove off. He never mentioned the incident when I saw him the following Saturday and I never discovered how he eventually found his way home.

I continued working Saturdays at the *Sunday Dispatch* for the next several months with the promise of a staff job as soon as a vacancy became available. One Saturday in May 1961 Ron Mogg called me into his office and said he hoped to be able to put me on the staff in a couple of weeks. I was, naturally, thrilled.

The following month the paper, which had been losing money for years, suddenly folded. Its closure had, it seemed, been on the cards for years although I was completely ignorant of the fact. It was presented as a merger with the *Sunday Express*, but no one was fooled. Once the biggest selling

Sunday newspaper in the country, the *Sunday Dispatch* was finished, along with my job prospects.

One curious outcome of my short time at the *Sunday Dispatch* was my unlikely debut as an actor and model. I was sitting in the newsroom minding my own business when I became aware of two people in Ron's office gesturing towards me. They turned out to be scouts from an advertising agency looking for a young reporter to feature in a cigarette newspaper and television campaign. Since none of the other reporters on the *Dispatch* could claim to be in the first flush of youth, I was the only candidate and they asked me if I would be willing to do it. It would not take more than a day and the fee would be £50, which to me was a fortune. Of course I said yes.

A couple of weeks later I turned up at a studio somewhere in West London where a rough replica of the *Sunday Dispatch* newsroom had been constructed. I had to sit at a desk in my shirtsleeves, type furiously, then rip a page from the typewriter and bellow "Copy!" to summon a copy boy. This was very roughly how it worked in a real newsroom, except I had to do it over and over again, for both movie and still cameras, until the director was satisfied. Sometimes I had a cigarette dangling from my mouth while I was typing, sometimes I shared one with the copy boy, sometimes I lit up after he had departed, pretending deep satisfaction with the first puff. Although I was a regular smoker at that time, the inside of my mouth was raw by the end of the day.

The launch advertising campaign for Olivier cigarettes, a brand that was destined to have a very short life, featured a range of thrusting young men in what were perceived to be glamorous jobs. Mine was: "Meet Russell Miller, 24-year-old Fleet Street reporter. He has the newsman's flair for a good story and the discriminating smoker's appreciation of a good cigarette…" The irony was that by the time the campaign was launched my brief career as a Fleet Street reporter was already over.

At the *Ilford Recorder* I had been promoted first to chief reporter and then news editor, which sounded very grand but in reality only meant keeping the diary and assigning reporters to various stories. I was called upon to deploy a little rat-like cunning when the local council refused to reveal, to the public or the media, details of grandiose plans, drawn up by Basil Spence, one of the country's leading architects, for redeveloping the town centre and building a new civic centre. It was to cost millions and was rumoured to involve the extensive compulsory purchases in surrounding streets.

I thought it was outrageous that all this was happening with very little public consultation; the council would not even indicate which streets would be affected. I learned that a model had been built of the proposed re-development, but it, too, was kept under wraps. This was long before the Freedom of Information Act came into law; local elected politicians in those days generally clung to the view that the public had no right to know what they were doing.

By lucky coincidence, Steph, my long-term girl friend and future wife, worked as a secretary for an architectural practice in London. When I asked her if she would call Basil Spence's office, architect to architect, to inquire if they could recommend a model maker, she was understandably reluctant but eventually succumbed after considerable pressure from me.

It was then a simple matter to send a photographer to the model maker's office. I was relying on him being unaware of the secrecy surrounding the scheme and my hunch was right. When the photographer turned up and said he had come to photograph the Ilford scheme the model maker was happy to show it to him. We were astonished by the pictures he brought back. The model clearly showed the extent of the council's ludicrous plan - hundreds of people would lose their homes if this municipal folly went ahead.

My story, accompanied by a picture of the model, filled the front page of the next edition of the *Recorder* and caused a public uproar. (The project was eventually abandoned.) No one was more furious than the councillors themselves. An inquiry was begun to find out how I had managed to get the information and I was accused of gutter journalism, employing duplicity (i.e. rat-like cunning) to circumvent the council's tight-lipped strategy. The next time I was in the Town Hall I was buttonholed by an outraged councillor, who shouted at me for a bit and concluded by spitting "Ilford can do without people like you!"

Ilford did, rather sooner than anyone, including me, expected. After the demise of the *Sunday Dispatch* I thought I would try my luck getting a job with the BBC, which was always advertising for young journalists to work in both radio and television, both in London and the provinces. I must have filled in 20 or so application forms without ever getting an interview. I concluded that I was probably being passed over because of my abysmal educational qualifications (three O-levels!) and my dodgy CV (a broken apprenticeship) although I later learned that some of the jobs did not, in reality, exist. The BBC charter required it to advertise all job vacancies, despite the fact that internal candidates had often already been earmarked for the post.

Thoroughly dispirited, and increasingly anxious to move on from Ilford, I applied for a job at an outfit grandly called Fleet Street News Agency and was invited to an interview with Tommy Bryant, the Fagin-like character who owned the agency. It was work very similar to what I had been doing at East London News Agency, but it was better paid, covered the whole of London and included the use of a car - a Volkswagen

Beetle. A week after my confrontation at the town hall I got a telephone call from Tommy asking me when I could start. I gave in my notice the same day and bade farewell to the *Recorder* four weeks later.

I was at last in Fleet Street, but not, in truth, where I wanted to be. Instead of being in the newsroom of one of the national papers, I was in a cramped, filthy, two-room office on the third floor of a decrepit building on the corner of Fetter Lane and Fleet Street. The young man who ran the office was Irish, with a rich brogue and literary pretensions, signalled by his penchant for velvet suits and paisley scarves dashingly knotted at the neck in lieu of a tie.

It was not long before I realised I had made a terrible mistake. Tommy was an even more difficult and demanding taskmaster than Harry Mitchell at East London. He employed three reporters, all of whom he treated like slaves. I worked six days a week and Tommy had no qualms asking me to work seven; he would think nothing of telephoning very early in the morning on my one day off to tell me I was needed in the office as soon as possible. At East London I had been happy to work all hours, but now I was a little older and a little wiser and I resented all the time I was putting in to make money for Tommy Bryant.

After a month of slavery at Fleet Street News Agency I began hunting for another job. Salvation arrived in the unlikely form of *Soldier,* the British Army magazine, which was looking for a feature writer. I had to apply through Civil Service channels, which were tedious and cumbersome - the magazine was owned by the Ministry of Defence - but at least I was not debarred by my lack of a degree and I had two big assets in my favour. First I had completed National Service in the army and second I had held a commission. I thought I would get the job and I did.

For me one of the main attractions was that it would involve travelling the world to wherever the Army was operating. But I got something out of it that was even more important for my subsequent career: I realised, working for *Soldier*, that I was capable of writing, with reasonable facility, more than just a couple of hundred words.

*   * * * *

I joined *Soldier* as a feature writer in the autumn of 1962 at a moment when it seemed to me, and many of my friends, that the Cuban missile crisis might lead to a full-scale nuclear war and the end of civilisation as we knew it. The US had discovered Soviet ballistic missiles deployed in Cuba, only 90 miles from Florida, and had set up a naval blockade of the island. For 13 tense days there was a stand-off between the United States and the Soviet Union, a confrontation historians now consider was the closest the Cold War came to escalating to a nuclear war likely to kill a third of humanity. I can clearly remember the relief I felt when I heard, via a BBC news flash, that Khrushchev had agreed to remove the missiles from Cuba. President Kennedy, already a hero to my generation at that time, became a super-hero.

Soldier magazine occupied offices in an unprepossessing warehouse just off the Holloway Road, in the drearier reaches of north London. Throughout my brief working life I had become accustomed to noisy communal offices with lots of banter; it was very different at *Soldier*, where we all had individual offices along a single corridor on the first floor of the warehouse and a sepulchral, Civil Service, calm reigned, apart from the occasional ringing of a distant telephone.

I spent my first few months at the magazine either re-writing Army PR handouts or covering military stories in the

UK, all the while itching for a foreign assignment. The editor, an amiable Yorkshireman called Peter Wood, organised what he called "tours" (it always struck me as a faintly incongruous description, being redolent of a "royal tour") during which a writer/photographer team would undertake a number of assignments in a particular area, usually travelling in a Land Rover on the ground or courtesy of the RAF in the air.

My first major tour, with a photographer, was to the Persian Gulf, covering stories in Aden, Bahrain, the Trucial States (now the United Arab Emirates) and Muscat and Oman. For a young man who had never left Europe it was a blast, particularly visiting Muscat and Oman, which at the time was virtually a closed country (my visa number was 0034!) and alleged to be one of the hottest places on earth. (In 1441 a Persian visitor claimed that the jewels on the hilt of his dagger had been turned to coal by the heat.)

I was to write about the Sultan's Armed Forces, a locally-raised army trained by British officers and NCOs on secondment and engaged in operations against an armed Communist insurgency from South Yemen. We flew into the country on a light aircraft from Aden and landed on an airstrip at the army base just outside the capital, Muscat, a port on the Gulf of Oman surrounded by a lunar landscape of bleak mountains and desert. Oil had recently been discovered in the area but its economic impact was yet to be felt - the only tarmac road in the entire country of 82,000 square miles was the 8-kilometre stretch leading from the base into town.

With history dating back to antiquity, Muscat was still virtually untouched by modern civilisation. (Now it boasts high-rise buildings, five-star hotels, high end shopping malls and even an opera house.) The city could only be entered through huge wooden gates which were closed at dusk every night. Inside the city walls, all citizens were obliged to carry a little oil lamp during the hours of darkness, an ordinance that was strictly enforced. One of the 16th century Portuguese forts guarding the harbour entrance had been converted into a prison and it was rumoured that no one knew how many people were incarcerated within its dank walls or why. Whenever I asked anyone about it they just shook their heads and changed the subject.

On the day we arrived in Muscat I had inquired if it might be possible to interview the Sultan. The absolute ruler of Muscat and Oman, Sultan Said bin Taimur, scion of a dynasty which had controlled the country since 1744, lived in a palace on the coast at Salalah, some five hundred miles to the south. To my surprise I got word a few days later that not only would he be pleased to receive us, but the RAF would fly us to Salalah. As far as *Soldier* magazine was concerned, there was absolutely no need for me to interview him, but I did not want to pass up the opportunity. I thought if I could persuade him to say something newsworthy I might sell a piece to one of the nationals.

In the event, it was a waste of time. The flight to Salalah took an hour and a half over a barren, rock-strewn wilderness, mountains topped with sinister watch towers and scattered mud hut villages clustered around wells. An ancient Rolls Royce was waiting at the airstrip to take us to the Sultan's palace, a white stone confection, glistening in the sun, on the shore of the Arabian Sea. Within the palace compound, which was enormous, was a blue-tiled mosque and a minaret. In the palace itself we were escorted past silent lines of uniformed retainers into an ante room, given a glass of mango juice, and told to wait.

After about half an hour we were informed the Sultan was ready to see us and we were ushered into a receiving room where a tall white-bearded figure wearing white robes trimmed with gold and a turban and with a traditional *khanjar* - curved dagger - at his waist, was lounging on a pile of beaded cushions. He welcomed us in perfect English and bade us to be seated on two chairs facing him. If I had any hope of wheedling any information out of him, it was soon dashed. I was hoping to get him to talk about the Communist insurgency, but he completely ignored my questions and offered anodyne answers to questions I had not asked. It was utterly bizarre. I asked him, for example, if he was confident the Sultan's Armed Forces would be able to defeat the rebels. This was his wily answer: "The Omanis are very peace-loving people, Mr Miller. My people have an old world politeness and are very hospitable. It is my sincere hope that we will retain the best of this old world while yet assimilating the best of the new."

After 45 minutes, an aide appeared and signalled the interview (such as it was) was over and we were escorted out. Later, I learned I had missed a very big story. Although we had no inkling of it, at the time of our visit the Sultan was deeply embroiled in a saga of typical Middle East intrigue. He suspected his eldest son, Prince Qaboos bin Said, was plotting to overthrow him and had imprisoned him somewhere in the palace. The old man was absolutely right. Qaboos, a reformer who wanted to end the country's isolation and use its oil revenues for modernisation and development, eventually escaped and ousted his father from the throne in 1970 after a successful coup supported, clandestinely, by MI6.

From Muscat and Oman we flew to Sharjah, on the Persian Gulf, headquarters of the Trucial Oman Scouts, a similar outfit to the Sultan's Armed Forces in Muscat, which was largely engaged in protecting oil exploration teams and suppressing tribal raiding. The greater part of the Trucial States was pure desert - mile after mile of rolling sand dunes - and the Scouts were equipped with Land Rovers fitted with huge balloon tyres capable of crossing the shifting sands.

The highlight of our visit was to be an expedition across the desert to Buraimi Oasis. We set off very early in the morning, before the sun was up, navigating by compass. We came across a long camel train as the dawn broke, but thereafter we saw nothing, not a living soul, for hours. As our long wheelbase Land Rover crested each dune you could see, momentarily, across the great expanse of desert and the billowing sand spreading away in every direction, before plunging down the reverse side of the dune and beginning to climb the next.

In the early afternoon we spotted another vehicle on the distant horizon apparently heading in our direction. We could only glimpse it when we were both on top of a dune, but there was no doubt, as the gap between us narrowed, that we would pass close by each other. We were just beginning to struggle up yet another dune when the other vehicle, another Scout Land Rover, appeared at the top and began to slither down the incline towards us more or less out of control. In the deep sand we were powerless to take avoiding action and there was a tremendous crash as the two Land Rovers - probably the only vehicles for hundreds of miles around - collided. Fortunately no one was hurt and neither vehicle was disabled, although the spare wheel had been torn off the side of our Land Rover. All the soldiers seemed to think it was a huge joke.

Buraimi Oasis had for many years been the subject of a bitter territorial dispute between Saudi Arabia and the Trucial States, both of whom claimed oil exploration rights in the area. Saudi Arabian soldiers occupied the oasis in 1952 and were kicked out by the Trucial Oman Scouts three years later. At the time of our visit the dispute was still unresolved and the Scouts had assumed responsibility for the security of the area.

I had naively expected Buraimi Oasis to look how cartoonists usually drew oases - a few date palms around a lagoon. In fact it was a collection of dusty villages and scattered historic forts and mosques. Our Arab hosts laid on a banquet in our honour, although I would later rather wish they had not done so. We all squatted on cushions in a large and stiflingly hot tent as huge steaming platters of rice and goat meat were brought in and laid before us. It would have been fine had not every platter been crawling with flies. Everyone ate with one hand, in the traditional manner, and a dubious green tea was served in small and dirty glasses. I was already feeling a little queasy when I went to bed and I spent that night and most of the next day on the lavatory, to the undisguised amusement of my Scout friends.

Our last assignment was back in Aden, which was reckoned, with every justification, to be one of the worst postings in the British Army. Built in the crater of an extinct volcano with no vegetation of any kind visible anywhere, the port was surrounded by grey hills of rock and slate shimmering in almost unbearable heat. Goats roamed the streets eating cardboard boxes, apparently obtaining nourishment from the glue. Aden, at the entrance to the Red Sea, had been a British protectorate for more than 100 years and we (the British) had more than worn out our welcome. An insurgency, supported by neighbouring Yemen, had begun a few months before we arrived and a state of emergency had been declared. Tension on the streets was palpable and the troops were under fire on a daily basis. We went out with a couple of patrols and managed to avoid being shot at, but I will not forget the looks of venomous hatred we generated from the locals. Even shopkeepers anxious to sell us duty-free goods could barely conceal their contempt for us. I was happy to leave.

Back in London *Soldier* magazine contrived to report on the appointment of a new Secretary of State for War, Joseph Godber, without a single mention of his predecessor. This was perhaps because his predecessor was John Profumo, the man at the centre of the biggest political scandal for decades, who had lied to the House about his relationship with 19-year-old Christine Keeler, been found out and was forced to resign in June 1963. The adventures of Keeler and her friend, Mandy Rice-Davies entertained and titillated the country for months. When told in court that Lord Astor denied an affair with her, Mandy famously replied, with a giggle, "Well he would, wouldn't he?" The dark side of the scandal was the persecution of the osteopath Stephen Ward, who introduced the girls to high society, was found guilty of living off immoral earnings and committed suicide.

I was by then married to Stephenie, my long-time girl friend. We both worked in London and drove in to work together from out flat in Chigwell Row, Essex. On the evening of 22 November, 1963, we were driving home - I can still remember exactly where we were on the route - when there was a news flash on the car radio announcing that President Kennedy had been shot during a motorcade in Dallas and was feared dead. That night, in the company of friends, we did our best to get drunk, but signally failed: the more we drank, the more sober and morose we seemed to become. We were all in our 20's and to our generation Kennedy had represented a beacon of hope in an increasingly alien world.

My next major trip was to the Far East - to Thailand, Singapore, Brunei, Malaya and Borneo, destinations quite as exotic and fascinating as those in the Persian Gulf. British soldiers in Borneo were engaged in a very nasty little jungle war, virtually ignored at home and euphemistically described as the "Indonesian confrontation." President Sukarno of

Indonesia had sworn to crush the newly-formed federation of Malaysia and had deployed his army along the border to mount raids into Borneo.

We travelled part of the time with Clare Hollingworth, then the *Guardian*'s formidable female defence correspondent. Clare was a large, florid-faced woman who had spent her life touring the world's trouble spots and was as tough as any man; she was the first correspondent to report the German invasion of Poland at the start of the Second World War. At one point we were travelling in a Land Rover along a jungle track close behind a three-ton truck packed with soldiers when one of them soldiers casually unzipped his trousers and pissed over the tailgate right in front of us. Clare, sitting in the front of the Land Rover, was not in the least bothered.

She had told me she was trying to confirm a rumour that British special forces were illegally crossing the border into Indonesia to carry out reprisal attacks. I knew it was true, but did not tell her. A few days earlier I had been shown a photograph in confidence of an SAS patrol that had returned from a month in the jungle. With their beards, straggly hair and ragged clothes they looked like cavemen. That photograph now hangs in the Special Forces Club in Knightsbridge.

While we were in Borneo, I was offered a flight in a little two-seater Auster aircraft to get a bird's eye view of the jungle. It turned out to be a hair-raising experience: first we got lost and then we ran out of fuel. I don't like light aircraft and I did not know at the time that the Army pilot was only recently qualified. We took off, rather shakily, but got safely into the air. Not many minutes passed before I could see, by the way he kept looking at the map folded into a pocket on his trouser leg and then peering out anxiously through the windscreen that he did not know where we were. He must have been exceptionally stupid - I could see ahead of us a long straight stretch of coastline and I could also clearly see it on the map.

With that problem solved, we continued our journey at about 1,000 feet over the jungle, which looked from the air like tightly packed heads of broccoli. We had just turned for home when the engine began to cough and splutter and then died. I looked down and knew that if we landed in the broccoli the plane would be torn apart and we would certainly die. With rising terror I looked at the pilot and saw he, too, was in a state of panic. "Christ!" he muttered, "Christ!" The propeller had completely stopped and we were gliding slowly down towards the jungle canopy. "Fuel!" he shouted, as if suddenly remembering his flight manual. "Gotta switch over." He leaned forward, flicked a switch to connect the reserve tank, pressed a button and, to my enormous relief, the engine clattered into life. When we got back to base, one of the grinning ground crew could see from my expression, as I stepped down from the Auster, that it had not been a fun trip. "Did he give you a fright, sir?" he inquired with a smirk. I could not speak.

Still metaphorically wearing my reporter's hat, in Brunei I interviewed the Sultan, Sir Omar Ali Saifuddin, but like his counterpart in Muscat he would not be drawn on anything remotely controversial. He introduced me to his sons, 19-year-old Crown Prince Hassanal and his younger brother, Prince Jefri. Both wore drainpipe trousers, Italian "bum-freezer" jackets and winkle-picker shoes and both looked absurd, if fashionable. They were said to race their Ferraris through the streets of the Brunei capital at midnight, a rumour the Sultan would neither confirm nor deny.

Prince Hassanal would succeed his father and in 1987, thanks to oil revenues, be named by *Forbes* magazine as the richest man in the world with a fortune in excess of $40 billion. Prince Jefri would become a notorious playboy, gambler and lothario, alleged to have blown more cash on hedonistic pursuits that any other human being on earth and the proud owner, among other trinkets, of a fleet of super yachts and a collection of 2,500 prestige cars.

Flying from Singapore to Ubon in northern Thailand we stopped to refuel at an American air base in Da Nang, Vietnam, where we were to spend the night. The disastrous Vietnam War was just getting under way and the Americans had launched Operation Rolling Thunder - the bombing of targets in North Vietnam. I was a bitter opponent of the war, as was most of my generation (35,000 people had joined an anti-war protest march on Washington in November 1965), but I could not help myself being thrilled by the raw power of what I witnessed that night. The base was buzzing with activity. Heavily-laden F105 Thunderchief bombers were roaring off every few minutes. At night, F16 Tomcat fighters took off in pairs, their after-burners flaring orange against the black sky. I caught a glimpse of little General Nguyen Ky, then head of the Vietnamese air force, swaggering about the PX in his black silk flying suit, with a pearl-handled revolver holstered on each hip.

In northern Thailand I was to write a story about a regiment of Royal Engineers which was building an airstrip in the jungle. It was allegedly a community project to help improve access to remoter areas of the country, but I knew, as I suspected everyone else did, that in reality it was to be used to support United States Air Force operations against North Vietnam.

What we found when we arrived was bizarre beyond belief. The news that there were several hundred bored, lonely - and randy - British soldiers holed up in a jungle encampment had spread to the red-light district of Bangkok and dozens of prostitutes had made their way to the area to ply their trade in the numerous bars which had sprouted up in the nearest village, Kok Tal Lat. Such was their success that the provincial government had been obliged to set up a sexually-transmitted disease clinic in the village, outside which the Thai national flag fluttered proudly from a makeshift flagpole.

The commanding officer of the unit, a Lieutenant Colonel, should by rights have sent the girls packing but I discovered, to my amazement, that he not only allowed his men to fraternise freely with them, but he had his own "special girl friend", who shared his hut. He cheerfully admitted she was a whore, but explained that she had temporarily forsaken the trade in return for his patronage. Some of the "girls" were not girls at all, but transvestites, although this did not seem to bother any of the squaddies, who assured me that "ladyboys" were better at sex than girls.

I was not able to write about any of this in *Soldier*, for obvious reasons, and was sorely tempted to offer the story to one of the tabloids, but I thought it would probably cost me my job if I did. I learned later that the opening ceremony for the airstrip was something of a disaster. A number of local dignitaries had been invited to watch the first aircraft land, which it did, safely, only to sink up to its axles in the tarmac after it had rolled to a stop. I remembered the colonel telling me that he had employed the same "fast track" technique for laying the tarmac that had been used on the M1 motorway, admitting that "it was a bit of a risk".

My last foreign assignment for the magazine was in South Africa and Swaziland. On board the aircraft bound for Johannesburg we were given immigration forms which required us to state our race - South Africa was still in the grip of apartheid - and the photographer, Frank Tompsett, and I both decided to write "human". We thought it was a huge joke. Unfortunately the white immigration officer at Jan Smuts Airport failed to see the funny side of it (other people may possibly have had the same idea) and made us go to the back of the queue and fill in new forms. We were delayed for so long that the guy sent to meet us assumed we had missed our flight and went home. That definitely was not funny.

In Mbabane, the capital of Swaziland, we were granted an audience with the King, Sobhuza 11, who would successfully steer his country towards independence from the UK in the next few years and would eventually reign for longer than any monarch in recorded history. He was an amiable chap, then nearing 70, wearing a feathered headdress, tiger skins and what looked like bits of carpet. He was said to have 70 wives and 210 children and looked remarkably cheerful. At the time of his death, in 1982, he had more than 1,000 grandchildren.

In August 1966 I got a call, out of the blue, from Beverley Hilton. Not the hotel, but the editor of *House Beautiful* magazine. (Although it was never one of my favourite hotels, I would occasionally stay at the Beverly Hilton when, years later, I was frequently on assignment in Los Angeles.) Beverley only knew of my existence because the magazine had earlier published a three-part series, written by me, about the renovation of a run-down Georgian house Steph and I had bought in Islington in the very early days of the area's "gentrification". On the strength of that, she wanted to know if I would be interested in a job as deputy editor.

Although I was still enjoying the travel offered by *Soldier*, I was getting bored with writing anodyne stuff about army exercises and operations. I discussed Beverly's offer with Steph, who was by then pregnant. It would mean more money, which we could certainly use, and an end, at least temporarily, to my globe-trotting, which would probably be sensible when the baby arrived. I decided to accept.

It was a good time to be working for a glossy magazine in central London - *House Beautiful* offices occupied an entire floor of a swank skyscraper in Victoria. In April that year an iconic cover story in *Time* magazine had declared London to be "the swinging city", the place, to use the argot of the age, where "it" was "at".

"The city is alive with birds (girls) and buzzing with mini cars and telly stars… London has burst into bloom. It swings; it is the scene…" the magazine reported. King's Road, the trendiest street on the planet at that time, was just a short walk from my new office, as were the Biba store in Abingdon Road, and Carnaby Street. Pop art and mini skirts were everywhere, rock and roll blared from pirate radio stations and a skinny kid with big eyes called Twiggy became one of the most recognised faces in the world. I'm faintly embarrassed to recall on my first day at *House Beautiful* I was wearing an on-trend grey flannel suit with a tight six-button double-breasted jacket and drainpipe hipster trousers, a pink shirt and Chelsea boots.

I liked my time at *House Beautiful*. I got on well Beverley, I was interested in interior design and I learned a lot about editing and magazine production, but after about a year I was beginning to get itchy feet and started looking around for another job. When I saw an advertisement for an editor to launch a new magazine called *Frontiers* I applied without much hope and was surprised to be invited for an interview at an address in Mayfair. There I learned the magazine was to be sponsored by a major financial institution called Investors Overseas Services (IOS) and distributed to their clients worldwide. It was to be a prestige, lifestyle publication full of seductive features about travel, sport, property, motoring, celebrities and the like. I was shown a dummy (a mock-up of how the magazine would look) and was impressed.

If I was surprised to get to the interview stage, I was even more surprised to be offered the job at a salary almost twice what I was earning at *House Beautiful*. What I did not know was that I was being conned. I knew nothing of Investors

Overseas Services at that time; had I done a little research I might have thought twice about accepting. Beverley was upset when I told her I was leaving. "I knew," she said, "that it was too good to last." I was touched, but not so touched that I was willing to extend my period of notice. I was anxious to be off, to be the editor of my own fabulous magazine.

I had been hired by the IOS director of public relations, a man called Graham Rushworth, and it was to him that I reported at the company's luxurious head office in Park Street, Mayfair, on my first day. The first bit of news he had for me was not good: the launch of the magazine had been delayed but I was not to worry, he said, as it would give me time to learn more about the company. The second bit of news was almost as bad: I was to be based at the administrative headquarters in Wembley, a dreary, soulless office block in a dreary, soulless London suburb with open plan offices on every floor filled by clerks sitting at desks in long lines and sifting through piles of paper. I hated it on sight.

Instead of planning the launch of a magazine, I was put to work writing articles for the annual report or little motivational handouts for the company's 25,000 salesmen, who sold mutual funds door to door on commission across Europe. Every time I inquired about the magazine I was fobbed off.

Meanwhile, I was certainly learning more about the company and the more I learned the less I liked. The founder was a flamboyant businessman/playboy by the name of Bernie Cornfeld who travelled by private jet between his château in France and his other homes in London, New York and Beverly Hills, who threw extravagant celebrity-filled parties and was said to maintain a stable of mistresses. He fired up his salesmen with the mantra "Do you sincerely want to be rich?" IOS was a classic pyramid-selling operation, with enormous pressure exerted on the sales force to recruit other salesman and take a cut from their commission. People who got in early were, it is true, getting sincerely rich and driving around in Rolls Royces by taking a percentage from everyone in their personal pyramid, but it was a different story for the poor devils at the bottom of the pyramid, who struggled to make a living. Greed was the driving force and company ethos.

I kept nagging Graham Rushworth about the magazine and he kept finding excuses for the delay. After two months of his prevarication I told him that unless he could give me a guarantee that the magazine would materialise I was going to quit. He was unable to do so and so I walked out.

(Three years later IOS collapsed, triggering an international financial crisis. Cornfeld was arrested, charged with fraud and spent 11 months in a Swiss prison, but was eventually acquitted. IOS never produced a magazine.)

It was foolish of me to resign before finding another job, but I hated what I was doing, hated Wembley and hated working for IOS. For the first time in my short career I would wake up in the morning and not look forward to going to work. Once I realised that the magazine I had supposedly been hired to edit was no more than a chimera, I could not stand it a moment longer.

Thus it was I found myself, shortly before Christmas 1967, with no income, no savings and no job. I had a large mortgage and a pregnant wife and a small child to support. There was no imminent prospect of walking into another job and there was no time to start looking. I needed to start earning. Immediately….

CHAPTER 6: FIRST FREELANCE FORAYS (Journalists love alliteration)

During my first few years as a freelance journalist I kept a meticulous workbook listing, day by day and month by month, what I had written, for whom and the fee. I still have it. Flicking through the pages today I am astonished by my output - the quality may not have been up to much, but the quantity was impressive. Rare was the month that I did not turn out at least ten articles; on average I filed a story every other day. I have no idea, now, how I found work so readily. This was years before e-mail and the internet; I can only suppose that I just sat on the telephone and kept calling round until commissions started coming in. In my first month I cleared £381, more than I had ever earned on a salary. Not only that, but I realised I was enjoying life more than I ever did when I had to go into an office. It was a revelation.

At the beginning I leaned heavily on my experience at *House Beautiful* to present myself, somewhat ingenuously, as a journalist with a special interest in, and knowledge of, design. I quickly obtained two regular weekly columns which generated sufficient regular income to pay the bills and put food on the table. One was called "Design For Living", which appeared in a group of local newspapers in Hertfordshire, and the other was about the new property market in London for the *Evening Standard* (which I suspect was a only published to generate advertising income from developers). The first paid ten guineas (yes guineas) a week, the second 15 guineas. My expertise and qualifications for both might have been questionable, but my ability to deliver copy on time was never faulted. I think editors greatly valued the latter over the former.

I also became a regular contributor a German magazine, *Schöner Wohnen* - a much glossier version of *House Beautiful*. I think the lady editor, whose name I regret I cannot now recall, took a motherly shine to me, invited me to visit the magazine's office in Hamburg, paid all my expenses and booked me into the *Vier Jahreszeiten* - the best hotel in town. I returned with a commission to write a monthly "London Letter" for the magazine, for which I was going to be paid the outrageous fee of £40 - more than twice what I was earning elsewhere.

London was still, in 1968, the centre of the universe as far as fashion and pop culture were concerned. Hippies and psychedelic art were everywhere; *Hair* was beginning its record-breaking run of 1,997 performances at the Shaftesbury Theatre; the Beatles and the Rolling Stones were the most popular bands in the world; Mary Quant followed up mini-skirts with hot pants and became a fashion icon ranked alongside Chanel and Dior. I remember on my visit to the *Schöner Wohnen* office I wore a floral Liberty print shirt which excited a certain amount of interest and perhaps boosted my doubtful credentials to be a chronicler of "the scene" for SW readers. It was as if I was a personal emissary from "Swinging London", which I guess was my intention.

The "London Letter" that I filed every month was supposed to be a mix of news and gossip, an insider's take on what was going on in what was generally acknowledged at the time to be the most exciting city in the world. It is possible that I might have given the impression that I was more of an insider than I really was, that I was out partying every night with artists and pop stars. (Actually, I was not an insider at all; I was a young married man struggling to make a living, as far from a fashionable party animal as it was possible to be, but I felt no need to share this with my readers at *SW*.) My copy was translated into German for the magazine then re-translated back into English for an insert that was included in editions destined for sale in the UK. It resulted in some tortuous renditions of the original. I mentioned in one letter a King's Road boutique called "Granny Takes a Trip" and it came back, stolidly re-translated, as "Your grandmother goes travelling."

On top of these regular commitments, I was picking up feature assignments here and there, wherever I could, mainly for my old employer, *House Beautiful*, but also for *Harper's Bazaar* and, most promisingly, for *Nova*, a ground-breaking feminist magazine which had only been launched a few years earlier and had become an influential must-read, certainly for the movers and shakers of "Swinging London". A torch-bearer for the burgeoning women's liberation movement, it was described in a review as "a politically radical, beautifully designed, intellectual women's magazine" (although it was read by almost as many men as women).

Nova had a reputation for publishing quirky, off-the-wall stories with an element of surprise - stuff that you would not find in other magazines. When I read a feature in the *Guardian* about the growing cryogenics movement in the United States - loons who were paying to have their bodies frozen after death in the hope that they could be brought back to life later, when medical science was sufficiently advanced - I thought it might appeal to *Nova* and it did. Sort of.

The features editor said yes, he might be interested in such a story, but the budget would not run to sending me to the United States. I would have to cover all my own expenses and take a risk that the story might not pan out, in which case the magazine would pay me nothing. The best case scenario would be a fee that might just about cover my expenses, always providing I could get the story and always providing Nova accepted it.

It was not a particularly alluring proposition, but there was another reason I wanted to go to New York. American magazines paid much more than their UK counterparts, were more exciting and interesting, there were more of them and they thus represented a potentially lucrative market for freelances. I thought if I could tout my portfolio and a bunch of ideas around the offices of magazines in New York I might pick up some work.

Getting to New York was no problem. Charter airlines of questionable repute were beginning to break into the Transatlantic market and were offering return flights, as part of fictional "package holidays" (which somehow circumvented regulations) for as little as £50. When I discovered that Michael Boys, a photographer who worked for *House Beautiful* and who had become a friend, was coincidentally in New York and willing to take the pictures for my story, I decided to go.

At not inconsiderable cost (Transatlantic telephone calls were very expensive in those days) I made contact with the secretary of the New York Cryonics Society, established he was around and willing to talk. Actually he was not just willing but desperately keen because he wanted as much publicity as possible. He promised to give me a tour of the arrangements for freezing bodies and explain the "science" behind the idea. They already had one corpse entombed, which he was ready to show me whenever I arrived. Before the call ended he gave me detailed instructions of how to find the Society's "Laboratory for Life Extension Research" on Long Island.

I would be lying if I said I was not excited about the prospect of visiting New York for the first time. (In later years

I would make many trips to the city, but I never tired of the place.) It turned out that my charter flight had been organised by some flower power/free love hippie group, as the entire aircraft seemed to be filled with black-eyed girls in mini skirts and long-haired freaks in velvet flares and psychedelic T-shirts. Long before the "no smoking" signs had been switched off joints were being handed round and a party atmosphere prevailed for the entire eight-hour flight, which included the cabin crew who quickly gave up their duties in favour of joining the party.

Michael met me at JFK in his rented convertible bright red Mustang - he had a lot of style - and drove me into Manhattan, where he had booked a room for me at his hotel - the Chelsea, on West 23rd Street, a home-from-home for innumerable writers, musicians, artists and actors for many years. (As I said, Michael had style.) Dylan Thomas died at the Chelsea in Room 205 in 1953; *Chelsea Girls*, a 1966 experimental film directed by Andy Warhol and Paul Morrissey was shot at the hotel; and Nancy Spungen (was that really her name?) would murder her boy friend, Sid Vicious, in a room at the Chelsea in 1978.

In truth, the hotel was quite run down, not to say shabby, when I registered as a guest for the first time in August 1968. I remember there was an oil drum lying on its side in the corridor outside my room, which no one seemed to think was unusual. In the bar that night I sat next to Divine, the grossly overweight drag queen who was already a notorious figure in the city's counter-culture. She asked me to buy her a drink - a Beefeater martini, straight up, with a twist - which I was shocked to discover cost $5. In retrospect I think she might have been trying to pick me up, but I beat a rapid retreat to my room to avoid the risk of having to buy her another drink.

Next morning we drove out to Long Island with the top down - it was the height of summer and very hot - and found the address I had been given with considerable difficulty (GPS and satnavs were still a long way away). Somehow I was expecting, perhaps foolishly, that the "Laboratory for Life Extension Research" would be, well, a laboratory. It was actually a garage, a small ramshackle garage in the back yard of a small wooden house in a faded suburb called Lindenhurst. All the members of the Society had assembled to meet me, all six of them - five young men and a woman with an Indian headband, geeky oddballs every one - wearing strange uniforms of black trousers, dark blue shirts with the Society badge stitched on one sleeve and "Cryonics of N.Y. Inc" embroidered on the back. The girl introduced herself to me saying "Hi, I'm a pop star."

They were all friends of the young man lying in a shiny steel capsule in a crematorium just down the road, immersed in liquid nitrogen and hooked up to various bits of machinery that maintained interior "cryopreservation" at below -130 degrees Centigrade. His name was Steven Mandell and he was still a student when he died at the age of 24. His demise was so sudden, the Society secretary explained, that they had to place a regular order for dry ice from Jolly Tim's Ice Cream Service across the street to preserve his body until he could be transferred to the capsule. All were utterly convinced that he would one day be brought back to life as indeed they would, when they, in turn, were frozen to await immortality.

(I was thrilled when my story made the cover of the January 1969 issue of *Nova* magazine with a picture of a model wrapped in tin foil and the cover line "If you want to stay alive FREEZE".)

The remainder of my trip to New York was rather less successful. I knew I had to try and pick up some work from

American magazines, but I had to steel myself to make the calls, explaining that I was a freelance journalist from London that I was in New York on an assignment and that I had some ideas I wanted to pitch. To their great credit, most of the "articles editors" I contacted agreed to see me (I had a feeling my English accent helped). The problem was that my portfolio, after only six months as a freelance, was pathetic, contained very little of substance and, I realised later, was very unlikely to impress an American editor sufficiently to entrust me with an assignment. One articles editor after another flipped through it with evident disinterest, listened to my ideas with similar disinterest, and then showed me the door. I did not pick up a single commission.

The worst moment, the very worst moment, was at the offices of *Eye*, a large-format magazine aimed at youth culture and considered at the time to be the epitome of chic, on the 33rd floor of an office block in Madison Avenue. When I arrived for my appointment I was greeted by a sleek secretary who led me through an open-plan office under the curious stares of the staff, who all seemed impossibly cool and good looking. I was probably not with the articles editor for more than five minutes before I was led out again through the same office, my ideas all disdained.

When I got back down on the street I discovered to my horror that I had left my portfolio behind. I would rather have walked over burning coals than go back into that office, but I knew I had to do it as I still had several more appointments. I retraced my steps and pressed the button for the 33rd floor in the elevator. I could feel my cheeks burning as the doors opened. I rushed through the office looking to neither left nor right, grabbed my portfolio from the bench where I had left it, then rushed back out again, saying nothing to anyone. It was possibly my imagination, but I got the impression everyone laughing at me.

I returned from New York with not a single commission from an American magazine. However, there was good news on the horizon. Dennis Hackett, the blunt Northerner who was the editor-in-chief of *Nova* and a justly exalted figure in the magazine world, was asked in the autumn of 1969 to launch a weekly colour magazine to be distributed with the *Daily Mirror*, then the biggest selling red-top tabloid in the country. Although I had never met him at that stage, on the basis of my contributions to Nova, he suggested that I should be hired as one of the regular writers.

The *Mirror Magazine* was brash, irreverent, innovative, great fun and doomed. No one, it seemed, had calculated the cost of printing 5 million copies of a high quality colour magazine every week and it closed exactly a year after its launch, not for lack of reader appeal - it was extraordinarily popular - but because it had exceeded its production budget by £7 million.

As far as I was concerned, it may have only lasted a year, but it was one hell of a year. I began earning serious money as a freelance for the first time, I had my own desk, typewriter and telephone in the magazine's offices on the eighth floor of the *Daily Mirror* building on Fetter Lane which I could use as and when I liked and I was introduced to the paper's lavish "expenses" culture, which mostly involved long, expensive lunches with innumerable bottles of wine, all paid for with what we casually called "Mirror Gold."

I always looked forward to "Mirror Gold" lunches but almost always regretted them afterwards, having drunk too much and frittered away an entire afternoon when I should have been working. One, at La Trattoria Terrazza in Soho, was unforgettable. "The Tratt" kicked-started the gastro revolution in the UK in the late 60s and numbered the Beatles, David Bailey, Michael Caine, Brigitte Bardot and Princess Margaret among its regular diners. We had gone with a gang from the magazine which included Jeffrey Bernard, who had also been hired as one of the regular writers. Jeff was better known as a Soho roué in those days than he was in the outside world. (He would become an almost legendary figure later through his "Low Life" columns in *The Spectator* and from Keith Waterhouse's play *Jeffrey Bernard Is Unwell*.)

Half way through the lunch, Jeff scribbled a note on a piece of paper, called one of the Italian waiters over and asked him to deliver it to an exceptionally pretty girl sitting with friends at a table in the corner. "Of course *signor*," he said, "straight away, *signor*." He bustled across the room and handed the note to the young lady with a discreet bow. She read it, blushed, then began to laugh and shake her head. The note said: "I know I am only a humble Italian waiter, but I have fallen in love with you. Can we meet later?"

Years later, many publishers tried to persuade Jeff to write his autobiography. While he was always ready to accept an advance he never wrote a word, although he was full of good intentions, as indicated by a letter published in *The Spectator*: "I am about to write my autobiography. Will anyone who knew what I was doing between the years 1955 and 1965 please get in touch?"

Jeff was a prodigious drinker - vodka was his tipple - yet it never seemed to affect him; I never saw him drunk. He often told me that doctors had warned him that if he continued drinking he would kill himself. Ultimately, he did: he died in 1997 at the age of 65 of renal failure.

Although I was unaware of it at the time, the *Mirror Magazine* assembled a formidable array of literary and journalistic talent, quite apart from Jeff. The editor, Mike

Molloy, went on to edit the paper and write successful children's books; the novelist and playwright Keith Waterhouse contributed a regular column; the cookery page was written by a shy young woman called Delia Smith; and the women's editor, Eve Pollard, would later become only the second woman in Britain to edit a national newspaper.

Along with conventional features, the magazine liked to stir it up. British pop stars - the Beatles, Lulu, Cilla Black, Cliff Richard, Sandie Shaw and Tom Jones - were conquering the world and making millions. One of my assignments was to play their latest albums to the head senior coach at Covent Garden Opera House and pose a simple question: could they really sing?

None passed muster. Cilla Black "made a kind of raucous sound", Sandie Shaw got "no marks", Cliff Richards' voice needed "straightening out", Lulu was "pathetic", Tom Jones "misused" his voice and as for the Beatles, well, as singers they "they emit noises on time when they want them. Emit is the word I would use rather than sing." His final verdict was scathing: "From what I heard, none of them would have a hope of making the chorus at Covent Garden, or any other chorus for that matter." (Two weeks after the publication of "Verdict on the Million Pound Voices" in the *Mirror Magazine* Paul McCartney announced he was leaving the band and the world went into mourning that the Beatles were no more. However, it is not thought my feature had anything to do with Macca's decision.)

The second part of the assignment was to play the albums of classical artists - Joan Sutherland, Tito Gobbi, Victoria de Los Angeles and Alfred Deller - to Mickie Most, Britain's most successful independent record producer. Unfortunately (for the piece) he liked them all and declared that they could all make best-selling hit records with the right material. He compared

Tiny Tim with the countertenor Alfred Deller and suggested that Deller could have had similar success with *Tiptoe Through The Tulips,* Tiny Tim's biggest hit. It is not known what Mr Deller, one of the most influential figures in the renaissance of early music and the founder of the Stour Music Festival, thought of this suggestion. Certainly a cover version of *Tiptoe Through The Tulips* never emerged.

Weekly editorial conferences at the Mirror Magazine usually ended in the White Hart, the pub across the road from the office, which Cassandra, (William Connor, the *Daily Mirror*'s acclaimed columnist) had re-christened "The Stab In The Back" and thus was always known as "The Stab". It was in "The Stab" one night that conversation turned to how difficult it was for ordinary people to get access to the country's movers and shakers. Journalists often could; ordinary Joes mainly could not.

Next morning Bill Hagerty, the features editor of the *Mirror Magazine,* buttonholed me and said he had a job for me. I was to pose as a member of the public and see how far I could get making contact with the country's "top drawer". He gave me a daunting list of potential candidates: a Minister of the Crown, the Lord Mayor of London, a member of the Royal Family, a leading actor or actress and a captain of industry.

This was not, in truth, journalism and was more suited to a television stunt (*Candid Camera* had been on British television screens for some years) but I had only been freelancing for about 18 months and I was still nervous about my ability to make a living. I was not going to turn down any assignment, even if it meant making a fool of myself which, unsurprisingly in this case, it did.

The fundamental flaw with the idea was that if I could not reveal myself to be a journalist I had to manufacture a pressing reason to try and see all these individuals without looking like a complete nutcase. It was not easy.

Richard Marsh, the Minister for Transport in the Wilson government, had always seemed to me to be an amiable cove; I had warmed to him when he publicly admitted that trying to teach his wife to drive had been such a "traumatic experience" that he had given up. He was my first target. I decided that if I could get to him I would complain about stringent new parking regulations which had been introduced in Bayswater, where I lived. It was pretty pathetic, but it was all I could come up with.

I realised that if I telephoned to try and make an appointment I would certainly be fobbed off, so I decided on a direct approach. First I needed to look respectable. My habitual working gear of jeans, T-shirt and a zip jacket was not going to impress and I badly needed a haircut. I have always believed that apparent confidence and an air of authority works wonders, particularly with bureaucracy, so when I turned up at the Houses of Parliament wearing a suit, a collar and tie, polished shoes, hair recently cut and carrying a briefcase, I bid the police officer at the gate a cheery "Good morning" and he waved me straight through. (This was two years before the first IRA bomb attack on London and, of course, long before the spectre of Islamic terrorism had materialised.)

I made for the only door I could see, as if I knew where I was going, and discovered a porter on duty just inside. He was more than happy to give me directions to the Minister of Transport's office, but I quickly became lost in a maze of corridors. I was debating whether I should return to the porter's lodge when a door further down the corridor opened and who should emerge but the Minister of Transport himself, carrying a sheaf of papers? As he hurried in my direction I said "Mr Marsh…"

"Sorry old chap," he interrupted. "Can't stop. Late for a meeting. Talk to my secretary." And with that he was gone.

It was, I suppose, a result of a kind inasmuch as I had actually got face-to-face with my target, but that was all.

I had less success at the Mansion House, the Palladian pile in the City of London which is the official residence of the Lord Mayor, then Sir Ian Bowater. With its six huge Corinthian columns the building is imposing rather than handsome. The architectural historian Sir John Summerson tartly pointed out that it was "a striking reminder that good taste was not a universal attribute in the eighteenth century". The Mansion House is not open to the public, but there is nothing to stop a member of the public entering the building through the front door, which is what I did, on the pretence that I wanted to deliver a petition to the Lord Mayor - personally

I was immediately confronted by a large, imperious, uniformed commissionaire who demanded, in a very loud voice, to know my business. His look of incredulity when I explained had to be seen to be believed. "Without an appointment?" he boomed. "You want to deliver a petition to Sir Ian *without an appointment*?"

I nodded. "I could wait," I offered helpfully.

He shook his head. "I am afraid you'll have to leave, sir…" - I got the impression that the "sir" was added with the greatest of reluctance, or perhaps a touch or sarcasm - "… all I can suggest is that you write in for an appointment, but you certainly can't wait here."

With that, he gently took hold of my elbow, turned me round and escorted me from the building.

The following night I could be found lurking outside the stage door of the Drury Lane Theatre, where Ginger Rogers was appearing in a successful production of the musical, *Mame*. Her star might have glowed less brightly from the days when she was dancing with Fred Astaire in the classic RKO musicals of the 30s, but she was still a star.

Thus it was that I was carrying a bunch of two dozen red roses which I was hoping to present to her as she left the theatre. I had already been warned by the stage doorkeeper that I would not be able to deliver them to Miss Rogers' dressing room and that she did not welcome visitors, either before the show or after the show, or between shows.

Half an hour after the audience had departed, a large black limousine drew up outside the stage door. Two minutes later, Ginger Rogers appeared, completely ignored my proffered bouquet, got into the back of the limousine and was driven away. We had not exchanged a word, or even a glance. She had treated me as if I was invisible and she did the same thing the following night. By then I was ready to throw the bouquet at her, but I resisted the temptation.

Making contact with a member of the Royal Family proved surprisingly easy. Princess Alexandra's husband, Angus Ogilvy, was in the telephone book. (Ah, those were gentle, innocent days; telephone books could supply a fund of information to diligent reporters.) When I called the number to ask if the Princess would be willing to open a fete, I was politely referred to her Household Office in Kensington Palace.

The policeman on duty at Kensington Palace directed me to a black-painted door in a huge brick wall with a sign that said "Household of HRH Princess Alexandra". I knocked. Nothing happened. I knocked again. Still nothing. I tried the handle. The door opened into a stone-flagged courtyard and another door with two bells - one for HRH The Duke of Kent and the other for HRH Princess Alexandra.

A pretty girl opened the door. After I had stated my case she said, as if she was really sorry about it, that Her Royal Highness did not normally open fetes or bazaars. The only thing I could do was to write to her Lady in Waiting, but she did not hold out much hope.

Perhaps, I said, if I could just get to see Her Royal Highness I might be able to persuade her? No, she replied, that was quite impossible.

My final port of call was the huge headquarters of the Ford Motor Company at Warley in Essex where I intended to complain to the chairman, Sir Leonard Crossland, about the reliability of my Ford Cortina. A beautiful but brittle receptionist arched her plucked eyebrows when I asked to see Sir Leonard. They rose even higher when I admitted I did not have an appointment.

"May I ask," she inquired, "what it is in connection with?"

"Yes, my car."

She swallowed visibly. "You want to see the chairman about your car?"

"Yes. It keeps breaking down."

"I don't honestly think Sir Leonard will be able to help you. You need a garage."

I was having some difficulty keeping a straight face, but I pressed on. "Yes, but if the chairman of the Ford Motor Company can't arrange for one of his cars to be mended, who can?"

"Just one moment please." She obviously thought, perhaps not unreasonably, that I was completely deranged. She picked up a telephone and whispered urgently into it, all the time eyeing me suspiciously.

Moments later, two uniformed security men appeared and I was being unceremoniously bundled out of the building.

It cannot be said that my feature, published under the headline "Somebody Up There Doesn't Want To See Me", broke any ground journalistically or did anything other than prove what everyone already knew, but it might have raised a few smiles.

My last assignment was to travel with two other writers and two photographers to Benidorm and then to Margate to put together two contrasting profiles of a British seaside resort and a Spanish one. It was while we were in Margate that we got a telephone call from Mike Molloy telling us to pack it in and return to London. The *Mirror Magazine* had folded.

I am certain there was some kind of party, but I can remember nothing of it, so I assume it was a good one. Jeff Bernard had the last word. He left a note on his typewriter: GRAVY TRAIN DERAILED. MANY HURT."

A week later I was called into the Mirror building to be interviewed by some grey-suited apparatchik who told me that unfortunately they were not able to offer me a job. I said that was fine by me because I did not want a job and had not even considered the possibility. I had actually forgotten that I had signed some kind of contract with the magazine and so when announced that the final figure would work out to eighteen seventy-six, I had no idea what he was talking about. He had to explain to me that it was my pay-off - £1,876, representing 40% of my total earnings from the magazine. I was walking on air when I left the building; not only was it completely unexpected, but it was more money than I had ever earned, in one lump sum, in my life to that date.

CHAPTER 7: COLDITZ CAPERS

Even in the golden light of a late autumn afternoon, Colditz Castle was not a pretty place. Perched atop a rocky promontory on a bend of the Mulde river, a tributary of the Elbe, it glowered bleakly over the small town of Colditz and the silver snake of water threading through featureless farmland of ploughed fields and sparse trees stripped of their leaves. Fifty kilometres east of Leipzig, in 1972 it was far behind the Iron Curtain which still divided Europe.

The castle has a melancholy history. During the Middle Ages it was used as a lookout post for the German Emperors. In 1504 it was accidentally burned down, then reconstructed in the Renaissance style as a hunting lodge for King Augustus the Strong of Poland. During the 19th century its condition was allowed to deteriorate and it was used as a workhouse for the poor and the sick, then as a mental institution. Between 1914 and 1918 no less than 912 patients died from malnutrition in Colditz. When the Nazis came to power in 1933 the castle was converted into a political prison for Communists, homosexuals, Jews and other so-called "undesirables" and on the outbreak of World War Two it became *Oflag IV-C*, a prisoner-of-war camp for officers deemed to be a high escape risk or particularly dangerous.

I am standing at the gates of Colditz Castle with four former inmates, who are returning to the place of their incarceration for the first time since the war. They are:

Captain Pat Reid, who successfully escaped from the castle in 1942 and subsequently wrote a best-selling book, *The Colditz Story*, that would be turned into a classic film with Sir John Mills playing Reid.

Dick Howe, who was escape officer at Colditz from 1942 to 1945 and organised many escapes, including eight successful "home runs".

Sir Rupert Barry, who proudly claimed to be the most frequent occupant of the castle's solitary confinement cells.

Jack Best, who was a prominent "ghost" - one of the PoWs who hid within the prison leading the Germans to believe they had escaped but in reality leaving them time to continue their tunnelling activities.

I am on assignment for the *Radio Times*, a magazine that has fortuitously plugged the breech left in my workload by the demise of the *Mirror Magazine*. Geoffrey Cannon, the new editor of the *Radio Times*, had somehow persuaded the BBC not only to increase the magazine's budget but to accept that it needed to be a first-rate publication in its own right, rather than just a somewhat staid programme guide. So it was that when the BBC was about to broadcast a television series that focussed on life at Colditz, featuring David McCallum, Edward Hardwicke and Robert Wagner, Cannon decided to find former inmates, take them back to the castle and record their reaction and memories for a feature in the *Radio Times*.

* * * *

The assignment was not without its logistical difficulties. It took a researcher five weeks of patient negotiation to get visas for us all to cross into the German Democratic Republic (GDR), then a Communist state which did not welcome visitors and whose isolation was symbolised by the hated Berlin Wall, which had been erected ten years earlier to prevent its citizens escaping to the West.

Foreigners were only allowed to cross the Wall at Checkpoint Charlie, in the American sector of West Berlin. Our group - the four ex-PoWs, Sarah Rock, the *Radio Times* researcher, photographer Alan Ballard and me - was waved past the Allied guard house, a little wooden hut behind a sandbag barrier. (The Allies did not want to install a more permanent structure as they refused to accept that the Wall represented an international border.)

Once we were past the famous sign warning, in four languages, that we were leaving the American sector, we were treated to the full Cold War experience: the menacing, shadowy figures in a watchtower, the unsmiling, suspicious soldiers in Soviet uniforms, the barbed wire, the concrete blocks preventing any vehicle from trying to charge through the checkpoint, the "death strip" behind the Wall - a mined area of raked sand and gravel offering clear fields of fire for the border guards.

A soldier relieved us of our passports and disappeared into a squat, single storey building. We waited. Ten minutes passed, then fifteen. We began to worry that something was wrong with our papers. Thirty minutes later, a young man in a cheap suit emerged carrying our passports. He smiled, introduced himself as our guide, said everything was in order and we could proceed. (It was a condition of granting our visas that we employ a "guide". In reality, he was a government informer who would report back on everything we said and did.)

It was a three hour drive to Colditz and we set off in two cars through the grey and cheerless streets of East Berlin and then out into the equally grey and cheerless countryside. Our visit to the castle was scheduled for the following day, so we stayed the night in a grim *Gasthaus* where the only choice on the menu for dinner was tinned meat and boiled potatoes.

Nevertheless, spirits were high, buoyed by our four elderly companions, whose excitement about re-visiting their former prison was palpable. Dick Howe told me that he was one of the very few prisoners who knew the exact location of a clandestine radio that was hidden in the roof; he thought there was a very good chance that it might still be there. The radio was just about the most important single piece of equipment in the castle, he said. Being able to tune in to the BBC enabled prisoners to keep in touch with the progress of the war and was a tremendous morale booster. While we were talking in the bar, I looked into the darkened dining room and saw rats scurrying about between the tables.

Colditz Castle had reverted to its previous role as a mental institution and as we approached the gates next morning, over a cobbled bridge which once spanned a moat, we could see pale faces at the windows staring out at us through rusting iron bars, many grinning vacantly. The stucco rendering on the towering walls had flaked away in great patches and the slate roof sagged under the weight of neglect. Pigeons were nesting in the clock tower.

All four returnees expressed shock at the extent to which the castle had deteriorated since they were in residence, although in truth they probably bore some responsibility. The PoWs tunnelled and burrowed and cut through so many rafters and joists and beams in their efforts to escape that the place became a warren of holes and secrets passages and tunnels and needed extensive reconstruction after the war. (One of their fellow prisoners, a captain in the Irish Guards called Harry

Elliott, spent much of his time cultivating wet-rot spores and implanting them in the timbers of the castle.)

We were met by the director, who was surprisingly friendly (he was the first East German we had met who did not view us with suspicion or overt hostility.) He explained that most of the wards were locked and as many of the patients were dangerous we would not be given access. We were, however, welcome to look around the rest of the castle.

In the courtyard, where the prisoners were exercised, the memories came flooding back. Sir Rupert Barry immediately identified the windows of the punishment cells. "They were quite nice actually," he said. "It was the only chance you got to get a room on your own."

Pat Reid found the grill in the base of the castle wall through which he had escaped disguised as a Flemish workman. On this return visit he discovered, much to his amusement, that alongside where he had lowered himself down a sheer rock face with a home-made rope there was a flight of steps, which would have made his getaway considerably less perilous. Reid made a "home run" and got to Switzerland, where he spent the remainder of the war as military attaché, working for the Secret Intelligence Service (MI6).

Jack Best, a former RAF pilot, was one of the architects of the most audacious of all the Colditz escape plans - to build a two-man glider with a 32-foot wing span and launch it from the castle roof by catapult. The castle was liberated before the attempt could be made, but Jack made it clear to me that ever after he was frustrated by suggestions that it was no more than a stunt, and never a serious escape idea. "Up there," he said, pointing to the roof of the chapel, "was where we would have taken off. The catapult would have been activated by dropping a bathtub filled with concrete from the top floor." He laughed.

"I always felt it was a shame we were liberated before we had the chance to give it a go." (He would be exonerated many years later when Channel 4 Television built an exact replica according to the Colditz plans for a documentary film and proved, without doubt, that it was airworthy and could have carried two men for at least a mile at 100 feet over the river and the town of Colditz.)

Dick Howe was anxious to see if the radio shack still existed. He led the way up a stone spiral staircase to an attic thick with dust, festooned with cobwebs and lit only by two small windows in each of the gable ends. He paced up and down in the half-light, looking for a particular floorboard. When he found it, he pressed down with his foot on one end and, lo and behold, the other end popped up. I helped him lift it out of the way and we shone a torch into the cavity under the floor. There, in the gloom, forgotten and untouched for 27 years, was a time capsule: the radio shack.

When he was a prisoner Dick weighed only nine stone and so squeezing through the gap in the floorboards was no problem. But by the time of our visit he was perhaps twice that weight and there was no question of him getting down there.

I was in my early 30s and I found I could just about wriggle through, feet first. A torch was passed down to me and when I switched it on it revealed an extraordinary sight: apart from a choking layer of thick dust over everything, it was exactly as it was when Colditz was liberated by US troops on 15 April, 1945.

The shack was tucked into the lower eaves of the castle roof. It was furnished with a makeshift bench and two stools and lined with grey blankets to prevent light shining through the roof tiles at night and giving away its location. In front of the bench was a wooden panel fitted with three light bulbs. These were controlled by three "stooges" in various parts of the castle with their fingers on buttons that kept the bulbs alight while it was safe. If any bulb went out, the radio operator shut everything down and got out.

"Don't step in between the stools," Dick Howe shouted from above."There is an escape hatch there - if you tread on it you'll go straight through into the room below."

I looked under the bench and saw a rope made from rolled strips of blue and white gingham sheeting, tightly sewn, tied to a beam above the hatch.

On the bench was a tin-lid ashtray overflowing with cigarette butts, the case of the radio on a wooden stand, three pencils and two exercise books filled, in neat handwriting, with news of the war and the latest football results obtained from the BBC. The last entry, dated April 14, 1945, noted that American troops, advancing rapidly from the east, were only 20 miles from the Castle.

(Although the case of the radio was still there, the radio itself, inexplicably, was missing. The components for it had originally been smuggled into the castle in 70 different food parcels.)

On shelves fixed to a wall behind the bench was a veritable treasure trove of escape equipment: stolen hacksaw blades; saws made from chopped razors capable of cutting through iron bars; a forged master key which could open most of the doors in the castle; makeshift tools of all kinds; plaster and soap moulds for making German badges; imitation bayonets carved from two wooden floorboards glued together.

There were rolls of fuse wire, tins of nuts and bolts, packets of razor blades, electric components of all kinds, a civilian raincoat "liberated" from some unsuspecting visitor and a bundle of forged German leave permits. In a yellowing packet of cigarettes I found an emergency escape kit comprising money, a compass and a map. It was all testimony to the ingenuity of the Colditz prisoners and their determination to escape.

While I was rooting around under the floor, there was a brief discussion in the attic about the next step. All four were adamant that the contents of the radio shack should return to the UK with them and be deposited in a museum. It was very unlikely, they argued, that anyone would ever find it again and it would be pointless just leaving everything in the roof to rot.

Alan, the photographer, was on the plump side and so he passed his camera down to me to take pictures showing exactly what we had found and how we had found it and I was then instructed to start handing everything up through the gap in the floorboards. By the time I emerged, the shack had been completely stripped, I was covered from head to foot in dust and there was a considerable pile of booty on the attic floor, which we would eventually distribute among our various suitcases to bring home.

That night, as I was preparing for bed, there was a soft knock on the door of my room in the *Gasthaus*. When I opened it I found our "guide" standing in the corridor outside. He put a finger to his lips and indicated he wanted to come in. I stepped aside. He closed the door quietly behind him, went to the bedside radio and turned it on, at the same time pointing to the walls and flicking his ear. The implication was obvious - the room was bugged. He then began whispering urgently to me in fractured English. At first I could not understand what he was saying but then I got the message - he wanted me to help him escape from East Germany into the West. There was no way I could help him and I told him so.

I was mainly concerned that it could have been a clumsy attempt at entrapment - a journalist implicated in helping a GDR citizen to escape would be in serious trouble and usefully in thrall to the regime. Oddly enough, exactly the same thing happened a year later when I was in Moscow to interview Oleg Popov, the famous clown of the Moscow State Circus (again for the *Radio Times*.) This time it was the State-assigned "interpreter" who wanted my help to get out of Russia. By then I had learned that attempts to entrap journalists were routine behind the Iron Curtain and so I showed him the door as soon as he started his spiel.

Our trip to Colditz had one last moment of drama to be played out as we were leaving East Germany through Checkpoint Charlie. Guards insisted on opening all our suitcases and discovered, to their mystification, that we were all carrying what looked to them like old rags and bits and pieces of junk, which they picked up and examined closely with perhaps understandable suspicion. We had agreed that honesty was the only way to explain what we had with us - that our four elderly travelling companions were former PoWs who wanted to take home "souvenirs" from their visit.

This did not satisfy the guards. An officer was called to inspect what they had found and he, too, was bemused. When they began gathering everything together it began to look as if they were going to confiscate everything. Sir Rupert Barry, the 4th Baronet, drew on his aristocratic pedigree and stepped forward, purple-faced and quivering with indignation. "I should warn you that Her Majesty's Government will not only consider these items to be historic artefacts," he announced, "but the property of Her Majesty's Government. There will be serious diplomatic consequences if we are not allowed to proceed."

The officer, who could clearly understand English, laughed unexpectedly. "Historic artefacts?" he sneered. "No, *Müll*, nothing but *Müll*. Take them."

"What's *Müll*?" I asked Sir Rupert as we were hastily re-packing our cases.

"Junk," he whispered. "Let's get out of here."

Everything we had brought back was put on display in the "Radio Times Colditz Escape Exhibition" at the Imperial War Museum in London which ran from January to September 1974 and proved so popular that the IWM was the only London museum to increase its attendance figures after the government had introduced entry charges at the beginning of that year.

* * * * *

Not long after my return from East Germany, the *Radio Times* handed me two plum (i.e. easy) jobs in the United States - spending a week travelling with André Previn and the London Symphony Orchestra on their US tour and then flying down to Florida to interview the volatile Romanian tennis super star, Ilie Năstase. The photographer was to be my Colditz friend, Alan Ballard.

We were due to pick up the LSO tour in Peoria, a city in Illinois with notably few claims to fame. These days (I am writing this in 2018) it seems to me that most transatlantic flights are full but in the early 70's there was not nearly as much traffic across the Atlantic. We flew to Peoria via Chicago in one of the new Boeing "jumbo jets" that had recently been introduced into service by BOAC and there were so few passengers on board that the flight attendants joined Alan and me with a bottle of champagne for a little party. When we had drunk that another was produced... It was hardly surprising we were pretty bladdered by the time we landed - not a bad condition to be in to arrive in a place like Peoria, which was best known for manufacturing earth-moving equipment and the production of maize and soybeans. Groucho Marx had a catch phrase, "Will it play in Peoria?", to check what appealed to mainstream America.

We had fortunately sobered up by the time we were introduced to André Previn the following morning. He was very welcoming, friendly and straightforward and conspicuously free from airs and graces. At the time he was married to Mia Farrow. (Their adopted Korean daughter, Soon-Yi Previn, would later be at the centre of a major scandal when it was revealed that she had entered into a relationship with Woody Allen, who was then living with Mia Farrow and was nominally her stepfather.)

The orchestra - flippantly known among the players as "Andy Previn's Band" - travelled from venue to venue by bus and played to largely packed concert halls. I was never able to anticipate the mood of the musicians when they left the stage at the end of a concert. If it had gone well, they would all be on a high, excited, ready to party into the small hours. If it had not gone well they would be depressed and moody and snap at each other. My difficulty was that as I had so little knowledge of classical music I could not tell whether the concert was going well or badly - it all sounded the same to me. (I did not admit this to Previn.)

After leaving the LSO in Chicago, we discovered when we checked in for our flight to Fort Lauderdale in Florida that we were booked in first class. That was the first surprise. The second was that The Breakers hotel in West Palm Beach, where Nastase was due to play in the Palm Beach Masters tennis tournament and where we would be staying, was one of the most expensive and exclusive hotels in the United States, built in the style of the Italian Renaissance and a place so posh that a jacket and tie were required *even for breakfast*. The third was a message waiting for us at the front desk saying that Nastase had been delayed and would not be arriving at The Breakers for another week.

Alan and I managed to solve the hotel's dress code by cutting my single tie in half and using safety pins to attach each half to our respective shirts, but we were really not enamoured by the stultifying formality of the hotel and called the *Radio Times* office in London to tell them we were going to find a cheaper, more relaxed, hotel somewhere nearby. The panicky response was to tell us that under no circumstances were we to check out of The Breakers; it was some BBC bureaucratic nonsense to do with our bill being met by a different budget. No matter what it costs, we were told, we were to stay put.

We took this as an invitation not to hold back. Sunbathing by the pool, sipping a Bloody Mary and trying to choose between a lobster or a filet steak for lunch without a worry in the world about the cost, it was hard not to reflect that life as a freelance journalist could, at times, be both weird and wonderful.

I had been warned that Nastase was difficult to interview - that he could be rude surly and short-tempered and that his nickname on the tennis circuit was "Nasty". None of these problems materialised - he was patient and charming and open and cheerfully admitted that his notorious temper tantrums on court were more to do with psyching out his opponent than genuine loss of control. I asked him if his ambition was to end his career winning Wimbledon and he grinned mischievously and shook his head. "No," he said, "I'd like to end my career smashing my racket over a linesman's head after a bad call."

Not long after my free week's holiday at The Breakers I found myself in Italy, a passenger in a Ferrari Dino 246 GTS being driven at ferocious speed along a highway on the outskirts of Modena by Clay Regazzoni, who was then leading the Formula One Drivers' Championship. I had spent the day at the Ferrari test track outside Modena to report on the rivalry between Ferrari's two team drivers - Regazzoni and Niki

Lauda. They were both brilliant drivers, but very different characters. Regazzoni was a handsome, laid back Swiss-Italian with a cad's moustache and a lust for life. Lauda was a humourless, uptight Austrian, obsessed with motor racing and winning. He made no secret of his frustration when Regazzoni set the fastest lap time on that day at the test track and insisted on taking a car out late in the afternoon to try and beat it.

He was still tearing round and round when Regazzoni shrugged, laughed at the absurdity of it, announced to the Ferrari mechanics that he was leaving and asked if I wanted a lift back to my hotel. There was little point in my staying any longer, so I accepted.

Both drivers had been supplied by Ferrari with the latest production model - the Dino 246 GTS was named after Enzo Ferrari's only son, Dino, who died of muscular dystrophy in 1956. I had no sooner clambered into the bright red two-seater than we were off with a squeal of tyres. I don't know if Regazzoni was in a tremendous hurry for some reason, or whether he was driving like a madman for my benefit, or whether it was the way he always drove on public roads, but it was certainly hair-raising. He was weaving in and out of the traffic with only one hand on the steering wheel, talking all the time and gesticulating with his spare hand.

I must admit that I was secretly relieved when flashing blue lights of the *polizia* appeared behind us and Regazzoni was obliged to pull over. Two policemen slowly stepped out of their squad car and approached the Ferrari. I could have sworn they were twirling their batons, although I might have imagined it. Regazzoni wound down his window and as the first policeman leaned over he instantly recognised the driver and his frown turned into a delighted smile.

"*Clay!*" he breathed, momentarily awestruck, and then, straightening up, he turned to his partner and whispered "*O mio Dio! È Clay Regazzoni!*" [Oh my God! It's Clay Reggazzoni!]

His partner leaned down to look in the car and confirmed that the driver was, indeed, one of the world's most famous racing drivers. The first thing he said was "*Posso avere il suo autografo?*" [Can I have your autograph?]

After Regazzoni had chatted for a while and signed autographs for the pair of them, they waved goodbye as we resumed our journey - at the same breakneck speed, with Regazzoni laughing his head off.

* * * * *

A trip to Moscow around this time resulted in my being declared *persona non grata* in the Soviet Union and which, years later, would cause me so many problems in Murmansk.

I was sent to Moscow with photographer Tony Evans to interview the famous Russian clown, Oleg Popov, for a feature in the *Radio Times*. Moscow before *glasnost* was surely one of the most depressing cities in the world, particularly in winter. We were booked into rooms on the thirteenth floor of the pre-Revolutionary Metropol hotel, a magnificent building with pink marble pillars and a huge domed roof of stained glass, which would have been wonderful except virtually nothing worked. You had to wait anything up to 20 minutes for an elevator and when you finally arrived at your floor you had to pass the scrutiny of a scowling old *babushka* who kept all the room keys and only handed them over with the greatest reluctance.

For some reason Tony had brought with him a Scrabble set and I was very glad he had because the service in the hotel restaurant was so slow that we would pass the time waiting for each course by playing several games. The food was awful and there was no fresh produce of any kind. One day a VIP party was dining in the restaurant and left behind a single tomato in a dish on their table. Both Tony and I made a grab for it: he got there first but generously shared half with me.

Fresh vegetables were virtually non-existent across the city. If you came across a queue stretching round an entire block you could be certain it would probably lead to a battered truck from which cabbages or carrots or some such were being sold on the black market.

Bureaucratic red tape was beyond belief. Without the right rubber stamps on the right piece of paper nothing happened. Even making a purchase in a shop was complicated. Once you had decided what you wanted to buy, you had to pay at a separate desk, then return to the counter with the receipt, then queue at a packing bench to collect your purchase.

As far as I could see, there was precious little evidence of what was supposed to be the Russians' natural gaiety: in fact the people looked pretty miserable most of the time. On the streets and in the shops I was struck by the uniformity of their sour demeanour. Even the students who gathered in a small park under the walls of the Kremlin at weekends were subdued both in their appearance and behaviour.

During the trip I stupidly got involved in a fractious argument with Rudi, our "guide", a young man from *Novosti*, the official agency which spied on visiting foreign journalists in the guise of providing them with facilities. Over lunch one day at the Metropol I mentioned my admiration for Alexander Solzhenitsyn, who had recently (1970) been awarded the Nobel Prize for literature. I viewed him as a hero for exposing the iniquities of Communism in his books; Rudi thought he was a traitor. "I think he was a man who only saw what he wanted to see," he said, glowering at me across the table. "Solzhenitsyn is not interesting. Why should I be interested in him?"

Rudi obviously faithfully reported our conversation to his masters. The next time I needed a visa to visit Russia it was refused, without explanation.

Postscript: my involvement with the Radio Times had a rather dramatic effect on my personal life. It was at the magazine that I met, and fell in love with, a beautiful young researcher by the name of Renate Kohler. We began an affair which resulted in both our marriages breaking up. Renate and I have now been happily married for more than 40 years.

CHAPTER 8: REPORTING THE TROUBLES

"The Toubles" began in August, 1969, when, after generations of sectarian conflict, a virtual civil war broke out and armed paramilitary groups representing either the Catholic minority or the Protestant majority began fighting. Hundreds of troops were poured in to try and keep the peace and stop the paramilitaries trying to kill each other. Republicans viewed the British Army as occupying combatants and thus a legitimate target. The violence continued for nearly three decades until the Good Friday agreement in 1998. More than 3,500 people were killed and 50,000 wounded. I made several trips to Northern Ireland in the early days of The Troubles.

The colonel is very solicitous about my safety and well-being. I am on a night patrol in November, 1972, with soldiers of the 3rd Battalion, The Parachute Regiment, through the bleak streets of the Ardoyne, a particularly troublesome Republican ghetto in Belfast. It is being led by the commanding officer and it is bitterly cold, but that is the least of my worries. We have reached one of many road junctions where the IRA have painted brick walls white so that snipers, usually stationed in an upstairs window, can get a better shot at the soldiers as they run across. There are an average of 30 shootings every night in the Ardoyne.

"OK Miller," the colonel whispers. "As we cross here, get between me and the wall. Use me as a shield." This is all very noble, except the colonel is not much more than 5 feet 6 inches tall and is as thin as a rake. I am six foot and 13 stone.

"Right," he says. "Let's go." We run hell for leather across the white wall and safely reach cover on the other side. My heart is thumping and I am gasping for breath.

I can see, even in the darkness, that the colonel is grinning. I get a strong feeling that he is enjoying himself. I am not.

In truth I was slightly wary of the good colonel from the start. When I arrived at 3 Para headquarters - a sandbagged factory in the centre of Belfast abandoned by its owner after too many bombings - to join the patrol he quickly discovered I had completed National Service in the Army. "Jolly good," he said. "Excellent. Do you want to carry a musket?"

A musket? No, I absolutely did not want to carry a musket, or any other weapon for that matter. A civilian with a gun accompanying a military patrol in the dark labyrinth of Ulster risked being marked out as either a member of the special forces or, even worse, an informer, and would thus be a prime target. What I really wanted to carry was a big placard that said "PRESS. DON'T SHOOT!"

I certainly did not get the impression that the colonel was joking. If he was serious it was not just surprising, it was highly irresponsible. If I had have been shot, he would have had a pretty hard time trying to explain why I had been carrying a weapon.

It was decided (not by me) that I should wear a beret and a flak jacket under a camouflage smock in the vague hope that I would meld unobtrusively with the soldiers, my long hair and flared trousers notwithstanding, and be viewed as some military lackey not worth shooting.

I was briefed by the Regimental Sergeant Major, who winced visibly at my appearance and the hair hanging out from under my beret. The RSM was a fine figure of a man with a bristling moustache, short cropped hair, penetrating grey eyes and a parade-ground voice. "Right, if I can explain the routine," he began. "When we move off, you will stay about a yard behind the CO. This man here…" he indicated a soldier, who smiled sheepishly, "…will cover you. He'll be on the opposite side of the road to you. If the shooting starts, don't try to cross the road, just take cover and wait." He pointed to two other soldiers waiting to set off on the patrol. "These two men here have to make sure no one shoots the CO, because he's important. My job…" he smiled thinly "…is to shoot any buggers that try and shoot us. Got it?"

Until the arrival of 3 Para, the Ardoyne had been virtually a "no go" area for the military. Among the grimmest and most obdurate of all the Republican strongholds, it was a warren of tightly packed streets and back alleys offering innumerable escape routes for gunmen. Army patrols were subjected to a constant barrage of hatred and abuse - gangs of teenage hoodlums pelted them with stones, housewives spat at them and cursed them, snipers shot at them from concealed positions. When 3 Para took over they began intensive foot patrolling through the area and kept at it despite the vituperation and numerous casualties. Within two months they had achieved a kind of uneasy peace after arresting a total of 323 people - almost a quarter of them active members of the IRA.

Setting an example, the CO and the RSM lead at least one foot patrol through the Ardoyne every night. The men call it "Sunray's walkabout", Sunray being the wireless code name for a commanding officer. It is "Sunray's walkabout" that I have been invited to join to get a taste of what soldiers in the war zone of Northern Ireland are obliged to endure.

Minutes into the patrol, my presence immediately attracts the unwelcome attention of the children and teenagers who seem to hang around the streets until close on midnight. They point and catcall and jeer and throw stones and race along back alleys in order to obtain vantage points for ridicule further along the way.

None of this worries the soldiers: they quickly become inured to verbal abuse and provocation. Weapons always at the ready, they dash from doorway to doorway, crouch behind cover whenever they can. They call it "hard target positions". A corner is never turned without first peering round the brickwork through the magnifying sights of a rifle, a gap in the houses is never crossed except at speed and covered by another member of the patrol; rifles are never lowered.

Every man is alert for any unusual movement. An upstairs window slightly raised could indicate the presence of a sniper. Sometimes the residents of an entire terrace will raise all their upstairs windows a fraction to spook an approaching patrol - a sniper could be behind any one, or none. It could be a game, except it can end with a soldier bleeding to death on the pavement.

Shadowing Sunray closely, I am amazed at his sangfroid. He offers a cheery "Good Evening" to everyone we pass, usually receiving nothing more than a sullen stare by way of reply, as if he is out for an after-dinner stroll. His equanimity is not even dented when a toddler no more than three years old picks up a stone and hurls it in our direction. "Oh, *that*'s not very nice," he says.

My suspicion that he is enjoying himself is confirmed when we return, safely, to headquarters. He divests himself of all his equipment and turns to me with a broad grin. "Well," he says. "Have fun?"

* * * * *

I was at last, at long last, on assignment for the *Sunday Times Magazine.* After knocking at the door for three years, it rankled then and it rankled for years afterwards that I only managed to get an entrée after meeting Robert Lacey, one of the editors, at a party. The assignment in Northern Ireland was a major project planned as a cover feature. Four pages were going to be devoted to thumbnail photos of all the soldiers who had so far lost their lives and I was to be accompanied by a gifted, and much more experienced, writer by the name of Roy Perrott. Roy was to report on the experience of young soldiers arriving in the tormented province for a first tour of duty; I was to report on the tactics of the IRA and how the Army was learning to respond. When I was informed I would be working with Roy I suspected his presence was an insurance in case, as a relatively new contributor, I made a cock-up, although I said nothing.

For some reason we travelled separately to Belfast and when I checked in at the Europa Hotel I found he had left me a note saying he had gone to bed and I was to give him a call at eight o'clock the following morning.

The international press corps covering "The Troubles" - dozens of reporters, photographers and camera crews from around the world - always used the five-star Europa Hotel, in the centre of the city, as a base. Despite the deteriorating security situation and the 15-foot high wire fence surrounding the car park and the fact that the majority of the clientele was irredeemably scruffy, the Europa strove to maintain the aura of a posh hotel. There were bellboys in the lobby, a concierge desk and smiling receptionists in smart suits. In the dining room on the first floor, tables were arranged around a small dance floor and every night a pianist in a dinner jacket sat at a white grand tinkling out selections from popular musicals, usually to the background accompaniment of flashes and bangs, clearly visible through the floor to ceiling plate glass windows, of bombs being set off all over the city and lighting up the night sky. It was surreal, like a scene from an avant-garde movie. (In all the times I stayed at the Europa I never once saw anyone dancing on the dance floor.)

When I knocked on Roy's door next day I was disconcerted, to say the least, to discover that he seemed to be drunk. He smelled strongly of alcohol and the contents of the mini-bar, a lot of little empty bottles, were spread over the top of a desk in his room. I was even more concerned when he announced that he could not see much point going out onto the streets; he reckoned he could get what he wanted on the telephone from his hotel room. I should get on with whatever it was I had to do (he seemed rather hazy about how we were to divide the assignment) and he'd see what he could get "on the blower". Very much the junior in our partnership, I said nothing, but I suspected the reality was that he had simply lost his nerve.

Northern Ireland was not inherently dangerous for reporters inasmuch as we were not deliberately targeted by either side, but it was, in effect, a war zone and there was always the possibility of getting hit by a stray bullet, or of wandering into the path of a bomb, or getting beaten up by the hoodlums who controlled the inner city streets and were not fond of the media.

I spent most of the day setting up interviews and driving around to get a feel for the place. I got back to the Europa at about seven o'clock and found Roy in the dining room, eating alone at a table on the edge of the dance floor. He was very drunk and having considerable difficulty getting his food - a Dover sole - into his mouth. He smiled woozily with a chunk of fish attached to his cheek and invited me to join him. I had no sooner sat down than he dropped his fork onto the floor. As he leaned over to retrieve it he began to fall forward, grabbed the tablecloth to try and save himself and pulled it off the table whereupon the entire contents - cutlery, glasses, plates, condiments, the remains of a Dover sole and a bottle of wine - scattered across the width of the dance floor.

Without a word, he slowly got to his feet and viewed the chaos he had created with some bemusement. Then, with amazing dignity considering he still had bits of fish around his mouth, he walked out, crunching the crockery underfoot as he went.

Next morning I found a handwritten note pushed under my door to say he had gone to Dublin. There was no explanation. I never saw him again.

* * * * *

Opposite the Europa are three historic pubs - Brennan's Bar, The Crown Liquor Saloon and Robinson's Bar - almost side by side and all dating back to the turn of the century with original interiors of gleaming brass and polished mahogany and elaborate ceramic tiles. All three are considered relatively safe and are popular with the press corps.

The Crown Liquor Saloon is crowded with reporters tonight because my friend Simon Hoggart is hosting his leaving party. Simon works for *The Guardian* and has been covering Northern Ireland for two years; he claims he has enjoyed it enormously (but what he really enjoys is getting something in the paper almost every day). He caused a rumpus when he exposed the brutal tactics being employed by the 1st Battalion, The Parachute Regiment, a few days before the same Battalion killed 13 unarmed civilians during a protest march in the Bogside area of Derry on 30 January, 1972, a day which became known as "Bloody Sunday".

As I was working for the magazine of a Sunday newspaper Simon did not consider me a rival and was extremely generous with advice and with his extensive list of contacts. He provided me with a vital telephone number for an insider in the Provisional IRA, then a proscribed terrorist organisation, although I nearly blew it when I first made contact. I had to call a number, leave a message and then wait for someone called Sean to ring me back. The call came at the worst possible moment.

I had been up all night with Simon and a BBC Television crew chasing through the dark streets of Belfast from one bomb explosion to another and I did not fall into my bed at the Europa until well after dawn. I was still asleep at midday when my bedside telephone rang. I picked it up groggily and heard a voice say "Sean." At first I could not think who it was and then, when I remembered, I asked possibly the most stupid question of my career.

"Oh hi Sean. Are you downstairs in the lobby?"

There was a silence at the other end and then the line went dead. I realised immediately what I had done. Obviously no terrorist is going to visit a reporter in a hotel crawling with media.

Ten minutes later Simon called. "You made a big impression with Sean," he said. "He just rang me and wanted to know…" Simon switched to an excellent imitation of an Ulster accent "… this fecking friend of yours, this fecking Russell Miller, or whatever his fecking name is, is he out of his fecking mind?"

* * * * *

I am in the operations room at the battalion headquarters of the Gordon Highlanders. It has taken over a derelict school at

Bessbrook, in the verdant rolling countryside of County Armagh, known to the troops as "cowboy country". When I arrived I saw there was a Provo bullet lodged two inches into the concrete at the side of the door and a warning scrawled in red crayon: "Don't loiter - shot from opposite!"

A bomb has been reported in a house in the village of Cullaville, 15 miles away and a few yards from the border with the Republic. A Gordon Highlanders patrol, accompanied by two members of a bomb disposal squad from the Royal Engineers, is already at the scene, approaching the house with extreme caution. Other soldiers are checking nearby houses.

There is considerable activity - and tension - in the operations room. A radio operator is in contact with the patrol, a medical team has been alerted and the intelligence section is checking through its records to find out what is known about the house and the people who live there. Clerks are standing by ready to deal with the mountain of paperwork that every incident generates.

A helicopter is on its way to search the area from above. In particular the crew will look for any signs of a wire leading from the house, concealed on the ground but visible from the air. (It is a forlorn hope - experienced bombers make a neat incision with a peat cutter, slip the wire in and carefully replace the soil.)

The helicopter will prove, in the event, to be unnecessary. This bomb can be set off with a remote-controlled device and at a vantage point on the other side of the border, safe from arrest, a man is waiting with his finger on the button, closely watching as the troops move in, closer and closer…

One soldier is looking through the window of the house and two others are crouched in the garden when the bomb explodes. The two men in the garden are killed instantly, but the third soldier miraculously survives: a wall crashes over him, but he emerges from the window alive.

The news is received in the operations room stoically. "When the first report comes in that there has been casualties," the Adjutant tells me, "I think the first reaction is a feeling of intense hate for the people responsible, but it doesn't last long."

It is hard not to sympathise with the troops in Northern Ireland. They arrive on four-month rotating tours, work 100-plus hours seven days a week, with seldom more than four hours of uninterrupted sleep. They are allocated two cans of beer a day and rarely venture outside their barracks - a young man with an English accent and a short haircut is unlikely to receive a welcome in any of Belfast's bars or clubs. Local girls are strictly off limits too - this is a place where girls act as decoys, pretend to be pregnant and carry explosive under their dresses or try to sweet talk their way through checkpoints carrying a parcel bomb under the mattress in a baby's pram. On top of everything, they are operating in what is effectively a war zone populated by families who seem, outwardly at least, to be just like their own.

Every soldier carries a yellow card which tells him when he can open fire, but the brief instructions are far from an insurance against civil prosecution. This is how it was explained to me by a senior officer at headquarters: "Before a soldier pulls the trigger he is expected to evaluate in a few seconds the legality of the circumstance in which he finds himself. At this time he may be under fire - not ideal conditions for legal analysis. In effect, he may either have to miss a chance of killing an enemy while he is working out all the pros and cons, or take a risk and shoot. If he shoots and finds he has made a mistake, he is liable to face a murder charge in a civilian court.

"This is one of the reasons there aren't more IRA terrorists killed: soldiers quite naturally don't want to take the risk. Take a classic example. A soldier in an observation post sees a man in the street below with a rifle under his jacket. He checks through his binoculars; yes, it's a rifle. He has no doubt about it, so he fires. The man falls and within seconds the street is full of people screaming that we are 'murdering bastards'. No rifle is found because by the time we get to the body, someone has spirited it away. Next thing the poor bloody soldier knows is that he is defending himself against a charge of murder."

A lance-corporal in the Royal Artillery articulated the dilemma very succinctly: "We wouldn't have no bother here if the Irish were wogs. If they was wogs we could just get stuck in and sort them out and no one would give a fuck. Instead of that, there's all this talk about us murdering them. What are we supposed to do? Stand here and smile while they murder us?"

* * * * *

Rosie is a very pretty and sweetly flirtatious waitress in the dining room at the Europa. I have got to like her a lot. This evening I am eating alone and the dining room is deserted except for two businessmen at a table on the other side of the dance floor. One of them is red-faced, grossly overweight and wearing a tight pinstripe suit. I guess the other, who is obviously subservient, is perhaps his solicitor or accountant.

As Rosie leans forward to put a plate in front of the fat man he whispers something to her. She gasps, bursts into tears and runs back into the kitchen. The fat man laughs. There is a short pause and then the restaurant manager appears, approaches their table and asks, politely, if he had said something to the waitress.

"Well," he booms, "I might have said something to her that I wouldn't say to you." He laughs again.

The restaurant manager does not know what to do. He clearly does not want to risk offending this customer and he retreats. By then I have had enough. I walk across the dance floor to their table. "I don't know what you said to that girl," I say, "but I can guess. The staff can't take you to task, but I can. You are a disgusting individual. The least you can do is apologise."

The fat man's face turns purple with rage. He clambers to his feet, jabs me in the chest and tells me to mind my own business. He was not going to apologise, he says, to some slip of a girl who should have been able to take a joke. His companion speaks up: "This is nothing to do with you. Go away."

I return to my table, happy to have embarrassed the fat man in front of his companion, but he keeps shouting insults at me across the room. By then a reporter and photographer from the *New York Times* have come into the dining room. They ask me what is going on and I explain. "We'll be around if there's trouble in the bar later on," the photographer says.

I am unbothered until the two men get up to leave and I can see from the corner of my eye that the fat man is talking earnestly to the restaurant manager and pointing to where I am sitting. He opens his wallet and passes a couple of banknotes to the manager. I feel a sudden chill. I have no idea who the fat man is, but if he is in contact with the paramilitaries it would be a simple matter to arrange for me to be "taught a lesson" that would almost certainly mean broken bones and the loss of a few teeth, if not worse.

Next morning, my increasing paranoia almost gets the better of me. Even though there is a wire fence barrier around the Europa car park, I always look under my rental car before I unlock it. This morning I can see some kind of package under the engine. I immediately think the fat man is taking his revenge. My heart lurches. I wonder what to do. I bend over to look again and it is gone. It was a screwed-up newspaper and it has been blown away in the wind.

* * * * *

It is July 12, the anniversary of the Battle of the Boyne when, in 1690, the forces of Prince William of Orange defeated those of the deposed King Edward 11 and ultimately ensured the Protestant ascendancy in Ireland. Today members of the Orange Order across Northern Ireland will take part in marches to celebrate the victory and, not coincidentally, rub the noses of their Catholic neighbours in the dirt.

I am covering the Drumcree march, which almost always causes trouble because its route takes it along the Garvaghy Road, a staunchly Republican enclave. It is being led today by the Reverend Ian Paisley, the firebrand leader of the recently formed Democratic Unionist Party and the founder of the Free Presbyterian Church - a man I profoundly despise as an extremist, a bigot and a racist, whose naked hatred for Catholics and Catholicism has done much to kindle the flame of sectarian violence in Northern Ireland.

While waiting for Paisley's arrival, the Orangemen are all kitted out in their absurd marching regalia - bowler hats, white gloves, rolled umbrellas and V-shaped orange "collarettes" over dark suits. The parade will be led by a uniformed flute and drum band, flag bearers and huge embroidered banners depicting William of Orange on a horse. Its pomp and triumphalism is guaranteed to enrage the Catholic community which is, in part, its purpose. The marches also attract posses of Protestant skinheads who tag along in the hope of a free-for-all with their Catholic counterparts somewhere along the way and there are plenty of them here today, despite the presence of hundreds of police and troops who will be deployed on the route to try and prevent violence.

When Paisley turns up he is greeted as a celebrity with much hand-shaking and back-slapping. It is the first time I have seen him in the flesh and I am struck by his curious shape: he is stooped and overweight and his too-big suit hangs off his strangely contorted upper body as if it had been made for someone else. He seems happy to be here and his wide grin exposes his protruding piano-key teeth.

Watching the march set off with flags waving, the band playing and drums beating it is hard not to conclude that its very purpose is to intimidate the Catholic minority with a show of strength and solidarity. As we approach the Garvaghy Road, Catholics are lined up to jeer and catcall, brandish V signs and lob the occasional brick, but the expected serious trouble fails to materialise this year.

At the end of the march, Paisley climbs up on a rostrum to deliver a typically rabble-rousing speech. He has a deep and powerful voice and the passion of an evangelist, which is what he is. He fulminates at length about the wickedness of the Papists and ends by bellowing, in a spray of spittle, the defiant mantra of the Ulster loyalists - "NO SURRENDER... NO SURRENDER... NO SURRENDER..." and the cry is enthusiastically taken up by the crowd.

In private Paisley is alleged to be a man of considerable charm and wit. I will never be able to assess this characterisation as he refuses to be interviewed by Sunday newspapers, believing that the publication of newspapers on a Sunday is a desecration of the Sabbath.

However, there is nothing to stop me attending a service at the Martyrs Memorial Free Presbyterian Church in Belfast, where he preaches every Sunday, which I do. The church, a recently constructed, nondescript redbrick building, is packed with families in their "Sunday best" long before the service is due to begin. Even from the pulpit Paisley does not dilute his fiery oratory and his sermon is full of gibes about "Papists" and the "Antichrist" - his name for the Pope. Every acerbic taunt is greeted with an audible murmur of appreciation from the congregation.

It is said that Ulster Protestants never forgive and never forget; I can believe it.

* * * * *

On the last day of my last job in Northern Ireland I experienced my first serious fright. I was booked on the final flight to London that evening from Aldergrove airport, a 30-minute drive from Belfast city centre. As I was checking out at the Europa, Ryan, the concierge, came up to me and asked if I needed any help with my bags, but I shook my head and said no I was fine.

"Would you be heading for the airport?" he asked quietly.

I nodded.

"You'd be best not taking the Falls," he muttered.

Ryan knew everything that was going on in Belfast, if not the whole of Ulster. I don't know if he had a direct line to the paramilitaries and I never asked, but he always seemed to know what was happening, often before it happened.

The Falls Road offered a shortcut to the motorway which led to the airport and if Ryan was warning me to find another route I should have listened. But I was tired, already late for my flight and very anxious to get home. I was also, perhaps, a little too cocky and self-confident for my own good. I decided to chance it. Big mistake.

No sooner than I had turned into the Falls Road than I encountered a barricade of car tyres across the road and a group of youths holding flaming torches. I slowed down, steering with one hand and holding my Press card up against the windscreen with the other. To my relief, they waved me through, but then I could see another barricade being constructed further up the road. I knew what was likely to happen: my car would be hi-jacked and torched - a popular pursuit among the young on both sides of the sectarian divide. I did not care about the car - it was an Avis rental - but I did want to leave that night.

The barricade in front of me was far from finished and so I accelerated towards the gap. As I did so, there was a loud bang and the window of the passenger door behind me shattered. I thought my heart was going to stop. I did not slow down, tore through the gap and hightailed up the road. Avis was not best pleased, but I made the flight.

Next day I telephoned Simon Hoggart to tell him what had happened and he laughed.

"What's so funny?" I protested. "I could have been killed."

"No, you couldn't," he replied.

"How do you know?"

"Russell, I can assure you that if they had wanted to kill you, they would certainly have killed you."

CHAPTER 9: THE RELUCTANT FEATURES EDITOR

In January 1974, at the height of the coal miners' strike, the disastrous Conservative government of Edward Heath imposed a three-day working week on the entire country in order to save energy and attempt to bring the miners to heel. By a strange coincidence I began working a three-day week in an office at precisely the moment, two months later, that the government abandoned its ludicrous strategy and called a general election, although my situation had nothing to do with energy-saving and everything to do with misplaced ego - mine.

At that time I had written quite a bit for *Nova* magazine but it came as a complete surprise when Gillian Cooke, then the editor, asked me, out of the blue, if I would be interested in becoming the features editor. The sensible answer should have been "No", because I was not really interested, but I was flattered and Gillian was persuasive and insisted I could do a great job…

There were plenty of reasons not to do it. Firstly, *Nova* had lost much of its glamour. At its launch it had been lauded as a ground-breaking, cutting edge magazine with an enviable reputation for graphic design, an ability to recruit top-name writers and a willingness to tackle controversial subjects. Its very size - it was bigger than almost every other publication on the market - proclaimed its self-confident stature. But it had never made much money and when the circulation began to fall the bean-counters had moved in to cut costs, notably by slashing the editorial budget and drastically reducing the page size. Whereas once it was impossible to miss Nova on the newsstands, it became, in its much reduced incarnation, nearly as impossible to find. The predictable result (predictable to everyone except the bean-counters) was that the circulation began to fall even more rapidly. (The magazine would fold in October 1975.)

Secondly, I had very little editing experience. In my time as deputy editor of *House Beautiful*, I was more involved in the production of the magazine than in editing its anodyne content. The features editor at Nova was responsible for acquiring and editing almost all the written editorial content, with the exception of the fashion pages. It meant commissioning articles from freelance writers, agreeing fees and ensuring the copy was not only delivered on time but that it fulfilled the brief. I had never done that. Indeed it was a task for which, I recognised in retrospect, I was almost entirely unsuited, both temperamentally and professionally.

Thirdly I did not want a full-time job that would jeopardise my career as a freelance. I put all these points (and more) to Gillian, but she persuaded me that none of them needed be a deal-breaker. She was convinced, despite my doubts, that I could do the job, mightily bolstered my ego with flattery and put a lot of pressure on me to accept. In the end I agreed on the basis that I would work three days a week, leaving me time to carry on at least some of my freelance activities.

I realised, almost immediately, that I had made a mistake and while Gillian Cooke welcomed me effusively to the magazine, no one else did. Apart from the art director, all the editorial staff at *Nova* were women, most of them early feminists and supporters of the recently emerged women's liberation movement. At least two coveted the job that had been handed to me, deeply resented the presence of this unwanted male interloper and made their resentment felt by completely ignoring me. Thus the atmosphere, when I arrived on my first day, was distinctly frosty. (One of the staff writers, a woman I shall only call Caroline, did not exchange a single word with me the whole time I was at the magazine.)

I had become accustomed to working at home, being my own boss rather than being beholden to some faceless organisation and I hated having to go into the office. I'd wake up on a *Nova* day thoroughly despondent at the prospect of having to spend the day sitting behind a desk. I commuted into the magazine's offices in Covent Garden by taxi (on the *Nova* account) and my spirits flagged ever lower the closer I got.

I did not even enjoy the work. The editorial content of the magazine was decided at regular conferences and once the plan for an upcoming issue was decided it was my responsibility to get the various features commissioned. This involved finding a suitable writer, persuading him or her to accept the modest fee that the budget allowed (as a freelance myself it was agony talking about money; my every inclination was to pay more, not less), then explaining in detail what we were looking for. Perhaps the problem was mine, that I had not sufficiently explained what was wanted, but I was often shocked at the poor standard of the copy that materialised and the number of times I had to ask for changes, or sometimes even a complete re-write. This usually caused hackles to rise. The rare occasions when a piece arrived beautifully written and entirely to the brief did not make up for the endless arguments with other contributors.

I stuck at *Nova* for about three months until I decided I could not stand it a moment longer and I walked out. I did, however, learn a very valuable lesson - that I never again wanted any job requiring me to show up in an office on a regular basis.

* * * * *

Being able to devote more of my time to the *Sunday Times Magazine* quickly paid off. Magnus Linklater, the amiable old-Etonian who was the editor and whom I liked enormously, obviously wanted to cement my relationship with the magazine and offered me an annual retainer of £20,000, over and above my usual fees. The only condition was that I would not be allowed to work for any of the other magazines in direct competition with the *Sunday Times*, notably *The Observer* and the *Sunday Telegraph*. That was fine by me and I accepted gratefully.

The vogue for "celebrity profiles", which would fill magazines for years to come, was just beginning and publicists and PR people had not yet acquired the power they would subsequently enjoy to dictate the terms of an interview. In those early days if a publicist had indicated that his or her client would not be willing to answer questions on certain, possibly embarrassing, subjects our response was simple: we would not bother with the interview. Today, sadly, publicists call the shots.

Over the years I would write many "celebrity profiles" and interview dozens of film stars, from James Mason to Arnold Schwarzenegger, and dozens of entertainers, from Ken Dodd to Max Wall (both, curiously, rather sad characters). Sometimes I would spend quite a bit of time in their company but I very rarely felt that I would ever want to be a friend to any of them - their need for attention and adoration was too desperate. The one exception was Adam Faith, the 60s' pop star turned actor and entrepreneur. Adam, whose real name was Terry Nelhams and was known to all his friends as "Tel", was a delight, largely because he was very, very funny and liked to tell self-deprecating stories about himself. The memory of his description of learning to fly a helicopter still makes me smile. Tel became a real friend and whenever our paths crossed - usually in Los Angeles - we would get together. His premature death in 2003 greatly saddened me.

At the other end of the spectrum was the incorrigible Jeffrey Archer, the writer, disgraced politician, ex-jailbird and insufferable self-publicist. I wrote a none-too-flattering profile of Jeffrey for the magazine, but its publication was delayed for some reason. As the weeks went by without its appearance, Jeffrey became more and more anxious and telephoned me frequently with reasons why it should be published soon - almost all blatant lies. Once he called to tell me that the film rights of his latest book had been bought by a major Hollywood studio for a record sum. It was nonsense.

"Archer," I wrote, "does not just hog the limelight, he *adores* it, blossoms in it, frolics in it, is never happier than when he is bathed in its full glare. Show him a television camera or a tape recorder and he will start talking. Confront him with a photographer and he'll smile. Reticent, reserved, modest he is not."

Jeffrey's tenuous relationship with the truth was described to me by his wife, Mary, as his "talent for inaccurate precis." It would eventually lead to his downfall. Jeffrey was accused by the *News of the World* of picking up a prostitute in Mayfair and later buying her silence when she threatened to go the newspapers. Jeffrey sued for libel, and in a famous High Court case Mary delivered a bravura performance in the witness box, completely convincing the judge that no man with such a "fragrant" wife would ever resort to acquiring the services of a "common prostitute". "Is he in need," the judge asked, "of cold, unloving, rubber-insulated sex in a seedy hotel?"

Jeffrey won the case but eventually received his come-uppance when, some years later, one of the principal witnesses admitted he had been lying about Jeffrey's alibi. Jeffrey was charged with perjury and perverting the course of justice, found guilty and sentenced to four years in prison.

Monica Coghlan, the prostitute who alleged she had had sex with Jeffrey, was unable to give evidence as she had been mysteriously killed in a traffic accident a few weeks before the trial. In the original High Court hearings she tried to prove that Jeffrey was indeed her client by saying she remembered him having a "spotty back", but Mary put paid to that by claiming that her husband had a "beautiful back". Unfortunately, no one asked Jeffrey to take off his shirt in court. Some time after he had been released from prison I ran into a mutual friend who played squash regularly with him at Dolphin Court in Pimlico. I asked him to try and get a look at Jeffrey's back when they went for a shower after the game. "Oh he never showers in Dolphin Square," was the reply. "He goes back to his apartment on the other side of the river."

In 1976 I was invited to contribute to a new series in the magazine called "Home Town" in which writers were intended to reminisce fondly about the places where they had grown up. My offering was rather different and began: "I think I was 20 years old, or perhaps 21, before I realised how intensely I disliked Ilford. I remember feeling rather guilty and mildly shocked at my own treachery...." My former employer, the *Ilford Recorder*, ignored it, but the *Ilford Pictorial* went to town, ran a front page splash under the headline "Storm as Russell writes off Ilford." It quoted the Mayor describing my piece as a "hypocritical and embittered attack".

(Years later, one of the editors at the *Sunday Times Magazine* was applying for a visa on my behalf and asked where I was born. "Ilford," I replied.

"Oh, hard luck," he said.)

Around this time I was working with Tony Snowdon on a major feature about the scandal of children in Britain being sent to prison. The Home Office described the institutions housing young offenders as "remand centres", but the uncomfortable truth was that they functioned as "children's prisons", this despite the fact that several years earlier Parliament had passed an act preventing the imprisonment of children under the age of 17.

Tony had begun working for the *Sunday Times Magazine* soon after his marriage to Princess Margaret in 1960. He was best known as a portrait photographer, but he enjoyed reportage, particularly on social issues, which was why we teamed up on a number of assignments. Tony was fun to work with, good company, very down to earth, and totally dedicated to the job.

One of the difficulties of his Royal status was his Royal status. When we were working on the "children in prison" story we visited a number of remand centres around the country. If word got out beforehand that the photographer accompanying reporter Russell Miller was Lord Snowdon (and we did everything we could to *prevent* word getting out) we would often arrive to be greeted by something like a reception committee. Tony always stayed in the background, leaving me to make introductions, but more than once the person we were meeting, anxious to ingratiate himself with the famous Lord Snowdon, would brush past my outstretched hand to welcome him with fawning effusion. He was unfailingly polite, but it drove him mad. He would divert unwelcome attention by interrupting and saying, mischievously, "Can I introduce you to my colleague Russell Miller?"

Tony's personal life was in turmoil. His marriage was falling apart and he was very bitter about the way he was being treated. One day we were working in London and stopped for a bite of lunch at his home, Kensington Palace - I think we had sausage and mash - and next morning he told me he had been presented with a bill for our food. His relationship with the Princess had deteriorated to such an extent that she was insisting he had to pay for all the facilities at the Palace that he had previously taken for granted. "Can you fucking believe it?" he asked me. Frankly, no, I couldn't.

"Children Behind Bars" ran as a cover story in the May 6, 1976 edition of the *Sunday Times Magazine*. The cover photo was a haunting image of a young boy barely visible behind the smoked glass of a barred window. A few months later it was announced that Her Royal Highness Princess Margaret and the Earl of Snowdon had agreed to separate.

One frisson of simple pleasure I got from my partnership with Tony was entirely frivolous. When we were working together I would usually pick him up in the morning at Kensington Palace. I'd take a taxi from my flat. "You mean the hotel, guv?" the cabbie would invariably ask when I told him my destination.

"No," I would invariably reply. "I mean the *palace*."

CHAPTER 10: UGANDA EPISODE

Of all the despots in Africa in the Seventies, none was worse than Idi Amin, the president of Uganda, and self-styled "His Excellency, President for Life, Field Marshal Doctor Amin, VC, DSO, MC, Lord of All the Beasts of the Earth and Fishes of the Sea and Conqueror of the British Empire in Africa in General and Uganda in Particular."

Idi Amin could neither read nor write when he was recruited into the British Colonial Army in 1946 as an assistant cook in the King's African Rifles. Despite his lack of education, he slowly rose through the ranks and by the time of Uganda's independence from the United Kingdom in 1962 he was, amazingly, deputy commander of the Ugandan army. When Prime Minister Milton Obote overthrew Kabaka (King) Mutesa 11 and declared himself executive president, he promoted his friend Amin to colonel and army commander.

Amin subsequently discovered Obote was planning to arrest him for misappropriating army funds, seized power in a military coup in January 1971 and began a reign seen as one of the bloodiest in African history. His regime would be characterised by appalling human rights abuses, political repression, ethnic-cleansing, extra-judicial killing of opponents, nepotism and corruption. By early 1972 at least 15,000 people had disappeared (the final figure of those murdered by the regime would be estimated at somewhere between 100,000 and

500,000). Victims included rival tribal groups, religious leaders, journalists, artists, senior bureaucrats, lawyers, intellectuals and foreign nationals. At one point there were so many bodies floating in the Nile that they clogged one of Uganda's hydro-electric dams. The US Embassy pulled out after Amin's leadership was described as "racist, erratic and unpredictable, brutal, inept, bellicose, irrational, ridiculous, and militaristic".

In June, 1976, Amin allowed an Air France airliner which had been hijacked en route from Tel Aviv to Paris to land at Entebbe airport in Uganda. The hi-jackers, members of the Popular Front for the Liberation of Palestine and a German terrorist group, released 156 non-Jewish passengers, but 83 Jews and Israeli citizens, as well as 20 others who refused to abandon them (including the captain and crew of the airliner) continued to be held hostage.

On the night of 3-4 July, a group of Israeli commandos flew in from Israel and seized control of Entebbe Airport, freeing nearly all the hostages. All the hi-jackers were killed, along with three hostages. A fourth hostage, 75-year-old **Dora Bloch**, an elderly Jewish Englishwoman who had been taken ill on the plane and had been transferred to **Mulago Hospital** in Kampala before the rescue operation, was subsequently murdered on Amin's orders in reprisal.

Almost exactly a year after the murder of Dora Bloch, I was offered a unique opportunity - an interview with Idi Amin. Journalists had not been able to enter Uganda for some years and so no one really knew what was going on, only that it was bad. An exclusive interview with the murderous president would be a worldwide scoop.

I cannot remember where or how I ran across Major Iain Grahame, but it is not important to the story. What was important was that he was probably as close to a friend as someone like Amin could have. Grahame was Amin's company commander in the King's African Rifles in the late 50's and recommended him for a commission. Their bond as fellow soldiers endured after Grahame retired from the army and became a farmer in Essex and he was asked by the Foreign Office to make several visits to Kampala to report back on what was going on. He was also included in the mission to plead for the life of Dennis Hill, a 61-year-old British teacher who had been sentenced to death by a military tribunal on a charge of espionage and sedition after describing Amin, in a book, as a "tyrant".

By the time my path crossed with that of Grahame in the spring of 1977 he was organising weekly flights to Kampala hauling luxury goods - whisky, cigars, premium wines - into Uganda for Amin and his cronies. The flights were known as "whisky runs". Grahame claimed to have an excellent relationship with Amin and suggested that it might be possible for him to arrange for me to interview the Ugandan president. I passed this on to the *Sunday Times* and several months of negotiations followed between Grahame and the newspaper about how an interview might be arranged. At the forefront of what was being discussed - certainly as far as I was concerned - was the question of my personal safety. Grahame was confident that so long as I remained under his aegis I would be safe. Eventually it was agreed - I would accompany Grahame on the next "whisky run" and meet Amin.

I never discovered what motivated Grahame to get involved with me, or indeed any journalist. He must have been aware that whatever I was going to write would certainly be unflattering and thus enrage the president and damage his relationship with him. I wondered if he thought that I would temper what I was going to write out of gratitude for his help in setting up an interview. If he did think that, he was going to be disappointed.

In the event, I never had the opportunity to find out. On the day before I was due to leave for Kampala, I got a call from the *Sunday Times*, from Joan, the editor's secretary, asking me to come into the office as soon as possible. "What's going on?" I asked her. "Something's come up," she replied. "Harry will explain when you get here." It was very unusual for Harry Evans, the editor of the newspaper, to deal directly with a contributor. My usual point of contact was Magnus, the editor of the magazine. At that time Harry had been editor of the paper for ten years and was already a legendary figure in journalism for his long-running campaign fighting for justice for the victims of thalidomide. It was under his leadership that the paper built an international reputation for campaigning and investigative journalism.

My flat was only a 15-minute cab ride from the *Sunday Times*' offices in Gray's Inn Road. As soon as I arrived at Harry's outer office Joan motioned me to go straight in, but Harry had seen me through the open door and came bustling out.

"Russell, you're due to leave for Uganda tomorrow, aren't you?"

I nodded.

"I'm sorry," Harry continued, "but I can't let you go."

I was stunned. "Why on earth not?" I protested. "All the arrangements have been made. It's taken months to sort it out and…"

Harry held up his hand to shut me up. "If you go," he said solemnly, "you'll be killed…"

I shook my head. "No…" I began, but Harry immediately interrupted, lowering his voice.

"Listen to me, Russell. Sitting in my office right now is the Ugandan Minister of Health. He has just defected. He knows everything about what has been going on in the Amin regime and he is ready to tell his story. Now do you see why I can't let you go? If you are found in Uganda when we publish, Amin will, without a shadow of doubt, have you killed."

I swallowed. There was no question he was right.

"You're up to speed with all the background and the current situation in Uganda, aren't you?" he continued, "so I want you to debrief him. Come in and I'll introduce you."

Henry Kyemba (pronounced "Chemba") was 37 years old, a tall, educated, urbane black man with a little toothbrush moustache and an infectious laugh. Henry first met Amin in the 50's when Amin was a sergeant in the army. He became a family friend and was a guest at Henry's wedding in 1965. After graduating from university, Henry joined the Ugandan civil service and was posted as an administrative assistant in the office of the prime minister from where he was quickly promoted to private secretary, then principal private secretary to the president, Milton Obote.

He was with Obote in Singapore at the Commonwealth Prime Ministers' Conference when Amin staged his military coup and appointed himself president. Obote by then was extremely unpopular and widely believed to be corrupt and Amin's coup was welcomed with fireworks and dancing in the streets. Few people in Uganda were aware of the horrors to come.

Henry was surprised when Amin asked him to stay in post as principal private secretary. By the time he was promoted to a cabinet minister in 1972 he knew a lot of what was going on but was too fearful for his own life, and that of his family, to resign. When Anglican Archbishop Janani Luwum and two of his cabinet colleagues were allegedly killed in a road accident,

Henry, as Minister of Health, visited the morgue when the bodies were being held and discovered all three were riddled with bullets. The Archbishop, still in his robes, had been shot in the mouth. It was then, realising that he might be next on the list to be killed, that he began making plans to defect.

The best opportunity presented itself when he was due to attend a World Health Organisation conference in Geneva. Henry was allowed to take his wife, Theresa, with him to Geneva but their two children Henry, 6, and Susan, 5, had to stay behind at the family home in Jinja. Once they had arrived in Switzerland the plan was for the children to be taken out of Uganda and across the border into Kenya.

Things quickly started going wrong. It seemed that word of his intentions had somehow reached Kampala. No sooner had Henry and Theresa reached Geneva than they heard that heavily-armed troops had surrounded their house in Jinja and all the adult occupants had been arrested. Henry, realising that his time was nearly up, tried a gamble. He knew well how Amin's mind worked and how susceptible he was to flattery: he called a press conference to reaffirm, vociferously, his loyalty and love for the Uganda president. Rumours of his defection were, he insisted, malicious and ill-founded.

It worked: the troops were withdrawn. As soon as Henry and Theresa learned that their children were safely in Kenya, they slipped out of the WTO conference and set off for London. Determined the world should hear his story, Henry had been advised to make contact with the famous editor of the *Sunday Times*.

* * * * *

The first priority for the *Sunday Times* was to ensure the Kyembas' safety. Henry was certain that once his defection was made public Amin would send agents to Britain to seek him out and kill him. Two suspicious Ugandans had already been detained at Heathrow airport. Harry had a house in the remote Essex countryside and it was agreed that I should take the Kyembas there for what Harry liked to call the "debriefing". (A secondary, unspoken, reason for spiriting Henry away was to prevent other newspapers getting to him and spoiling our exclusive.)

I went home to pick up the bag I was planning to take to Uganda the following day while a secretary was sent out to buy sufficient food and drink for three people for a week. (Theresa had kindly offered to cook for us.) Then we all piled into an office car and were driven to Harry's modest country cottage outside Alphamstone, a nondescript village in rural Essex. I didn't want to start formal interviewing until we were set up in the house and so we chatted idly about this and that en route. For a man who would soon be hunted by professional assassins he was remarkably cheerful.

We began work next morning and established a pattern that would last for a week. I would sit down with Henry after breakfast, a tape recorder on the table between us, and question him intently about every aspect of life in his home country. We would work until lunchtime and after lunch I would transcribe the audio tapes on my portable typewriter (home computers were only just beginning to appear on the market).

The story he had to tell was horrific - of a regime ruled by sheer terror, of indiscriminate killings, of bodies lying unburied in the streets, of a paranoid, lunatic president to whom human life had no value. "If he is provoked," Henry said, "he reacts like a wild animal and goes berserk. No one around him is safe."

Fortunately, Henry had a remarkable memory for dates, names and places and, most importantly, he knew exactly what had happened to Dora Bloch. Up until that time her fate was a mystery; all anyone knew was that she had disappeared. Henry felt a keen sense of responsibility for her fate: she could have been discharged the day before the raid to join the other hostages, but Henry agreed she could stay on in her private room at Mulago Hospital in Kampala. "I thought it was an act of kindness," he explained. "She was, after all, 75 years old and the hostages were sleeping on the concrete floor of an airport building. Had she been discharged she would probably have been rescued with the other hostages."

A matter of hours after the Israeli commandos flew out of Entebbe with the hostages, two agents from Amin's feared State Research Bureau carrying pistols burst into Mrs Bloch's room on the sixth floor of the hospital. Shouting at staff to stand aside, they dragged her, struggling and screaming, out of bed and frogmarched her down three flights of stairs. None of the staff dared to lift a finger to help her. Watched by horrified nurses and patients, she was bundled through the Casualty department and out into the street, where two cars were waiting. Mrs Bloch, still screaming, was put into the back of the first car and both drove off at high speed.

Henry was having dinner at his official residence in Kampala when he received a telephone call from the hospital to tell him what had happened. He immediately called the president to ask what was going on. Amin expressed surprise, even though Henry knew that State Research Bureau agents only operated on the express orders of the president. Half an hour later Amin called back. He made small talk for a couple of minutes and then said "Oh, by the way, you know that woman? Forget her. They have already finished her."

The following day, in response to international concern about the fate of Mrs Bloch, Radio Uganda announced that she had been discharged from hospital and rejoined the other hostages at Entebbe before the raid. The day after that a spokesman for the president confirmed that there was no one by the name of Bloch anywhere in Uganda. This at least was true - her body was lying in a forest outside Kampala.

One of the most moving moments of my sessions with Henry was when I asked him if he would write down the names and positions of those friends and colleagues who had disappeared. He began writing: Brigadier Smuto Guweddeko, former commander of the Air Force; Yekosofatl, former Minister of Culture; Frank Kalimuzo, former vice-chancellor of Makerere University; Joseph Mubiru, former governor of the Bank of Uganda… When there were 40 names on the list I asked him how many more there would be. "Oh, I could keep writing all day," he replied.

Harry Evans visited us several times, riding out to Essex on his BMW motor cycle from Gray's Inn Road, to see how things were going. He said that the whole of Fleet Street and London correspondents from many international newspapers were frantically searching for Henry, but no one had any inkling of where he might be.

When I decided I had extracted every scrap of information I could from Henry and when I thought there were no more questions I could possibly ask, I suggested that we pack up. Henry looked troubled for a moment, then said, rather plaintively, "But you haven't asked me about Amin's cannibalism?" I wondered if I had heard right, but I had. Yes, Henry said, Amin had told him on several occasions, quite proudly, that he had eaten the organs or the flesh of many of his human victims and kept human body parts in his refrigerator. He once made this admission in the presence both of Henry and a woman doctor, who almost fainted in horror.

The defection of the Ugandan Health Minister and the story he had to tell made the front page of the *Sunday Times* for two weeks running in June, 1977, and was followed up by hundreds of other newspapers around the world. It was the first authoritative account of the terrible things that were happening in Uganda and hastened the day when Amin's monstrous regime was brought to an ignominious end in 1979 when he was forced to flee into exile in Saudi Arabia, where he remained, with his four wives, until his death in 2003.

Harry Evans, like all good editors, loved a scoop and he included an account of Henry Kyemba's defection in his autobiography, *My Paper Chase*, mentioning my "good fortune" at not flying to Kampala the day after Henry defected. "Had he been there representing the *Sunday Times* when we published Kyemba's story," Harry wrote, "he would not have survived."

(Personally, I would have hoped that had I been in Uganda at the time Harry would have done everything possible to get me out before publishing, but as he explained it in his autobiography it rather seemed as if he was ready to sacrifice me in order to avoid delay in publication.)

CHAPTER 11: ATTICUS & THE 'SOME-DAY TIMES"

Atticus was the popular upmarket gossip column that appeared on the back page of the *Sunday Times*. In the late 70's, the column was written by Anthony Holden, but whenever Tony took a break I was invited to take over as the "Guest Writer." The joy of Atticus was that you could write pretty much whatever you wanted, however you wanted. Like this, from February 5, 1978, when two hucksters came to town:

"Susan and Stephen Schmaltz…
    no that is not
quite right. I will start
again.
Susan and Stephen *Schutz*
are staying at the
Dorchester Hotel
in London this weekend.
Their press release says
that Susan
is America's best selling
poet
although personally
I have never heard of her.
I am writing in this
strange way

to give you an idea
what her poems are like.
Here is one:
'you know how I feel
you listen to how I think
you understand…
    you're
        my
            friend.'
I don't think I will be
her friend;
'specially after she reads
this.
But as her books have
sold 1½ million copies,
why should she
worry?
Her work is now on sale
here. Which is why she is
in London
talking to people like me.
She says people
"identify"
with her poems; that is
why they are successful.
Stephen does not say very
much. He has a big moustache.
He is responsible
for all the illustrations
in Susan's books.
They met at Princeton:
he was from the Bronx;
she was from upstate New York.

Now they live in a cabin
in Colorado.
Their press release
says they spend
24 hours a day
together,
creating, loving and
living.
Susan says she spends
a long time
thinking
about her poems.
Stephen says he gets
his inspiration
from nature.
The trouble is,
he can't draw
and she can't write.
Still, they are a nice
young couple.
Although I did notice,
they do
bite their fingernails.

Under my temporary stewardship, Atticus took on an anti-establishment twist, largely driven by my freedom to poke fun at hallowed British institutions:

"Thursday, to Henley for lunch at the Leander Club, on the opening day of the Royal Regatta. I am the guest of the club president and directors of Pimm's Limited, who have kindly supplied apparently limitless quantities of the beverage they manufacture.

It is raining and lowering clouds of dark grey are banked up all around. Nevertheless, a lot of chaps are perambulating, like crumpled peacocks, between the marquees. Lank little curls sprout from under their straw boaters and their mouths hang slackly above where their chins should be. They wear blazers of many hues, some gorgeously piped with satin and braid, and white flannel trousers with black shoes.

In comparison, their womenfolk are a dowdy lot in their floppy hats and unhappy floral frills and flounces.

Lunch is served in a large marquee lined with ruched pink and white fabric and lit by plastic chandeliers. Pink is the colour of the Leander Club and its members sport surprising pink socks between their black shoes and white flannels, pink ties and pink schoolboy caps. It is popular to wear the cap several sizes too small, so as to appear like a pimple crowning their ruddy complexions.

The emblem of the Club, established in 1818, is a pink hippopotamus. Its origin is obscure. 'There is a story,' a member chortles, 'that the hippopotamus was chosen because it is the only other aquatic creature other than oarsmen, to go round with its nose stuck in the air.'

Conversation round the lunch table continues in similar vein. 'We keep up standards at Henley,' says a member to my right. 'It may be Edwardian, but we are proud of it.'

'Standards' may be interpreted as the anachronistic rules which forbid men to remove their jackets or ties in the Stewards' enclosure and bar admittance to women wearing trousers.

The lady opposite me is not wearing trousers, but a black straw hat which I believe milliners describe as 'off the face'. She is a dead ringer for Kathy Kirby and giggles prettily as her neighbour brays something about

'…he is always going down to Monte Carlo, and that sort of thing, and getting smashed out of his mind…'

To my left is a Leander member who turns out to be a cleric. He has to preach the sermon at the Regatta service. 'Oh, you're from the *Sunday Times*,' he says, beaming. "I think your sportswriters are far too lyrical, you know. They need stuffing. Do you think you could get them stuffed?'

'A wife is table d'hôte,' someone else is saying, 'lovers are à la carte.'

There is a lot of chat about 'oarsmen' and I innocently inquire if a cox is considered an oarsman? We all haw-haw and then I am treated to an explanation of the special relationship between a cox and his crew. ''He's the chap, you know, who will laugh if you throw a custard pie in his face. I mean you can break his leg and if he is a good sport you can lift him into the boat and he can still do his job.'

They are a jolly lot, rowers. In the clubhouse there are many cartoons. 'I say I do hope that one about the Etonian has been turned to the wall,' says a chap with a Leander-pink cherubic face and a white moustache. It is really frightfully naughty. I couldn't possibly tell you the caption in front of the ladies.'

We all haw-haw. Outside, on the river, I believe there are some chaps rowing. But I am not sure."

I learned later that Frank Giles, the well-connected deputy editor of the newspaper (his wife, Lady Kitty, was the daughter of an earl), hated my sarcastic piece about the Leander Club (possibly because he was a member or he had friends who were members), but to his credit he made no attempt to suppress it. There was a wonderful, probably apocryphal, story about Giles in William Shawcross' biography of Rupert Murdoch, the media mogul who had bought Times Newspapers in 1981. When he was fired as editor of the *Sunday Times* in 1983,

Murdoch proposed he should take the title "editor emeritus" for the two years remaining before his retirement. Giles, mystified, asked what the title meant. "It's Latin, Frank,'" Murdoch allegedly replied. "E means exit and meritus means you deserve it."

My lack of education came to bite me one day when I was writing the Atticus column. I was working in the office to a very tight deadline with only a few minutes left to file my copy. For some reason (I cannot remember now why) I needed to know the title of one of the most obscure of Shakespeare's plays and I asked a secretary if she could get the answer from the arts department. She returned with a scribbled note: "Timothy of Athenea". I stuck it in the piece and forgot about it. When I returned home later that day I showed a proof of the column to Renate (we had married a few months earlier) and she immediately saw the mistake. "What's this Timothy of Athenea?" she asked. "Do you mean Timon of Athens?"

Aghast, I telephoned the managing editor to see if it was too late to make a change. It was. I was left to suffer the possible ridicule of my better-educated graduate colleagues. Actually no one said anything directly to my face, but I could imagine there was plenty of gossip behind my back about my then well-established ignorance.

The column I most enjoyed was the one published on August 20, 1978. The lead interview was with Beverly Nichols, a writer and notorious name-dropper who had just published his autobiography. "I arrived at his white-painted cottage on Ham Common," I wrote, "straight from the hospital where my wife had given birth to a son. 'Have you chosen a name yet?' he inquired with a sly grin when he heard the news, 'or shall I drop some for you?'" In the regular "Birthdays" panel which featured in every column, I added, after the usual celebrities, "Barnaby Miller, whose arrival at dawn on Thursday made writing Atticus this week even more hectic than usual, is three days old."

When Tony Holden moved on from Atticus I was told the column was mine if I wanted it, but I did not. I had been happy to stand in for Tony, temporarily, but I was anxious to get back to proper journalism full time, writing features for the magazine.

The only trouble was, the magazine was soon to disappear for a year - along with the newspaper.

* * * * *

The production of the *Sunday Times* was so often disrupted by militant print unions throughout the 70's that it had earned the unwelcome soubriquet "The Some Day Times." It was irritating for readers not knowing whether or not their paper would appear at their corner shop or in their letter box; but it was infuriating for all the journalists, me included, to see their work disappear without being published.

The heart of the matter was that the print unions had held the employers to ransom for years. Their unique ability to halt publication on a whim gave them extraordinary power and they did not hesitate to make use of it, with frequent slowdowns and wildcat strikes at Times Newspapers' plant in Gray's Inn Road and the promulgation of restrictive practices. (When I was writing Atticus I occasionally had to make a last-minute change to the column on "the stone", where the pages were made up, and I was warned under no circumstances was I to touch anything. A non-printer having the temerity to touch a piece of type would risk an immediate walk-out.)

The unions insisted that 540 casual workers were needed to get the paper out every Saturday, but only about half bothered to show up for work, even though all 540 pay packets were collected and signed for, often under false names: "M.Mouse" of "Sunset Boulevard, Hollywood" was one of the regulars.

Exacerbating the problem was the unions' stubborn resistance to the introduction of new technology. In the United States most newspapers were composed electronically, which was cheaper, faster, cleaner and less labour intensive. Times Newspapers in the UK were still being printed using hot metal typesetting and linotype machines, which were largely unchanged since their invention nearly 100 years earlier. (Times Newspapers executives, on a tour of the United States, got very excited when they encountered a linotype machine at the *Boston Globe*. "What department is this?" one of the visitors asked. "It's the museum" was the reply.)

Every attempt by Ken Thomson, the chairman of the company, to allow the phased introduction of new technology was rejected by the unions. The difficulty was that new technology rendered traditional printing skills valueless overnight and would inevitably mean hundreds of redundancies. Thomson offered to invest millions of dollars to buy out restrictive practices and overmanning, along with higher pay and longer holidays, all to no effect. In November, 1978, he finally lost patience and closed down both titles. It was expected the stoppage would only be temporary; in fact it lasted an entire year. When printing resumed, virtually nothing had been resolved.

The suspension of *The Times* and the *Sunday Times* was a significant factor in the notorious "winter of discontent" of 1978-79, during which there were widespread strikes by public sector trade unions demanding bigger pay rises following pay caps imposed by the Labour government of James Callaghan in an attempt to control inflation. (The phrase was lifted from the first line of Shakespeare's *Richard 111* - "Now is the winter of our discontent/Made glorious summer by this son of York…")

The weather turned very cold in the early months of 1979, with blizzards and deep snow across the country, further worsening the economy. The government's inability to control the strikes would help propel Margaret Thatcher to victory in the general election later that year.

Throughout the stoppage Harry Evans had worked tirelessly to bring unions and management together, to no avail. For Harry, who would be voted the greatest British newspaper editor of all time in 2001 (and knighted in 2004), one of the worst moments was the inability to report the culmination of the long-running campaign to get justice for the victims of Thalidomide with the newspaper's victory in the European courts.

All the journalists, including me, were paid during the stoppage, leading to the following exchange with the Scottish teller at my bank in Piccadilly:

"I hope ye don't mind me askin' Mr Miller, but ye work for the *Sunday Times*, don't ye?"

"Yes, I do."

"And it's no' being published is it?"

"No, it's not."

"And yet ye're still being paid?"

I agreed I was and he shook his head in a mixture of utter mystification and awe at the weird ways of Fleet Street.

I had plenty to keep me busy while the paper was suspended. Although under the terms of my contract I could not write for any competing publications, I had been supplementing my income for some time with hack work - writing captions and editing chapters for a Time-Life Books series, "The World's Wild Places", which was being put together in its London office. Some ingenuity was required. I remember I was required to write a caption for a book on the Australian outback. The picture was of Ayers Rock and showed a coach park with "Welcome to Ayers Rock" in large letters above the entrance - not exactly convincing as one of the world's wildest places.

Time-Life Books was enjoying considerable success at that time with its heavily illustrated historical series marketed around the world by direct mail, with all kinds of inducements to persuade potential subscribers to sign up. When it launched a series on the Second World War I nagged to be entrusted with a book of my own and was eventually offered the chance to write "The Resistance" for a flat fee of $24,000. I was delighted to accept.

All Time-Life books stuck to a rigid format - six chapters on a single theme, interspersed with photo essays. By and large it was the pictures that sold the books, although I was enjoined to do my best to seek out original unpublished material and first-person interviews for each of the chapters. This was a pretty tall order on a subject that had been endlessly researched by dozens of authors, many of them professional historians. The difficulties were exacerbated by the fact that three of the six chapters were to be devoted to the French Resistance and my French hovered between non-existent and execrable.

I dragooned Renate in to help (her French was excellent) and we set off for France to track down survivors of the Resistance willing to tell their stories. Somewhat to my surprise we made good headway and I was happy with how the project was going when I got a call from the series editor, a genial chap by the name of Tom Flaherty, asking me to fly to the United States to meet the executives working on the series and report on my research thus far. Although Time-Life Books had swank offices in London's Bond Street, its headquarters were in Alexandria, Virginia, just outside Washington DC, and it was the US operation which was handling the World War Two series.

Time-Life was paying, so I was happy enough to make the trip and meet with Flaherty and other editors over several Martini-fuelled lunches in a nearby restaurant. On the flight home I wondered idly what was the point of the trip - it had all been very amiable, but a bit of a waste of time as far as I was concerned. I made two more visits to Alexandria before I figured out what was going on. "Getting the author in" on the pretext that there were problems to be sorted out was a way for Flaherty and his colleagues to convince the top brass at Time-Life Books that they were on top of everything, that they were keeping close tabs on the progress of the book, that deadlines would be met. The cost of flying me back and forth and putting me up in the local Holiday Inn was of no consequence to a massive organisation like Time-Life.

When I realised that nothing was actually achieved by these visits, at least nothing that could not be resolved on the telephone, I turned down Flaherty's fourth invitation, claiming to be frantically busy, and suggested that we could perhaps discuss whatever he wanted to discuss on the telephone. It took about 20 minutes.

Once I had delivered all six chapters, the dreaded "fact checkers" moved in, combing through the manuscript line by line. I quickly discovered that if I could source information to a previous publication - title, author and page number - they were happy. It did not bother them that previous publication did not necessarily vouchsafe for accuracy. My chapters immediately presented them with a quandary. They were obviously unaware that I had been tasked to seek out original material and so there was often no previous publication to which I could refer and thus satisfy them.

This led to bizarre exchanges between me and the fact checkers.

Fact checker: "How do you know that Mr X was the radio operator on this mission?"

Me: "Because he told me he was and showed me a photo of him with the radio."

Fact checker: "How do you know that Miss Y was 19 years old at the time of the attack?"

Me: "Because she told me she was."

Fact checker: "How do you know Mr Z was injured?"

Me: "Because he showed me the scars."

None of these answers satisfied the fact checkers and in the end I was obliged to send them transcripts of all my interviews. Even then they were not particularly happy. The whole process would have been a lot simpler if I had not bothered to dig up original material and had simply lifted information from existing books.

The Resistance by "Russell Miller and the editors of Time-Life Books" was published in 1979, the 17th of 39 volumes in the World War Two series. I would go on to write four further books for Time-Life - another in the World War Two series, *The Commandos*, and three for other series - but it was unsatisfactory, highly restrictive, work and I was not sorry when it came to an end.

Years later I was wandering around a gun show in rural Texas (on assignment for the Sunday Times) and to my surprise I found a copy of *The Resistance* on a bookstall, along with many books and lurid magazines devoted to weapons and armament of all kinds. I explained to the owner of the stall that I was the author of *The Resistance* and stupidly asked if he would like me to sign it.

"No," he replied. He could not have been less interested. Perhaps I should have bought a gun and shot him.

CHAPTER 12: BASHING THE BUNNY

I was at a party at the Playboy Mansion in Los Angeles when the destroyer, *HMS Sheffield*, was sunk during the Falklands War in May, 1982. A waiter came up to me, asked me if I was English, and gave me the news. I did not believe it. We had been fed so much propaganda about "tin-pot military juntas" and "banana republics" since Argentina had occupied the Falklands in March that it was inconceivable to me that a "tin-pot military junta" could attack, let alone sink, one of the ships of the Royal Navy Task Force that Margaret Thatcher had dispatched to the South Atlantic the previous month to eject the invaders.

But when I got back to my hotel room and turned on the television, the first picture to appear was that of *HMS Sheffield* with black smoke billowing from her superstructure. She had been hit by an air-launched Exocet missile and 20 members of the crew had been killed. For me the interest was personal - my nephew, Jonathan, was one of the young officers on board. By the time I got through to my sister at her home in Chester on a bad transatlantic telephone line, the Ministry of Defence, to its credit, had already confirmed to the family that Jon was not among the casualties. [Jon, who joined the Royal Navy as an apprentice and retired as a Rear Admiral, has never talked about his experiences in the Falklands.]

Greatly relieved that he was safe, I spent the rest of the evening making notes about the day's weird events (in Los Angeles, not the South Atlantic). I was among 500 guests who had been invited to the annual lunch at the Playboy Mansion to celebrate the announcement of the "Playmate of the Year" - an important event in the Playboy calendar, although perhaps less so in the real world. It was part of my research for a profile of Hugh Hefner, the founder of the Playboy empire and chairman of Playboy Enterprises Inc, a man known throughout the world as "Hef" and for whom the word "hedonism" could have been invented. All the definitions applied perfectly to him: self-indulgence; pleasure-seeking; self-gratification; lotus-eating; sybaritism; intemperance; immoderation; extravagance; luxury; high living…

The guests had been asked to gather at a parking lot on Sunset Boulevard, from where a fleet of limousines with faintly sinister black windows had been hired to transport us to the mansion in nearby Holmby Hills. I was ushered into a limousine with three pneumatic blondes who made no secret of their disappointment that I was not a celebrity.

We swept through a large pair of iron gates up a steep winding drive, past terraced lawns where flamingos and peacocks picked superciliously across the emerald turf, past fragrant lemon groves, past tame black rabbits with shining pelts scampering through clusters of flowering shrubs, past distant stands of redwood trees which shut off the outside world and the traffic on Sunset Boulevard.

The car pulled up outside a large grey stone house with mullioned windows, built in the style of a Victorian Gothic vicarage. Behind the house was a huge marquee where the lunch was to be held. On the Astroturf within there were round tables covered with pink linen tablecloths. In the centre of each table was a bowl of pink roses and an ice bucket containing several bottles of premier cru chablis. A pink folder on each chair revealed the identity of the Playmate of the Year 1982: none other than Shannon Tweed, a 25-year-old Canadian with large surgically-enhanced breasts, who just happened to be 56-year-old Hefner's current girl friend! Among the rewards were a $45,000 Porsche sports car and $100,000 in cash.

Miss Tweed hailed from Placentia, Newfoundland, and apparently wanted to be a Playmate because she thought the women in Playboy were "the epitome of beauty, class, taste and femininity." Shannon Tweed, the file asserted, really was her name, unlikely as that might seem. (Still, they said that about the first Playmate, "Janet Pilgrim", in 1955, when all her friends knew her as Charlene Drain.)

Guests were encouraged to wander the grounds and marvel at the many facilities: the swimming pool artfully contrived to resemble a natural rockpool fed by a tumbling waterfall which appeared to connect, under a stone bridge, with a pond full of brightly coloured koi; swimmers who ventured through the waterfall found themselves in the "woo grotto", with a scented lagoon discreetly screened by ferns and tropical flowers. It could have been described as a veritable Garden of Eden were it not for the piped music wafting unexpectedly from fake rocks wired with stereo speakers and spread around the property.

I thought I would take a look inside the mansion itself, but as I entered the "Great Hall", with its lofty beamed ceiling, white marble floor and sweeping staircase, a television crew rushed in to film the emergence of our host from the bedroom he shared with Ms Tweed on the first floor. As the lights went up, a door opened and Hef stepped out wearing a white three-piece suit, brown shirt and black shoes, his famous pipe gripped between his teeth. At the bottom of the stairs he was greeted by a posse of former Playmates, some no longer young but instantly recognisable by their magnificent décolletages, and swept into the marquee where he was hailed like a demi-god.

After this, the entrance of the Playmate of the Year a few minutes later, was something of an anti-climax. The television crew was still on hand to record Miss Tweed's appearance, in a long white dress shot with gold lurex, from Hefner's private quarters, but fans and well-wishers were notably absent. She progressed down the stairs, smiling bravely, but lingered hesitantly at the bottom, apparently unsure of whether to venture into the party alone or run back upstairs. Eventually she glared at two Playboy secretaries who had been checking the guest list and screeched "Help me!"

This contretemps was quickly resolved and Miss Tweed was soon installed by Hefner's side in the marquee so that the two of them could canoodle for the benefit of the photographers. The speeches were mercifully short (Hefner: "I've, uh, gotta a couple of things to give you, Shannon." Shannon: "First the money.") and soon we were all tucking into fresh lobsters and swilling Chablis.

* * * * *

Three days later I sat down in the Great Hall for a one-to-one interview with Hefner. By then I knew a lot about him and I knew that his carefully cultivated public image was a myth. Instead of living the kind of beguiling lifestyle notoriously espoused by his magazine, the founder of Playboy played Monopoly - yes, *Monopoly* - every Tuesday, Thursday and Saturday, usually with the same four male friends. They liked to have girls around during the game to watch or shake the dice or move the pieces, but girls were rarely allowed to play.

Hefner eschewed fine dining and ate virtually nothing but fried chicken, pot roast and sandwiches and drank nothing but Pepsi. In the kitchen of the mansion there was a book detailing precisely how everything had to be cooked, particularly the gravy. If, God forbid, his gravy was lumpy Hefner was likely to throw a tantrum. There were also detailed instructions for how his breakfast tray had to be laid out. Everything had to be *just so*, even down to the placing of the personalised matchbooks, which had to be propped up in an ashtray with the side bearing the name Hugh M. Hefner faced upwards, not the side featuring the Bunny logo.

Friday and Sunday nights were party nights at the mansion and girls always had to outnumber boys, but it was getting so difficult to attract sufficient numbers of pretty girls that a limousine was regularly sent out to tour the nearby UCLA [University of California, Los Angeles] campus looking for suitable candidates and handing out invitations. One of the problems was that girls were not allowed to bring their boyfriends, except with a special dispensation, rarely given, from Hefner himself. So why would any young woman choose to spend the evening with a bunch of lecherous, middle-aged men in a ludicrous environment? It was true that the occasional film star could be found at the Playboy Mansion, but by and large they were overwhelmingly B-team and hangers-on.

It was, then, not too surprising that Hefner often did not turn up for his own parties, preferring to remain closeted in his private quarters. This could lead to surreal situations: a "party night" with everyone just sitting around, bored, waiting for something to happen, drinking Hefner's drink and eating Hefner's food with no Hefner present. Suddenly, around midnight, a secretary appears on the gallery overlooking the "Great Hall", scurries down the stairs and says: "Quick, everybody, make like it's a party. Hef's decided to come down." So everyone jumps to their feet, the music is turned up, people start dancing and laughing loudly, so that when Hef appears in his trademark silk pyjamas it looks like a great party is in full swing.

My interview was scheduled for five o'clock in the afternoon (Hefner was proud to claim that he never got out of bed before four). It was to take place in the "library", which boasted very few books with the exception of the Encyclopaedia Britannica and bound volumes of *Playboy* magazine. Framed pictures of Hefner on the front cover of various magazines dominated one wall and over the door was a framed needlepoint worked by one of Hefner's multitude of long-departed lovers reading, satirically, "Be it ever so humble, there is no place like home."

He appeared on time wearing blue silk pyjamas, a velvet bathrobe and maroon velvet slippers with the HMH monogram worked in gold on each toecap. They were, he explained, his working clothes. He was shorter than he appeared in photographs, slight of frame and etiolated in complexion, with grey-tinged hair combed rather too carefully across the top of his head.

It quickly became clear during the course of the interview that he took himself very seriously indeed, as a major social reformer and philosopher and a man who, through the power of his unique magazine, created a climate in which it was possible to liberate the world from the shackles of puritanism and launch the so-called "sexual revolution. It was tricky to equate this image of himself with the image of the man sitting before me who lived in a fantasy world, who rarely stepped outside his mansion unless exceptional circumstances forced him to do so, who had never ridden a bus or entered a shop for 20 years, who devoted much of his energy to playing kids' games, who fell in and out of love like a teenager and who was cross when his gravy was lumpy.

He almost swallowed his pipe when I suggested that he might perhaps be a little out of touch. "*Me*? Out of touch? How can you remain highly successful in the communications and entertainment industry and not be in touch? I have a very clear picture of what's going on out there, I can assure you. What I have tried to do, 'smatter of fact, is to take a lot of time-wasting out of my life, so I can spend *more* time staying in touch. I don't need to go out to do that. Most of one's real understanding of what is going on comes from various forms of the media, not waiting for a bus or going shopping."

But what did he do, I asked him mischievously, when he needed new pyjamas? He looked at me as if I was completely mad. "I have them sent in, *of course,* the notion of me, heh-heh, *shopping*, heh-heh, it boggles my mind!"

* * * * *

While I was writing Atticus for the *Sunday Times* I shared an office with Philip Norman and we became close friends. Philip was one of the few writers on the Magazine who had arrived there by sheer talent: he won an assignment for the Magazine in a competition for young writers and moved seamlessly onto the staff. At the time we met he was already the author of several books and would soon be starting work on *Shout, The True Story of The Beatles*, which was an immediate best-seller, was lauded around the world as the definitive biography of the group and was published less than a year after the shocking murder of John Lennon on the steps of the Dakota Building in New York in December 1980.

It was Philip who suggested that the whole Playboy saga would make a good book (it had not occurred to me!) and introduced me to his agent, Michael Sissons at A.D.Peters. Michael took me on as a client solely on Philip's recommendation and, to my surprise and delight, was enthusiastic about a biography of Hefner. On the strength of a detailed synopsis for a book titled "Bunny, The Real Story of Playboy", he secured publishing deals with Michael Joseph in the UK and Holt Rhinehart in the United States. (Philip, who remains a close friend, suggested the title and much later would suggest the subjects - Field Marshal Slim and Arthur Conan Doyle - for two other biographies in my modest oeuvre.)

I was well-placed to start research. I was very often in the United States in those days and so I usually managed to slot a couple of interviews for my book into my magazine assignments. (The whole time I worked for the *Sunday Times* on foreign assignments no one ever, ever, questioned my travel plans. I could ask for a flight, a rental car and a hotel to be booked and it would just happen.)

The main problem was getting co-operation from the Playboy organisation for my book. It seems my faintly mocking profile of Hefner, which had appeared in August, 1982, had done me no favours, because no one in the organisation would talk to me. I needed access to senior executives, the magazine archives, Hefner's friends and, of course, Hefner himself. (I had not covered any of the historical stuff in my interview with him for the magazine.)

All my letters were ignored. None of my telephone messages was returned. The fact that I had a contract to write a book apparently meant nothing. No one at Playboy was interested.

At home I was having better luck. Victor Lownes, Hefner's former best friend, was more than willing to talk. Victor had met Hefner at a party in Chicago in the early 50's and was soon hired as the magazine's promotions director. He ended up in

London, running Playboy's lucrative casinos at a time when other parts of the empire were suffering - in fiscal 1980, gaming contributed $31 million to the corporate profits of $32 million. His big mistake was to get into what he described as a "pissing war" with another big casino operator which ended up with Playboy being investigated and Hefner panicking that its gaming license was at risk.

His decision to fire his friend was a disastrous move. It simply indicated that ultimate control of the Playboy's gaming operation was vested in the United States, which was against the rules laid down by the Gaming Board. By sacking Victor, Hefner ensured that Playboy would lose its licence.

Victor was more than happy to talk about all this, and much else, when he invited me for the weekend to Stocks, his country house in the Chilterns. Word of our meeting must somehow have penetrated the fastness of the Playboy Mansion in Los Angeles.

In the summer of 1983 I was staying with Renate and our two small children in a house in Tiverton, Rhode Island. (Exchanging houses was a way of being able to work in the United States without being separated from the family). In the middle of a violent thunderstorm one evening the telephone rang unexpectedly. I picked up the receiver and a voice said "Mr Miller? This is Hugh Hefner." I almost dropped the receiver in surprise. How on earth had he found me?

I grabbed a notepaper and pencil as Hefner began ranting on about the terrible injustice that had been done to Playboy in London by the loss of its gaming licences, hinting darkly at political conspiracies and right-wing cabals dedicated to the destruction of his company. Twice the call was cut off by bolts of lightning, twice he came back on the line to continue the tirade. At the end of a wild and rambling monologue lasting more than an hour, Hefner agreed to cooperate and promised to let me talk to any of his executives. All he wanted, he said, was for me to be "straight".

"How shall I set it up?" I asked. "Through Rich Nelson?"

"Who's he?" said Hef.

I swallowed. Hefner did not know that Rich Nelson was his director of public relations. I enlightened him.

I had been trying to talk to Rich Nelson for months, but he was always in a meeting and always too busy to return my calls. Next morning I put a call through to the Playboy headquarters in Chicago and asked to speak to Rich Nelson. I got the same standard message, from the same female voice, that he was in a meeting. This was the conversation that ensued:

Me: "I think you should get him out."

Girl: "I'm sorry, what did you say?"

"I said that if Mr Nelson really is in a meeting, you should probably get him out."

"Who is this?"

"You know who it is. You know I have been trying to talk to Mr Nelson for months. I spoke to Mr Hefner last night and he said I should talk to Mr Nelson without delay."

I did not point out that Hefner had no idea who Rich Nelson was. There was a long silence. "You spoke to Hef?"

"That's right."

"Last night?"

"That's right."

"Just a minute. Please hold on."

There was another long pause. Not exactly a silence, as I could hear whispering and the muted clatter of an office. Finally a male voice came on the line. "Hi Russ, this is Rich. Good to talk to you at last…"

Once Hefner really understood that there was going be a book about Playboy he realised that it was in his best interests to cooperate; he eventually gave me hours of his time at the mansion and was always friendly, charming and courteous. I was able to interview many of his senior executives, including his smart daughter, Christie, who had taken over the day-to-day running of the company.

I was even given permission to look round the original Playboy mansion in Chicago, which was kept in a constant state of readiness in case Hefner ever decided to return (which he never did). It was a bizarre experience. A maintenance man in blue overalls opened the door when I rang the bell at 1340 North State Parkway, a large brick and stone townhouse with a mansard roof and a façade of lavish beaux arts detail. Screwed to the massive oak door was a small brass plate engraved in copperplate with the legend SI NON OSCILLAS, NOLI TINTINNARE (If you don't swing, don't ring.)

In the enormous oak-panelled ballroom, where Hefner held his famous Friday night parties, the walls were hung with modern paintings by Jackson Pollock, Franz Kline and Willem de Kooning. Picasso's *Nude Reclining* was over the marble fireplace, flanked by medieval suits of armour, at the far end of the room. The bar was fully stocked with bottles, glasses polished. There was a Frank Sinatra record on the stereo turntable. Once this room was filled with music, chatter and laughter; now the only sound was the faint hiss of the air conditioning.

In the basement, the water in the heated swimming pool glistened silkily, through the lisping waterfall I could see the changing coloured lights of the Woo Grotto and a psychedelic array of pinball machines clicked and throbbed anxiously in the Games Room. I rolled a ball down the bowling alley and the automatic pin spotter whirred into action. "It's a bit freaky, isn't?" I asked the maintenance man. He rolled his eyes and shrugged his shoulders.

Up in Hefner's private quarters, his fabled round bed, eight and a half feet in diameter, was still able to rotate 360 degrees at the press of a switch (was there ever a more pointless mechanism?). The en-suite bathroom was enormous and featured a marble "Roman" bath, a jacuzzi able to accommodate a dozen people in companionable comfort and a velvet covered water bed with mirrors fixed to the ceiling above and the wall behind.

A brass and oak spiral staircase connected the private quarters with an executive suite on the floor above. Neat piles of paper were stacked alongside electric typewriters on the desks once used by the secretaries. Everything was ready for work to begin, except for the telephone directories, which were years out of date. The front page headline on a ten-year-old copy of the *Chicago Sun-Times*, left on one of the desks, shrieked NIXON - I WON'T RESIGN.

As a rule of thumb it seemed the guest suites tended to become less luxurious in proportion to their distance from Hefner's quarters, but none of them approached the spartan conditions of the Bunny dormitories on the third and fourth floors. In stark contrast to the gross extravagance below, the dormitories took on the aspect of a rather parsimonious girls' boarding school - thin cord carpets, bunk beds, wooden lockers and communal washrooms. The pigeonholes for the Bunnies' mail were all forlornly empty; on the wall nearby were the telltale holes where their payphone, long since removed, was mounted.

I had an absurd vision of all the Bunnies sitting on their bunk beds and studying their Bunny Manuals, a 44-page document beyond parody and issued to all new recruits. "Always remember, your proudest possession is your Bunny tail," it preached. "You must make sure it is white and fluffy."

Guests at the Chicago mansion were said to be able to order up any food or drink they wanted from the kitchen at any time. There was also a persistent rumour, vigorously denied, that they could also order up a Bunny from the dormitory. I was assured it never happened, although certainly no eyebrows would have been raised if any guest was able to sweet-talk a Bunny into bed, and presumably they often did.

One of the last interviews I conducted for the book was with Linda Lovelace, star of the 1972 pornographic film, *Deep Throat,* who was then living in obscurity and poverty on a trailer park in Long Island. Linda was a frequent visitor to the mansion with Chuck Traynor, her controlling and abusive husband and manager, whose presence was only tolerated because he would not allow Linda to go anywhere without him. In a soft and hesitant voice she told me a story that exposed the seamy underbelly of life in the Mansion. Traynor convinced Hefner that his wife enjoyed sex with animals and offered to lay on a demonstration. On pain of a beating, Linda agreed to take part. Hefner and few cronies gathered in the woo grotto to watch as Linda, naked, got down on all fours and Traynor encouraged a large dog to mount her. To his frustration the dog refused to co-operate and after several failed attempts the demonstration was abandoned. Linda got a beating later that night anyway, for embarrassing Traynor in front of his "friend", Hef.

Through the winter of 83/84, in between assignments for the *Sunday Times Magazine*, I worked assiduously on my manuscript, thumping the keys of a small portable Olivetti typewriter day and night in the study we had had built in the garden of our cottage in Buckinghamshire. Word-processing computers were still some way away and so it was a physical labour as well as literary one, particularly as I had a fetish that each time I started work the first page I typed had to be without errors. If I made a single typo I would rip the page out of the typewriter, screw it up, throw it on the floor and start again. Sometimes the floor was almost covered with screwed up balls of paper.

Bunny, The Real Story of Playboy was published in the autumn of 1984 and to my great delight garnered favourable reviews, both in the UK and the US. Jonathan Yardley, the *Washington Post*'s revered book critic, called it "Marvellously entertaining... Thorough, incisive, unsparing and deliciously funny... a thumpingly good book." Julie Burchill in the *Literary Review* described it as "Brilliant, the best study of American success encapsulated in one sad, shell-shocked shell since Albert Goldman's Elvis" and *The Times Literary Supplement* declared it to be a "witty and meticulous piece of reporting". Only the *New York Times* was unimpressed, its reviewer claiming that my book had stirred in him a feeling he did not know he was capable of: sympathy for Hugh Hefner. I got the feeling that his irritation stemmed from the impudence of a British writer taking on such a quintessentially American subject. It was also voted "Book of the Year" - but that was by Penthouse magazine.

By the time the reviews came out I was already embarked on a second book, and one that would cause me considerable grief.

CHAPTER 13: TWO BOOKS "ONE RICH, ONE POOR"

In April 1983 the *Sunday Times Magazine* published a three-part series which I had written about the fabulously wealthy oilman, Paul Getty, and which became an effective synopsis for my second book, *The House of Getty*. This is how the series was introduced:

"The tormented saga of the Getty family reads like the script of a television soap opera, with all the ludicrous improbabilities of the genre, interweaving sex, money, drugs, power, crime tragedy and family intrigue.

Central to the plot is an eccentric old man, said to be the richest in the world. To judge by his lugubrious countenance wealth has not brought him happiness: the underlying moral, essential to every soap. He is notorious for his miserly behaviour (standing outside a restaurant with his guests until the band stops playing to avoid paying a cover charge for music!)

He marries, and rapidly divorces, five times. Women are his weakness and for the rest of this life he maintains a bizarre coterie of mistresses, sometimes simultaneously, who deeply loathe one another.

He has five sons. The youngest, Timothy, is a delicate child and spends much of his young life in hospital, where he dies, blind and wasted, at 12, while Daddy is too busy to visit him. Only his eldest son shows any talent for the old man's business - oil. On his shoulders rests the old man's hope for founding a dynasty. In 1973 he dies of an overdose of barbiturates and alcohol in mysterious circumstances.

Soon afterwards the old man's eldest grandson and namesake, Paul Getty 111, is kidnapped in Italy. The ransom is not paid until the kidnappers cut off the boy's ear and post it to a newspaper in Rome.

Three years later, a few weeks before his death, surrounded by his brawling mistresses, the old man signs a last codicil to his will, removing control of his vast wealth from his own family.

Most of his money goes to his museum, a huge replica of a Roman villa in California. Intended as his legacy, the museum is so rich that it threatens the stability of the world's art market.

The bitter wrangling of the old man's will is not resolved when there is a further tragedy. Paul 111, deeply scarred by his kidnapping, suffers a severe stroke - aggravated by drugs and alcohol - that leaves him blind and paralysed at the age of 24.

Today the *Sunday Times Magazine* begins a major three-part series by writer Russell Miller which for the first time penetrates the veil of secrecy erected by the Getty family and tells the inside story of all three generations.

Our series begins with the almost unbelievable final act of the Getty story: young Paul's father, living as a recluse in London after the death by heroin overdose of his second wife, refuses to pay his son's medical bills until the boy's mother, his first wife, takes him to court. His income from the Getty fortune is estimated at $20 million a year.

"It is as if," says a friend of the Gettys, "the money brought a curse on the family."

* * * * *

The extensive research I had carried out - both at home and in the United States - for the magazine project provided a solid basis for the book and I made rapid progress. One of my principal sources was an American writer by the name of Bela von Block who had ghosted Getty's autobiography and thoughtfully copied hundreds of pages of the oil man's private diaries - a wonderfully rich seam for any biographer to mine. Von Block lived in Barcelona, was willing to talk to me and part with the diaries for a fee of £500, which the *Sunday Times* was happy to pay.

I thought I had acquired biographical manna from heaven. What I did not consider, and was too stupid to check, was the possibility that Getty would l*ie in his own diary*. It would cause me no end of trouble.

Meanwhile, I soon discovered that an American journalist, Robert Lenzner, was also working on a biography of Getty and was well advanced with his research. Lenzner was the New York bureau chief of the *Boston Globe* and a regular contributor to *The Economist*. As it happened, one of my closest friends, David Nyhan, was a columnist on the *Globe* and he told me that Lenzner was mightily displeased to find a parvenu - me - encroaching on his territory. Dave made some inquiries on my behalf and let me know that Lenzner was within a year of finishing his manuscript.

What I should have done, what any sensible writer would have done, would have been to ignore Lenzner, continue with my research and not fret if my book was published after his. But I simply could not resist the challenge - all my old cutthroat instincts nurtured at East London News Agency came flooding back. I was damned if I was going to be beaten to publication by a rival author and I determined to pull out all the stops and get my book out, if not before Lenzner, then at the same time.

I had two major factors in my favour: I had the old man's diaries (and Lenzner didn't) and I had managed to track down Robina Lund, a well-connected young woman who had been Getty's private lawyer and close friend (and, I later discovered, one of his many lovers). Robina knew everything that had been going on and was willing to talk. Almost more importantly, she had refused Lenzner's request for an interview. (In her quaint English way, she had taken exception to his letter seeking her co-operation because it was both undated and badly typed.)

When the old man was generating headlines around the world for refusing to pay a ransom for his kidnapped grandson - RICHEST MAN IN WORLD WON'T PAY RANSOM - , it was Robina who negotiated the secret loan he made to his son, the boy's father, (naturally at an agreed rate of interest) which finally led to the boy's release, although not until he had had one ear cut off.

Dave Nyhan, who I think was enjoying being a go-between, kept me abreast of Lenzner's progress. He told me that Lenzner was having difficulty ordering his material and that he was furious when he learned that the *Sunday Times* had chosen to serialise my book instead of his. (Some people might have thought that it would have been surprising if Andrew Neil, then the editor of the paper, had snubbed one of his own contributors, but Andrew was a hard-nosed bugger and if he had thought that Lenzner's book was significantly better I am certain he would have gone for it.)

So it was that I approached publication day in November, 1985, with a certain amount of confidence. I felt I had done a pretty good job of pulling together the story of three generations of Gettys and I thought that my efforts - *The House of Getty* - would stand up reasonably well when compared with the rival book - *Getty, The Richest Man In the World*.

Early reviews of both books were generally favourable, but then came a bombshell - an absolutely lacerating hatchet job in the Economist by an anonymous reviewer which lavished extravagant praise on Lenzner's work and trashed mine without, shamefully, any mention of the fact that Lenzner was a correspondent for the very publication in which the review appeared.

Getty, The Richest Man In The World was a "splendid book that gets to the heart of a complicated, inconsistent man". *The House of Getty*, in stark contrast, was "scrappy, under researched, jerkily written, in parts erroneous and, frankly, dull." It went on to talk about "glaring omissions", failures and errors of fact.

To say I was devastated would have been an understatement, but I was also angry. It was quite evident to me that if the review had not actually been written by Lenzner himself, his fingerprints were all over it. It quoted from an interview I had given to the *Sydney Morning Herald* in which I had unwisely admitted rushing to finish my manuscript and wishing I had had more time. Who would have known about that interview? Lenzner.

I was accused of "relying heavily" on Getty's ghosted autobiography which "in parts was pure fiction." Who would know that? Lenzner.

I was further accused, falsely, of drawing material from *The Getty I Knew*, a book written by Robina Lund. Curiously, *The Getty I Knew* was the American title. (It was published in the UK under *Getty: The Stately Gnome*.) Who would know it by the American title? Lenzner.

In an attempt to drive the final nails into the coffin of my credibility, the review stooped to blatant lies and claimed I was perpetuating "Getty-inspired myths", which had been exposed by Lenzner. Two of the so-called "myths" did not appear anywhere in my book.

None of this would have matter much if the review had appeared in, say, the *Daily Mail*, but it was in the august *Economist*, a journal of considerable prestige, respected around the world. Nevertheless, I have no hesitation in saying that the Getty reviews represented a lapse in its usual high standards. At the very least, it should have noted that the author praised so effusively was one of its own correspondents.

I readily admit I made mistakes in my haste to get my book out. The most damning was to believe numerous entries in Getty's diaries; it just never occurred to me that anyone would lie in a personal, private diary. He claimed, for example, that Gettysburg in Pennsylvania, the site of the most famous battle of the Civil War, was named after his family. I swallowed it whole because I had no reason to doubt it. Had Google existed then I would have immediately discovered that the town was named after a family called Gettys, but of course Google did not exist then.

I also erred in not including source notes and a bibliography, which would have added authority and prevented some of the sneering disdain exhibited in *The Economist*. Source notes would have shown that information provided by Robina Lund was from a one-on-one interview and not from her book.

The magazine did have the decency to publish my letter the following week:

"Dear Sir,

"Authors should not whine about critical reviews and thus I do not intend to take issue with your description of my book, *The House of Getty*, which your reviewer found 'scrappy, under-researched, jerkily written, in parts erroneous and, frankly, dull.'

"This was in marked contrast to a rival book, by a Mr Robert Lenzner, which was both 'sensitive' and 'splendid' and apparently got to the heart of the subject in a way that highlighted the failure of my own miserable efforts.

"Mr Lenzner must be a wonderful writer, which is, I suppose why he is an American correspondent for *The Economist*.

"Yours faithfully…"

The magazine added a footnote agreeing that Lenzner was, indeed, an "occasional contributor", but by then the damage was done.

Signet, Lenzner's US publisher, photocopied *The Economist* cutting and circulated it with review copies of his book, which was both shabby and vengeful and done for no other reason than to discredit me. Despite this, many reviewers maintained their independence. In a syndicated review originally appearing in the *Los Angeles Times* Bevis Hillier plumped for *The House of Getty*. "For the casual reader, who just wants to find out what sort of man Getty was and what kind of life he led, I would still recommend Miller's book in preference to Lenzner's. It is a much more relaxing and entertaining read."

Mostly the reviews were split about 50-50, with half preferring Lenzner's book and half preferring mine. But for some the temptation to ride on the Economist's back and savage my work was too tempting to resist.

I was haunted for months by a nightmarish headline in the Bookworld section of the *Chicago Tribune*: TWO BIOGRAPHIES OF GETTY: ONE RICH, ONE POOR. Lenzner's book was described as "better written and more thoroughly researched", while mine was "slapdash and full of glaring omissions." The reviewer, Gerald Nemanic, went on to make exactly same points as were made in *The Economist*.

In order to limit the damage, Henry Holt, my American publisher, sent me on a four-week book tour of the United States, which started with an appearance on one of the big breakfast televisions shows in New York - either NBC's *Today* or ABC's *Good Morning America*, I can't remember which now - and ended up in a little radio shack in rural Kansas on a local Christian broadcasting station.

Let no one persuade you that a book tour is fun, because it is not. The publisher wants to get maxim media exposure in return for the considerable cost, so that the author is rushed from pillar to post, from television studio, to newspaper office, to radio station and back again, to talk to interviewers who almost certainly have not read your book and sometimes can't even be bothered to pretend they have. It is exhausting - a different city every day, very long distances to travel and you are never in one place long enough to get any clean laundry.

I managed to get by with a little fund of the same anecdotes that I trotted out at every interview but I was so tired by the third week that things started to go wrong, I was doing a live television interview- I can't remember where it was, somewhere on the west coast I think - when I suddenly realised I was repeating the same anecdote that I had related just a few minutes before. The horrified woman presenter was staring at me with her mouth open and clearly did not know what to do. I had the choice of stopping and asking "Haven't I just said this?" or ploughing on; I chose the latter. At the end of four weeks, Holt asked me if I would do another week, but I absolutely refused and went home.

Although the year was blighted by bloody Robert Lenzner and *The Economist*, it wasn't all bad. In 1985 I won my first award when I was nominated as "Writer of the Year" by the British Society of Magazine Editors.

CHAPTER 14: THE SAGA OF BARE-FACED MESSIAH

I expected to be sued by the Church of Scientology when I wrote a biography exposing L Ron Hubbard, its founder, as a liar, a crook and a charlatan, but I did not expect to be subjected to an orchestrated campaign of harassment and dirty tricks, to be followed day after day in the United States, to have my reputation traduced, to be dragged through the courts and accused of a murder in East Berlin…

I was shaving in the bathroom of our house in Buckinghamshire on the morning of January 24, 1986, when I heard on the radio that L. Ron Hubbard, the founder of Scientology, had died. "Inconsiderate bastard" I muttered to myself.

Hubbard had disappeared from public view some five years earlier; no one knew where he had gone or why. About a year before he died I had suggested to Philip Clarke, then the editor of the *Sunday Times Magazine,* that we should look for him, not really as an assignment, but more of a project to fill in time when I was in the United States. There was always waiting time on foreign assignments, nothing ever slotted in back to back, and I could use that time making inquiries about Hubbard's whereabouts. My reasoning was that if we were able to find him we would have a world-wide scoop; if we failed, we would have an even greater mystery. Philip agreed (probably because it was not going to cost him any money).

I made some progress. I knew, for example, that he was somewhere in California, between Los Angeles and San Francisco. I learned this because a mole at the Scientology headquarters in Los Angeles told me that a motor cycle courier made a daily delivery to Hubbard - mail and other papers, presumably. The courier left at 9 a.m., headed north out of the city, and rarely returned before three in the afternoon. By my reckoning he could probably reach the area around San Luis Obispo, which was 200 miles north of Los Angeles, in that time.

But that was as far as I had got when the bugger died. I was gratified to learn, however, that I had been on the right track. At the time of his death, Hubbard was living in a remote ranch in the hills outside the little town of Creston, which is in San Luis Obispo County. There was obviously not going to be any story about the mystery, or the possible discovery, of his whereabouts, but by then I knew so much about him that he was an obvious candidate for another biography, which would complete a neat little American trilogy - sex, money and religion.

Burned by the Getty experience, I resolved this time around that my research would be faultless and my sources impeccable and that I would take however long it needed. (I would be grateful for this later, when the Scientologists did everything in their power, using every possible device, legal and illegal, to stop publication of my book.)

I expected trouble from the Church, which had a long history of animosity towards journalists. Church leaders knew that a web of lies had been spun around Hubbard's background and career and that it was very likely I would uncover the truth. Nevertheless, I was surprised when, early on in my research in

Los Angeles, a disaffected former Scientologist I had been interviewing in Pasadena casually asked me if I was being followed. I remember I laughed: such a thing had never occurred to me. But on the way home from that interview I kept checking in my rear view mirror and it did seem that there was a particular car constantly behind me. Just to make sure I was not being paranoid, I pulled into the car park of a shopping mall. The car also pulled in and stopped on the other side of the lot. I got out of my car, locked it and walked around the mall for bit, then returned to my car. As I drove away, back onto to the Santa Monica Freeway, the car was right behind me. So I was being followed.

Renate and I had arranged a long-term house exchange and were living in Pacific Palisades, on a dead end street off Sunset Boulevard, and so anyone who wanted to tail me had only to wait at the end of the street for me to come along. It also became evident after a few days that they *wanted* me to know I was being followed because they started using a bright red sports car with huge red wing mirrors that was impossible to miss, even several cars behind me.

I was unsure whether the church was simply trying to intimidate me or wanted to keep a check on what I was doing - probably a little of both. One day I decided to drive out to Gilman Hot Springs, about 80 miles east of Los Angeles, on the other side of the San Jacinto Mountains, where the church had set up some kind of base in an abandoned health spa. I knew I would not be allowed into the place, but I could check it out from the outside.

As I approached the mountains, the red car some way behind me, I could see up ahead there was a road works reducing the carriageway to a single lane and a man holding a "Stop/Go" sign. I accelerated slightly to put a little more distance between myself and my tail and as I passed the "Go" sign, the guy holding it swivelled to "Stop". I laughed out loud. If it had been a scene from a Hollywood chase movie it could not have worked better. Further up the road I found a place where I could pull off and shelter behind a ravine. I heard the red car before I saw it, tearing along and obviously determined to catch up with me. I gave it ten minutes before I continued on my way, feeling very cocky and whistling cheerfully.

Slowly, step by cautious step, I began to discover that virtually everything the Church of Scientology claimed about the exotic life of its founder was a lie.

It was said that he grew up on his grandfather's huge cattle ranch, which covered a quarter of the state of Montana. He did not; it did not.

It was said he wandered the Orient as a teenager, learning the secrets of life from gurus and wise men. He did not.

It was said he was an explorer. He was not.

It was said he graduated in mathematics and engineering from George Washington University. He did not.

It was said he was a World War Two hero, served behind the lines in all five theatres of war, was wounded several times and ended the war half blind and crippled. All lies. He was in fact a malingerer, an incompetent and a coward who did his best to avoid seeing any action. He never saw action and was not wounded.

Through the blessed US Freedom of Information Act I was able to obtain, from the National Archives, a complete copy of Hubbard's disastrous war record. (More than ten years would pass before the UK introduced similar legalisation.) Hundreds of pages listed numerous adverse reports and documented his misadventures as an officer in the US Navy, among them fighting a battle against imaginary Japanese submarines off the

West Coast and firing by mistake on Mexico, thereby generating an official complaint.

Since Scientologists viewed Hubbard as the greatest man who had ever lived, the truth about him was going to hit them very hard and my book was going to be extremely damaging, so it was no surprise that Scientology lawyers began firing off a barrage of letters to my publishers warning of dire consequences if publication went ahead without the church being given an opportunity to "approve" my manuscript.

When legal threats fell on stoney ground, they turned to attacking me personally. Both Michael Joseph and Henry Holt were informed that I was a completely unscrupulous journalist intent on defaming Hubbard for my own malicious purposes and that I had frequently been accused of libel - a total lie. Mallory Rintoul, Holt's feisty counsel, would have no truck with such behaviour. "We didn't reply to your first letter," he wrote to the church, "we don't intend to reply to your second letter. Don't read anything into our failure to reply except we don't choose to reply."

Increasingly desperate to stop publication, at least in the United States, the church offered Holt $1 million for the rights to my book, a proposition it rejected, unequivocally, to its great credit. The buy-out offer was certainly not motivated by a high appreciation of my work - during a legal deposition the executor of the Hubbard Estates is on record as describing *Bare-Faced Messiah* as a "scumbag book, full of bullshit."

Back home in Buckinghamshire, events started to take a slightly more sinister turn when the police were informed that I was responsible for the savage murder of a private detective in the car park of a South London pub. I learned later that the tip-off was unusually detailed and was thus taken very seriously. Two CID officers turned up on my doorstep and demanded to know my whereabouts on March 10, 1987, a few months previously. I looked in my diary and saw the page for that day was completely blank, so I was unable to explain where I was. The questioning continued. Had I ever used the services of a private detective? No. Had I ever been in the Golden Lion pub in Sydenham? No. Did I know an individual called Daniel Morgan? No.

Eventually, exasperated, I asked "What is all this about?" The officer explained that Morgan was a private detective who had been hacked to death with an axe in the car park of the Golden Lion in March. I vaguely remembered the story. "What's it got to do with me?" I asked, although I had a suspicion of what was coming.

"Well sir," he replied cautiously, "we have been given information that you are responsible for the gentleman's death."

After I had explained I was an author working on a biography of L.Ron Hubbard and that this was probably not unconnected with being falsely accused, he seemed satisfied and willing to believe my innocence. Two weeks later I had another call from a different CID officer, this time in Yorkshire, investigating an arson attack on a helicopter factory in which I was also allegedly implicated.

It was obvious that someone was going through a whole list of unsolved crimes and pointing the finger of blame at me, which was irritating and time-wasting both for the authorities and me. In the end, I was given a name and telephone number to which I could refer investigating officers who would then be told what was going on.

Meanwhile, friends and colleagues were calling to warn me that they had received a strange visit from a private detective making inquiries about me. The detective always identified himself as "Eugene Ingram", but I began to suspect there might have been a team of Eugene Ingrams because they were popping up on doorsteps all over the place, not just in the UK but right across the United States. I had a lot of friends in America and it seemed that Eugene had tracked down most of them. He was apparently polite and persistent and most of those people he visited were left with the strong impression that he was looking to uncover dirt about me.

He even knocked on the door of a former neighbour at a small flat in central London where I had once lived nearly ten years ago. The neighbour, I think his name was Tony, called me late one night to tell me of the visit and ask what was going on. After I had explained he gave me the telephone number of the hotel where Ingram was staying - Ingram had left it with him in the event that Tony might later remember something useful.

As soon as I had finished talking to Tony, I called the hotel and asked to be put through to Mr Ingram's room. A gruff American voice answered with a grunted "Yes?"

"I understand you are making inquiries about someone called Russell Miller," I said. "Is that right?"

"Yes, I am," he replied without hesitation, perhaps hoping that someone was at last ready to dish the dirt. "Who is this?"

"This is Russell Miller," I said.

I could imagine him at the other end of line trying to think how he should respond, but for a moment there was silence.

"If you want to know about me," I continued. "Why don't you come and talk to me? I'll tell you anything you want to know."

Silence.

"What is it you want anyway? What are you trying to prove?"

"I know your wife was born in East Germany," he said at last, "and I suspect you are in the pay of the intelligence services. Furthermore, I think you murdered Dean Reed."

For the first time I felt a distinct chill in my spine. His suggestion that I was a murderer was too risible to be considered seriously, but how the hell had he discovered that Renate had, indeed, been born in East Germany? It was not something she broadcast and she was certain she had never mentioned it in anything she had written, but it was a disturbing indication of the extent to which our lives were being probed.

Dean Reed was a singer, small-time actor and political activist from Colorado who had defected to East Germany in 1973. He always claimed it was for ideological reasons, but it was hard not to observe that he enjoyed a great deal more success in East Germany and Russia than he had ever had in the United States. In June, 1986, I was sent to East Berlin to interview him for a profile the *Sunday Times Magazine*. Renate came with me to act as interpreter and help deal with all bureaucratic hassle about getting across the Wall into East Berlin, where Reed had made his home.

We arrived in West Berlin on Friday, June 13, checked into a hotel and, as arranged, Renate telephoned Reed's German manager to arrange a time and place to meet for the interview the following day. The plan was to go through Checkpoint Charlie into the East early next morning, but it was quickly evident there was a problem. The manager told Renate that Reed was unwell and had been taken to hospital, although it was not serious. He suggested she call back later, which she did. Same story: Reed was still unwell, ring again in the morning.

By Sunday morning with the manager still prevaricating, I did not think it was worth while hanging around any longer. I asked Renate to tell him we were returning to London and would re-arrange the interview for another date when his client was completely recovered. He agreed.

On Monday morning, back home, I was astonished to read in *The Guardian* that Dean Reed, the 48-year-old American pop star who had defected to East Germany in 1973, had been found drowned in the Zeuthener Lake near his home in East Berlin three days previously - *the day we got to Berlin*.

Reed was not ill when we called, he was not in hospital - his body was being fished out of the lake. The official explanation was that it was a tragic accident, but there were persistent rumours that he had committed suicide or been murdered by the Stasi, the East German secret police, perhaps because he was planning to return to the United States. Reed - an American who had chosen to live behind the Iron Curtain - was a major propaganda asset for the German Democratic Republic and his return home would have been a serious embarrassment.

Eugene Ingram had discovered that I was in Berlin with my wife on the day that Reed died. He had discovered my wife was born in East Germany. He already suspected that my work as a journalist was no more than a cover for my employment by the intelligence services and so it made perfect sense to him that I was responsible for killing Reed.

I did not bother to challenge him. What was the point? It was all nonsense, of course, but it did ratchet up the pressure on Renate and me. We were warned that our house in Buckinghamshire was under constant surveillance, that our mail was being intercepted and that our telephone line was tapped. I am not sure I believed any of it, but at the same time we were all too aware that the Church of Scientology would go to any lengths to destroy its perceived enemies.

An American journalist called Paulette Cooper was driven to the very brink of a nervous breakdown after she had written a critical book about Scientology in 1971. Her home telephone number was scrawled on pay phones across New York with the message "Want a good time? Call Paulette." Neighbours in her apartment block were warned she had a dreadful infectious disease and that they should avoid getting into an elevator with her. The church somehow got hold of her personal stationary, covered with her fingerprints, used it to forge bomb threats and reported her to the FBI. The vicious campaign mounted against her was only discovered when the FBI raided Scientology offices in 1977 and recovered documents relating to Operation Freakout, the baldly stated aim of which was to have Cooper "incarcerated in a mental institution or jail."

I learned later, through the reporting of others, the extent of the "dirty tricks" campaign launched against me. Two Scientology "investigators" had been sent from Los Angeles to London in the summer of 1987 with orders to use any means to smear my reputation and to obtain either a copy of my manuscript or advance page proofs of the book. They rented an apartment in Abingdon Mews, Kensington, where, every night, garbage sacks stolen from outside the offices of Michael Joseph were tipped into the bathtub and searched in the hope of finding page proofs. In the end, their perseverance paid off since a woman was seen in a copy shop in East Grinstead - where the Church of Scientology's UK operations were based - making seven copies of an advance proof of my book which, it was subsequently discovered, had been stolen from the printers in Bungay, Norfolk.

Meanwhile, both Michael Joseph and the *Sunday Times*, which had announced it would be serialising *Bare-Faced Messiah*, were deluged with threatening letters and telephone calls warning that publication would result in dire consequences. Two men - one of them Eugene Ingram! - used a fake business card to obtain access to the *Sunday Times* headquarters in Wapping - a considerable feat since it was not known as "Fortress Wapping" for nothing - and talked their way into the office of Brian MacArthur, the paper's executive editor. He threw them out when he realised who they were.

Later that day the same team tried, and failed, to get into Michael Joseph offices in Kensington.

At Frankfurt Book Fair - the publishing industry's most important showcase - a man approached the Michael Joseph stand and asked Alan Brooke, the director, how much he was being paid by the CIA to publish *Bare-Faced Messiah*.

Just four weeks before my book was due to go on sale, the Church of Scientology sought an injunction in the High Court to ban publication on the basis of breach of copyright and confidentiality - the use of two photographs and extracts from Hubbard's diaries and letters. (It was interesting, to me at least, that the Church never claimed, in any litigation anywhere in the world, that my book was libellous. They always relied on obscure legal issues.)

I was named as co-defendant along with Michael Joseph and was thus obliged to attend. Almost the first words spoken by the learned counsel for the plaintiff on day one in Court 18 tempted me to snort loudly and shake my head in disbelief. Mr Alan Newman, whose beaky little nose and enormous spectacles made him look like a barn owl, assured the court that the litigation was certainly not aimed at preventing publication of my book - his clients simply wanted to protect their legal rights. What nonsense! I knew, and everyone in the court knew, that the action was being brought precisely to stop my book being published.

Four days of rather wearisome legal arguments followed in the august surroundings of the High Court at the end of which the judge, Mr Justice Vinelott, gave the Church's lawyers short shrift, described the application as "mischievous and misconceived" and dismissed it.

The Church immediately applied to take the case to the Appeals Court where, three weeks later, it was similarly dismissed, that court deciding that publication of my book was desirable in "the public interest", which outweighed any minor technical infringements. An application to appeal to the House off Lords was refused.

The *Sunday Times* planned to start serialisation in the same week as publication and assigned a reporter, Richard Palmer, to write a news story about the struggle to overcome the Church's antagonism as a way of promoting the serialisation. Richard unearthed a private detective based in Bristol who seemed to know a great deal about what had been going on. His name was Jarl Grieve Einar Cynewulf and he claimed he had been paid £2,500 by the Church to find information to smear me; he had apparently been told he could "name his price" if he could prove that that I was a CIA agent. He claimed, to Richard, that my house in Buckinghamshire was under surveillance for 16 hours every day and that the Church's file on me was already more than 100 pages thick.

Richard agreed to return to Cynewulf's house the following day with a photographer but in the interim something happened. The co-operative and helpful individual of the previous day had been transformed into a malevolent lunatic. Cynewulf answered the door carrying a revolver. "You'd better leave unless you want to end up in a box," he snarled, pointing his gun at Richard. The photographer snapped a quick picture and then both of them ran for it as Cynewulf fired. (It turned out later that he was firing blanks, but as Richard sensibly pointed out: "I did not know that at the time.")

The photograph on the front page of the next issue of the *Sunday Times* of Cynewulf brandishing a gun and the story inside under the headline "Cult's private detective fires at journalists" did nothing to harm the sales of my book.

The book promotion tour organised by Michael Joseph included a half-hour live television debate on Granada at which the Church was invited to provide representatives to defend

Scientology against the accusations in my book. They provided three young people - two men and a woman - who were highly personable and articulate and did a good job under difficult circumstances. When the debate turned to the thorny subject of Hubbard's war record, they insisted the record had been "sheep-dipped" and that what I had obtained from Washington was no more than a cover to conceal his real activities behind the lines. My response was that if that was the case, surely the cover record would be seamless and anodyne, not a thick document that exposed Hubbard as a reckless, arrogant and incompetent officer who was shifted from post to post, leaving in his wake a trail of unpaid tailors' bills.

In the Green Room after the broadcast I found myself alone in a corner with one of the Scientologists and I asked him, sotto voce, if he really believed my book was full of malicious lies. He looked me straight in the eye and nodded. I despaired.

Legal attempts were made to block publication of *Bare-Faced Messiah* in South Africa, Canada and Australia but none prevailed. Only in America, where I might reasonably have expected the biggest sales, were we stymied. In the United States a ferocious litigant with access to unlimited sums of money is a formidable opponent and Henry Holt found itself bogged down in seemingly endless litigation in one court or another for almost three years.

The case finally ended up in the Supreme Court, which decided I had infringed copyright, effectively ending any hope that *Bare-Faced Messiah* could be published in the United States. It was a ruling, the *Washington Post* declared, that had "caused alarm and dismay among publishers, historians and writers."

Holt had fought valiantly and honourably, but in the end was forced to admit defeat. Legal costs were approaching $1 million, its insurers were kicking up a fuss and it was increasingly hard to justify the expense for a book that was never going to generate massive sales and income. When Holt told me that they were throwing in the towel I did not blame them one bit and thanked them for everything they had done to try and get the book out.

Fourteen thousand copies of *Bare-Faced Messiah* were distributed in the United States, mainly to libraries, before the Church obtained an injunction. They soon began to disappear mysteriously from the shelves when large numbers of borrowers failed to return them. It was rumoured there was a storage facility somewhere outside Los Angeles that was slowly being filled by unreturned copies. I never discovered if it was true, but I certainly would not discount it

There was a sad postscript to the saga of *Bare-Faced Messiah*. I began receiving heartbreaking letters from parents who had lost their sons or daughters to Scientology asking me for help or advice to try and rescue them from the cult.

The truth was, even with the best will in the world, there was not a damn thing I could do.

CHAPTER 15: THE INTERVIEW THAT MADE ME WEEP

It is strange how a chance encounter, or a casual remark, can sometimes lead to a story. I was at a dinner party in North Oxford given by the poet and playwright Jenny Lewis when she happened to mention that her husband, Simon, a barrister, was representing one of the families caught up in what had become known as the Cleveland Child Abuse Scandal and was utterly shocked by what they had endured.

During the latter part of 1987 the Cleveland Child Abuse Scandal had become a major news story. A doctor at Middlesborough Hospital, Marietta Higgs, had caused 121 children to be removed from their families after deciding that they had been sexually abused. An inquiry later revealed that her diagnostic technique was faulty and that almost none of the children had been harmed. The anguish and stigma she created lingered for a long time as many parents faced a lengthy battle with the social services to regain custody of their children.

Simon Lewis was representing a family which had had all three of its children taken away. While the story had been extensively covered - and Higgs had been widely vilified - no one had actually sat down with one of the families to document in detail exactly what had happened to them. Simon told me that the mother had kept a meticulous diary of the horrific events as they unfolded and I asked him if she might be willing to talk to me. He was strongly of the opinion that the world should know what had happened to them and agreed to contact her on my behalf. Weeks of negotiations followed, during which I made several trips to Cleveland to gain the family's trust. The parents insisted that their identities should never be revealed and I assured them that this would not be a problem. In the end, they agreed.

I interviewed the mother at her home over a period of several days. It was protracted because I frequently had to call a halt to compose myself: it was the first and only time in my career that I was often close to tears during an interview. I was a father to four children myself and could empathise with the distress she endured: like hearing her children screaming as she and her husband crossed the car park outside a hospital where they had been kept overnight at the insistence of the social services. It would be many months before they were allowed home. Her story was like something out of Kafka, every parent's worst nightmare.

The more she told me the more outraged I became that such a thing could happen in Britain, that loving parents could be subjected to an ordeal almost beyond belief by social workers and police officers oblivious to what they could see with their own eyes - that this was a normal family just like any other. It was as if common sense had been suspended and replaced by a police state.

It all began when she took her youngest child - an 18-month-old boy - to her GP with a sore rectum. The GP referred them to a consultant at Middlesborough Hospital - Marietta Higgs. Higgs examined the boy without comment and asked to see his siblings - a girl aged 10 and her brother aged 8. She then said she wanted all three children to stay in the hospital overnight. The parents were mystified but bowed to her authority and made no objection. When they returned to the hospital the following morning to collect their children, they were met by representatives from the social services with a court order to take the children into care. Dr Higgs had decided that all three children had been sexually abused and presumed their father, a teacher, was the abuser.

In the face of the full might of the social services, backed by the courts, the parents were powerless to do a thing. They tried to explain to the children what was going on, that they would have to go away for a few days, but of course they (the children) did not understand. Why would they? "The worst thing was that the only way they could see it," their mother told me, "was that Mummy and Daddy were going to let people take them away and we were not stopping it. They thought we were abandoning them; it was awful."

Both parents assumed that they would be able to sort out the problem in a few days, a week at the outside, and that their children would be quickly returned to them. In fact it was 18 months before the family was reunited - eighteen months of anguish and misery. The children were separated from one another and put into foster homes. Their parents were not allowed to know where they were and were only allowed a "supervised visit" in the office of the social services once a week for just an hour. It always ended in tears with the sobbing children pleading to be allowed to return home.

Social workers constantly pressed the parents to "accept responsibility" for what had happened. They protested they could not accept responsibility for something they did not believe had happened. "You're in a no-win situation," they were told. "Until you accept responsibility you won't get your children back."

At one point the parents thought that if they separated they might have a greater chance of the children being allowed to return home. The father telephoned his brother and asked if he could stay with him for a while. The brother hesitated, then said he was sorry but he could not take the risk - he had children of his own. It was one of their lowest moments. A few days later the father was suspended from his job as a teacher "as a result of allegations of misconduct" and his weekly access visits to his children were terminated with immediate effect.

A maelstrom of fear, suspicion and hostility had engulfed the family. In the end, they had to accept that the only way to recover their children was through the courts - a long and draining process which was eventually successful. In the final hearing at Middlesborough High Court the judge was scathing about the way the family had been treated: "I am satisfied that these children were not sexually abused by their father; I am satisfied that they were not sexually abused at all...I am satisfied that they have caring and loving parents who have not harmed them in any way whatsoever... and I sincerely hope that whatever tongues may have been wagging in the locality may now be stilled and that this family will be left to pick up the pieces after their awful experience."

The mother never for a moment believed that her husband was abusing their children. Don't you think, she asked me, that I would know if that was happening? That I would spot there was something amiss in his relationship with them? If he was abusing them, why did they wait so impatiently for him to come home from school and then argue about who would get a bedtime story? I agreed that it defied belief.

What she did not know was that Higgs had returned from a medical conference the previous year utterly convinced that a condition called Reflex Anal Dilation (RAD) was evidence of sexual abuse - buggery, not to put too fine a point on it. It was subsequently confirmed that RAD can appear in any child quite normally and spontaneously. More importantly, Higgs ignored psychological pointers that might flag up abuse - behavioural problems, self-harm, and the rest - and tore perfectly happy, well-adjusted families apart on the basis of a single, misguided diagnosis.

I never viewed her as "evil" - as did the more hysterical elements of the tabloid press - but deeply misguided and catastrophically impervious to doubt. I also suspected that she might have hoped her single-minded pioneering of a new diagnostic technique might eventually be recognised as perhaps the "Higgs syndrome". It was not to be - instead of being recognised by her peers as a pioneer she was denounced and discredited.

Initially the family had no idea that they were not alone or that Higgs had been similarly diagnosing many other children as abuse victims. They only discovered what was going on when they were invited to a meeting and discovered the venue packed with other parents with exactly the same experience as their own. One father, shocked to be told by Higgs that his son exhibited RAD and was thus being abused, said the boy's cousin was in his car outside the hospital. Could he bring him in so that Higgs could show him what a normal anus looked like. Higgs agreed; the father brought in the other boy. Higgs examined him and announced that he, too, was being abused.

By the time I interviewed the parents their children were all at home and it seemed they had pretty much recovered from their ordeal, but there was no question that the family was scarred by the experience and the mother was very concerned about long-term psychological damage manifesting itself in the future.

When I came to write my piece I had to restrain my outrage. I just laid out the events chronologically and soberly, without any embellishment, making extensive use of the mother's diary.

It ran to some 20,000 words, was the longest article ever published by the *Sunday Times Magazine* at that time, and covered 13 pages. The response from readers was extraordinary. No parent could fail to be moved by their ordeal and hundreds wanted to express their sympathy and anger that such a thing could happen in a modern, civilised society. Mail arrived, literally, by the sackful and it kept coming for weeks. Many people sent money, although it was the last thing the family wanted; it was all donated to children's charities.

A few months later the editor of the Magazine telephoned me at home to say that I had been "Commended" in the British Press Awards, largely on the strength of my Cleveland feature. It heralded quite a little run for me - in 1989 and 1992 I was a voted Magazine Writer of the Year, with another "Commended" in between.

I would not have won the award, nor would I have got the story, had I not been at that North Oxford dinner party that night.

CHAPTER 16: A DAY IN HELL'S KITCHEN

(Sunday Times Magazine, July 30, 1989 - one of three features submitted to the British Press Awards when I was named Magazine Writer of the Year for the first time.)

It is eight o'clock on a Thursday morning and the boys in the kitchen at Harvey's restaurant in Wandsworth are already at work, rattling the pots and pans, chopping and slicing and whisking and kneading and mixing. Every working day begins in the same way, preparing every sauce, every garnish, every ingredient on today's menu from scratch.

If the young men in their white aprons and blue gingham trousers appear a little bleary-eyed, in rather less than blooming good health, it can perhaps be explained by the fact that they did not finish their previous day's work until three o'clock this morning. It was quite a bit later than usual: normally they get away by two.

The chef-patron, Marco Pierre White, has not yet made an appearance, but this is only because he is making a detour on the way from his house in Kensington. He is calling at a butcher's in Belgravia to pick up a tray of pigeons which will make their succulent debut on the dinner menu tonight, accompanied by a ravioli of cèpes and confit of garlic.

Shortly before nine o'clock Marco strides into the restaurant carrying the tray of pigeons under one arm. He pulls an upturned chair from a table, slumps into it, shouts for coffee and makes a scissors movement with two fingers which indicates that he wants a cigarette and he wants it now. Marco survives on cigarettes and coffee.

It would not be an exaggeration to say that he looks truly terrible. His skin is pasty and prone to pimples; his face is gaunt and his hollow eye sockets are grey. Several days' growth of wispy beard sprouts from his chin and top lip. His horrible long hair hangs over his ears in lacklustre lank curls apparently unfamiliar with shampoo.

Lest it appear that I am being somewhat ungenerous about Marco's consumptive appearance, I should point out that one of his *friends*, a photographer, recently asked him if he would model for an advertisement designed to illustrate the ravages brought about by drug addiction. Marco, who likes to think of himself as a Byronic figure rather than a junkie, indignantly refused.

For reasons that are not immediately apparent to your reporter, women fawn over Marco. A smouldering stare from the brown eyes somewhere in those grey sockets starts female knees weakening; his wolfish smile brings on hot flushes.

One lady restaurant critic who should have known better breathlessly described how the intensity of his gaze could "glaze a crème brûlée from ten yards away." A reporterette on a glossy magazine was almost, but regrettably not quite, lost for words to describe his beauty: "His looks should never have been allowed. His looks are champagne and oysters, tiger skin rugs and blazing fires…"

Before he starts work Marco downs three or four cups of coffee and smokes a similar number of cigarettes, lighting one from the other. He likes to talk, likes to shock. He views himself as something of a philosopher, offering curiously Thatcherite homilies about the need to lead from the front and only getting out of life what you put in, etcetera. Unfortunately, unlike Mrs Thatcher, Marco is incapable of opening his mouth without the liberal use of certain Anglo-Saxon expletives and dreadful clichés.

Here, for example, is Marco holding forth on being a chef: "Any chef who says he does it for love is a fucking liar. At the end of the day it's all about money. I never thought I would ever think that but I do now. I don't enjoy it. I don't enjoy having to kill myself six days a week to pay the bank. But if you don't want to cut the mustard you're finished at the end of the day. If you've got no money you can't do anything; you're a prisoner of society. At the end of the day it's just another job. It's all sweat and toil and dirt; it's fucking misery."

While Marco is expanding on this theme, one of his "boys" appears from the kitchen to say that someone has telephoned to make a reservation for a table for one. They are full, of course (they are full every night), but Marco's boy is worried that the call is from an inspector for one of the food guides and so perhaps they should somehow squeeze him in.

Marco snorts at the notion. "Tell him to piss off," he says. Marco's boy smiles nervously and returns to the kitchen to deliver the patron's succinct message, possibly more discreetly. "The way I look at it," Marco explains, "is that if I accept a table reservation for one I have one empty chair and that's going to cost me fifty quid."

His keen appreciation of finance stems from his hefty overdraft which, he says, costs him £45,000 a year in interest alone. He borrowed the money for a £200,000 refurbishment of the restaurant last year and now he needs to make £15,000 a week to break even; most weeks he turns over between £23,000 and £25,000. It is not bad money for a 27-year-old who claims he only had £7.36 in his pocket when he arrived in London seven years ago.

Marco is uncharacteristically reticent about his background. He admits to being half Italian and coming from "somewhere around" Leeds. His mother died when he was six years old and he is now effectively estranged from his family; he has not seen his father or three brothers for 10 years. He was bored at school and hated catering college so much that he only endured it for three days. All they taught him, he recalls with disgust, was how to make an apple pie. He decided to try his luck in London and got a job for £70 a week in the kitchen at Le Gavroche where he assiduously learned his trade; four years ago he opened his own restaurant in a run-down wine bar on Wandsworth Common called Harvey's. Last year he became one of the youngest chefs ever to have been awarded a Michelin star.

"Because I used my brain and worked hard I got somewhere. You've got to have intelligence; if you don't have intelligence you're a fucking non-runner. But you've also got to work hard; if you don't put any effort in, you get fuck all out."

As if to prove the point, Marco suddenly stubs out his cigarette, gets up and literally runs into the kitchen, calling over to his shoulder that I should join him when I have finished my coffee. He has explained that ten o'clock is the very latest time for him to be at his station in the kitchen in order to get everything ready for the lunch service. It is a quarter to 10.

The white-tiled kitchen at Harvey's is small, cramped and hot. Marco, naturally, occupies centre stage, standing at a steel-topped table in the middle of the kitchen. Behind him is a range of ovens and gas-fired hotplates and to his right the three trainee chefs, Gordon, Stephen and Clive, work at a long bench above a series of refrigerated cabinets. John, an amiable Irishman with a wonderful Fifties "DA" haircut, washes plates, dishes and pans all day long at a sink in front of Marco's table. The two pastry chefs, Patrick and Roy, are tucked away in a finger-like extension off the main kitchen.

At this hour the atmosphere is reasonably relaxed, although Marco ensures everyone is kept busy by rapping out orders every few minutes. Only John is occasionally allowed to slip out through the back door for a quick smoke in the alley behind the restaurant; everyone else in the kitchen has to bustle ceaselessly.

Marco is meticulously chopping and paring the choicest little fillets and cutlets out of great slabs of meat laid along the front of his table. He works very fast, only pausing to push hair out of his face. When the meat is all prepared he starts on the tray of pigeons, banging and slapping the tiny creatures with gusto. His bony, scarred fingers are covered with blood and gore, which now also spatters the front of his apron. There are angry red burn marks along both his forearms.

No one is allowed to interrupt the work of the kitchen; there is, quite literally, no time to spare. Gordon, at 22 the most senior of the sous-chefs. usually answers the telephone, but anyone who wants to speak to Marco is out of luck. Whenever Gordon tells Marco there is someone who wants to talk to him, Marco snaps: "Tell him to piss off."

Out in the restaurant the waiters are setting the tables with crisp white linen, silver cutlery and crystal glasses. A small bowl of fresh flowers goes on each table. All of the front-of-house staff are French, with ludicrously thick accents. At one point in the morning the assistant manager calls into the kitchen: "Marco, zee Gourmet Cooking Club of Great Britain is on zee telephone. Zey wish to speak wiz you urgently."

"Tell 'em," Marco bellows as he wrestles with the last of the pigeons, "to fuck off."

Shortly after 11 o'clock Marco starts on the shellfish: first a crate of enormous scallops. He opens each shell with a twist of his knife and scrapes the contents into a large stainless-steel bowl. An enormous turbot, two sea bass and two salmon are waiting for his attention.

It is evident that he expects whatever implement he requires to be put into his hand instantly, rather in the manner of a surgeon. "Carving knife," he snaps, holding out a hand. No one, it appears, has heard him. "WHERE'S MY FUCKING CARVING KNIFE?" he shouts. "COME ON, FUCKING WAKE UP! WHEN I ASK FOR SOMETHING I WANT IT AND I WANT IT NOW."

There are now seven different pans bubbling and steaming on the hotplates behind Marco. In between cleaning and filleting the sea bass he plunges his fingers into one pan after another and sucks on them speculatively. When more salt is required he throws it into the pan with a curious pecking motion from the height of his outstretched arm. It is a technique I notice is copied by the sous-chefs, but with rather less dexterity.

The temperature in the kitchen is rising steadily and so is the tension. In less than an hour the first customers for lunch will arrive and there is still much to do. Marco demands constant time checks and instant answers. "How long for the Madeira?" "Thirty seconds, Marco." "How long for the trotters?" "Ten minutes." "How long for the brains?" "Two minutes, Marco." Every now and again Marco bellows "SERVICE!" to summon a waiter to bring him a bottle of mineral water, which he gulps straight from the bottle.

The assistant manager, changed now from jeans and T-shirt into a dark grey suit with ridiculously wide shoulders, appears in the kitchen to inquire what Marco proposes to offer for the special lunchtime menu. Marco is helping Gordon roll out fresh pasta for the lobster ravioli, to be served with a purée of truffles on the à la carte menu. "Do we have any red mullet?" he asks. "No, Marco." "OK, here's the menu. Salad of scallops or fresh fish à la nage, followed by escalope of salmon with oysters and chives, or roast rump of lamb with spring vegetables, followed by a passion fruit soufflé."

The arrival of the first customers is only signified in the kitchen by the first order, which is slipped under a bar fixed to the wall just inside the door. Marco looks at it and says, "Right give me two rav, quickly now. QUICKLY." More orders follow in rapid succession. Marco is everywhere, bouncing about the kitchen with his hair flying, barking instructions, urging on the boys, bellowing for this and that.

At the height of the hurry-scurry Marco's temper snaps. Stephen, a wan young man with perspiration pouring down his cheeks, has not produced the chopped coriander at the right moment. "What the fuck have you been doing for the last five minutes?" Marco demands. Stephen starts to open his mouth, but Marco is not in a listening mood. "Don't insult me boy. How old are you? Twenty one? And you are insulting me already. When I want something I want something and if you don't want to give it to me you know where the fucking door is. DO YOU UNDERSTAND?"

"Yes, Marco," Stephen mumbles meekly, his eyes fixed on Marco like a startled fawn. A few seconds later Marco demands a whisk and Stephen jumps forward, but it is, of course, the wrong whisk that he proffers. Marco naturally assumes this is deliberate insubordination and hurls the whisk at Stephen with the advice that it is "fucking useless". The whisk bounces off Stephen's chest and clatters to the floor.

At this moment the telephone rings. Marco snatches it up and discovers to his displeasure that it is a supplier who has not delivered on time. "WHERE THE FUCK'S MY ORDER?" he snarls. "I've been stitched up. I've got fuck all. You better pull your fucking finger out." He slams down the receiver with considerable satisfaction.

"I give all my suppliers a fucking hard time," he will explain later. "It's the only way to keep up the quality. When you're spending £125,000 with a butcher you want the best and you want it at a certain time. If I don't get the best I send it all back. Why should I take insults?"

The tempo of the kitchen has a curious lilting pace during service. Most of the time the young chefs are rushing about, squeezing past each other, bending to reach into ovens, jiggling pans, dancing to Marco's frenzied tune. But then comes the moment when the food is ready to put on the plate and there is a sudden lull as everyone bends over the serving trays, rapt with concentration. The ingredients are arranged by hand with great delicacy and precision. If a drop of sauce falls on the rim of a plate it is carefully wiped away.

When Marco tells a waiter he can take the tray away - usually by telling him to "Piss off!" - the frantic activity begins again.

"We've got three and a half minutes for three beef, one lamb, one trotter, OK?"

"I've got no garlic."

"Clive, can you get your finger out, OK?"

"Let's move it. Quickly. QUICKLY!"

"Thirty seconds for the rav."

"SERVICE!"

The salad of scallops is served in thin slices which Marco balances in a precarious tower on the plate. In the hectic, confined conditions of the kitchen it is a miracle that the waiters can get such delicate dishes to the table intact, but it becomes clear they do not always succeed. One of them sweeps up a tray of three scallop salads and bumps into Marco, collapsing all three. For one terrible moment it seems that Marco, who has a knife in one hand, is going to disembowel the waiter and to judge by the waiter's expression he thinks so too.

John, stoically washing dishes at the sink, has been providing me with a sotto voce running commentary about what has been going on in the kitchen. He rolls his eyes and murmurs: "It'll be hell now." He is right.

"Why are you so fucking clumsy?" Marco roars at last. "What's the matter with you? Last night you tried to burn me, now you keep walking into me. Do you think I work 100 hours a week for you to walk into me? DO YOU?"

"No, Marco."

Within a few minutes it is Clive's turn for a tongue-lashing. He has been cooking little patties of shredded potato but he has not done them to Marco's satisfaction. Marco contemptuously throws one of them into the dustbin. "I know you were working in a shithouse before you came here," he says, "but I don't do shit." Clive tries to edge away, but Marco jabs a finger into his cheek and pushes him against the wall. "If you're going to do something for me, you do it fucking right. DO YOU UNDERSTAND?" Clive nods as best he can with a finger hooked under his cheekbone.

Out front, in the air-conditioned restaurant, the diners are, of course, blithely unaware of all this passion and drama. An automatic door effectively sound-proofs the kitchen and protects the customers' sensibilities, so who would ever guess that the sublime food served at Harvey's is created in a neurotic sweatshop fraught with hostility? There are 18 for lunch today, mostly businessmen and presumably on expense accounts. For them, lunch at Harvey's is a quiet, elegant and pleasurable occasion, a time to relax, enjoy the food and wine and perhaps discuss a deal or two.

In the kitchen the lunch service is turning into a nightmare, at least for Stephen, who is clearly today's favourite whipping boy. Marco discovers that Stephen has not confirmed an order for truffles. It is an opportunity too good to miss. As he works, whisking sauces, slicing meat, constantly tasting everything, Marco addresses the kitchen on Stephen's multitude of failings. "Is he fucking stupid, or is he not? What a dickhead. What a fucking doughnut. What a plonker. What's the matter with him? Why does he insult me every fucking day?"

Stephen shakes some salt into a pan on a hotplate. "What the fuck are you doing that for?" Marco shrieks. "You're not helping me. Don't you want to help me? Well why are you fucking around? Get out of my fucking way. Next time you're out. Do you understand? OUT!"

Shortly after three o'clock the last order in the restaurant has been filled and the lunch service ends. "That's it," says Marco. "Clean down." The tension in the air suddenly subsides, fizzing out like air from a deflating balloon. Everyone looks washed out, particularly poor Stephen. Marco goes out the back door and down the alley and perches on a brick parapet behind the restaurant. He lights up a Marlboro and draws the smoke deep into his lungs. John brings him a cup of coffee.

I am suspicious that all the extraordinary histrionics were a show put on for my benefit and I suggest as much to him, but he absolutely denies it. "If you don't whip a horse it won't win, will it? I shout at the boys to keep them motivated, stop them falling asleep. You know what makes the food good at Harvey's. It's the bollocking. If I didn't bollock them they'd send any old shit out. I have to move twice as quick as everyone else because I'm the boss and when I turn round and say 'Fucking move your arse baby' they can't question it because I do it. If any boy answered me back I'd sack him instantly.

"The boys know that if they want to get to the top they've got to take the shit. Harvey's is the hardest kitchen in Britain. It's the SAS of kitchens. But you don't get to the top in this business by being pampered. When a boy comes to me he is putting his career in my hands; if he really wants to learn he'll accept everything that comes his way. He'll leave as a good cook and in a few years he could have his own restaurant with a Michelin star."

Gordon, who will soon be going to the Gavroche, has cooked pigeons for us [me and the photographer] and a table has been set in the now empty restaurant. Marco joins us, bringing with him a crate of morale mushrooms to prepare for dinner. He himself never eats; on Sundays he might go out to a restaurant with friends, but for the remaining six days of the weeks he never sits down for a meal. He does not have the time, he says simply. Neither does he drink. He likes to taste a wine, but would never drink a glass of the stuff. He subsists on Mars bars and coffee.

When the coffee and petits fours arrive Marco nibbles at a couple and distractedly crunches the remainder between his fingers as he talks about the future. His plan, he says with a wicked grin, is to be free to live a life of decadence by the time he is 35. He'll keep Harvey's as a flagship restaurant, open a couple of others serving very simple, very good food, and then he'll be making a lot of money. "If I cut the mustard I'll be a very rich boy, a very rich boy indeed."

Some afternoons the boys in the kitchen can take a break, sometimes as long as an hour, but today they are out of luck. They will be doing 59 covers tonight and the preparation keeps everyone, including Marco, busy.

None of the boys has any interest in enjoying the food which costs them so much in terms of time and energy and adrenalin. Roy, the assistant pastry chef, reckons he has made about one and a quarter million petits fours in the two years he has been at Harvey's. He didn't like them much at the beginning and now he'd never touch them.

With an hour still to go before the restaurant is due to open for dinner, the mood in the kitchen is decidedly more relaxed than it was at lunchtime. Marco is arranging brains and artichokes on lamb cutlets and holding forth on a subject close to his heart - women. He is describing in considerable detail what he likes to do to women and what he likes women to do to him and the boys are smirking happily as they work. No one, of course, interrupts; no one offers any views of their own lest they upstage Marco and incur his formidable wrath.

At 7.20 Marco takes a break for a cigarette. He lounges on a small sofa at the front of the restaurant, from where he can watch girls go by and pass judgement upon them. At precisely 7.30 he spots his first customers approaching along the pavement, all dressed up for a night out. "Oh gawd," he sighs. "Here they come. Nouveau riche written all over them, darling. Naf, naf. The one on the left's got a nice little bum, but look at that one on the right. Last time I saw a mouth like that it had a hook in it. And look at her nose - it's like a cormorant's. She shouldn't be allowed out until after midnight."

It would be true to say that Marco does not have a particularly high regard for his customers and he quotes with relish the incident when the orders for two tables were accidentally transposed. Each table contentedly chomped through dishes quite different from those they had ordered, without apparently realising it and certainly without a word of complaint.

"I don't ever want to see my customers," he says. "They're all ugly bastards anyway. I'm not the kind of chef that goes poncing round the tables with my name on my jacket, fishing for compliments. That's passé. The only kind of people who would appreciate that are people without style or class. I've got enough problems as it is, without sitting down at the end of the day to have pseudo-intellectual conversation with some naf customer."

After a pleasurable few minutes insulting his customers Marco returns to the kitchen through the restaurant, completely ignoring the few tables already occupied. As he enters his domain he calls out: "Clive, sweep the floor." Clive instantly picks up a broom.

The first order, from a table for eight, materialises within a few minutes. Marco looks at it, mutters "Fucking hell" and starts shouting instructions.

Soon everyone is scrambling to keep up with the orders as they stack up along the bar and Marco is urging greater and greater effort. "Let's move it," he says. "Move it, quickly, quickly." At the hotplate he works two-handed and each time he prepares a sauce he goes through a ritual of whisk, taste, season, whisk and taste again, with a spoon that moves in a blur between the pan and his mouth. By nine o'clock the heat is so intense that Gordon's tunic is stuck to his back and the perspiration is beginning to soak through his trousers.

So far Marco has managed to keep his temper, apart from the odd gibe directed at the hapless Stephen; "Did you taste the sauce? Did you take any notice? Why did you serve that shit then? Remember - absorb! A few minutes later Marco grabs a waiter struggling out with a single dish on a tray. "Are you fucking stupid or something?" he inquires. "You've got one plate and you want to carry it on a 25-pound fucking tray. What's the matter with you?"

233

When Clive fails to hear a waiter calling "Backs!" to clear a path for a tray, Marco gives Clive a hefty shove which sends him reeling and then loudly conducts an inquest above the noise of the kitchen. "Did you hear him, Gordon? Did you hear him Stephen? I heard him. Why didn't you, Clive?"

Occasionally, as the door to the restaurant opens, it is possible to hear the low buzz of conversation, bursts of soft laughter and the chink of glasses. It is a comforting reminder that there is still a civilised world out there outside Marco's hellish kitchen.

As the evening wears on, Marco's temper shortens. "Gordon, I told you to put the mushrooms on top, so why didn't you fucking do it? If you don't want to do what I ask, fucking tell me and I'll do it myself."

At eleven o'clock the tantrum that has been fermenting all evening is suddenly ignited. The manager comes into the kitchen with news that the gentleman with the party on table nine would like Marco to join them for a drink. Marco's eyes bulge.

"UN-FUCKING-BEL-IEV-ABLE!" he exclaims to the kitchen at large. "Fucking unbelievable. I'm in the middle of service and this dickhead thinks I can take time off for a drink. Unbelievable." He shakes his head at the ignorance and thoughtlessness of his customers. "Go back and tell him to fuck off," he orders, presumably expecting it to be the end to the matter.

But the manager is back in two minutes with a new request from table nine. Would it be possible for them to visit him in the kitchen? "WHAT?" Marco screams. "Do you think I want a fucking army trooping through here? Tell 'em to come back at one o'clock. Unbelievable!"

When the manager appears for a third time to say that table nine would only like to pop in for a few seconds to express their gratitude for his cooking, it seems Marco has to restrain himself from storming into the restaurant and pushing the occupants of table nine out into the street. It would not be the first time he had turned customers out. Instead he says between gritted teeth: "Just go out there and say NO! NO! NO! Do you understand?"

It is a few minutes after midnight before the service finishes. The restaurant is still two-thirds full, but the only requests now will be for more coffee or drinks, which the waiters can handle. As Marco says: "OK, clean down!" once again the tension drains away. Stephen smiles for the first time all day and there is a moment for the boys to relax, exchange a little chit-chat, before they start to clear up.

It takes nearly two hours to stack everything away and clean the kitchen ready for the next day. Marco is last to leave."

(In 1994 Marco became the first British chef to be awarded three Michelin stars. In 1999 he retired from cooking and became a restaurateur and television celebrity chef. The "Gordon" referred to in the text was Gordon Ramsay.)

CHAPTER 17: THE MOVIE I DID NOT WRITE

I have already mentioned that journalism is a craft which feeds upon itself; innumerable magazine features owe their genesis to often overlooked news stories that can be profitably followed up and expanded. In the summer of 1990 I was flicking through *The Guardian* over breakfast at home one morning and my eye was caught by a little story, no more than three paragraphs, on the foreign page. It stated that a couple with no medical training, resident in Washington DC, had concocted an experimental medicine which seemed to be slowing the progress of the rare neurological disease affecting their desperately ill son, Lorenzo.

Augusto Odone, an Italian-born economist working for the World Bank, and his American born wife, Michaela, a linguist, had refused to accept that Lorenzo's illness - adrenoleukodystrophy, or ALD - was terminal and set about trying to find a cure.

It was obvious there was much more to the story than three paragraphs in *The Guardian* and later that day I telephoned the World Bank headquarters in Washington, asked to speak to Augusto Odone and to my great surprise was put straight through. Augusto did not seem to be surprised by my call and confirmed that he and his wife would be happy to talk to me. The following day I was on a flight to Washington.

The Odones' story was tragic. They first began noticing changes in their son when he was about four years old and the family was living in the Coromo Islands, off the coast of Mozambique, where Augusto was working on a project for the World Bank. A high-spirited and precocious child who could speak three languages fluently, Lorenzo suddenly began slurring his speech, stumbling and having temper tantrums at school. Doctors initially ascribed the symptoms to some tropical disease.

But when they returned to Washington, Lorenzo's condition steadily worsened. After two years of testing, doctors told the Odones that Lorenzo had ALD, a rare genetic disorder that strikes apparently healthy boys between the ages of five and 12. There was no cure, no hope. The progress of the disease would be rapid. Lorenzo would quickly lose his sight, hearing, speech and ability to walk. He would probably be dead within two years.

"It was like descending into hell," Augusto told me. "Basically we were being told to go home and watch Lorenzo die. We couldn't and we didn't."

When Augusto asked how they could find out more about the disease the doctor airily advised them not to bother, because there wasn't much written on the subject and they "wouldn't be able to understand it anyway."

Nothing could have been more calculated to enrage a couple like the Odones. Undeterred by their lack of medical knowledge, Augusto and Michaela set out on an extraordinary odyssey to save their son. They spent weeks in medical libraries, studying the biochemistry of the nervous system and combing through textbooks to learn everything they could about the disease. They tracked down every doctor, every specialist, every consultant who had ever expressed an interest in ALD and pursued them relentlessly. They re-checked everything that was known, wheedled raw data from research institutes and re-calculated it. They exposed fundamental flaws in existing theories. They telephoned around the world in search of answers, they experimented on members of their own family. Driven by an obsession to save Lorenzo, they simply never gave up.

They soon ran into opposition from the medical establishment, which was at first deeply sceptical of their efforts and then openly hostile. No one could believe - or, indeed, wanted to believe - that two amateurs could succeed where the finest scientific brains had thus far failed. But the Odones, spurred on by the horror of watching their son's decline, would not be deterred. They called doctors, biologists and other researchers around the world to assemble the few far-flung experts on ALD for a symposium, at which some learned of the others' work for the first time.

Despite many dead ends and despite being surrounded by sceptics, by distilling what they had learned through "doggedness, serendipity and ignorance of our own limits" (Augusto's words) they became world experts on the disease. The outcome of their extraordinary venture into the sequestered realms of high-level medical research was the discovery of a treatment for ALD which not only halts the progress of the disease but prevents susceptible children developing its terrible symptoms. It is officially registered as the invention of Mr and Mrs A Odone and is called "Lorenzo's Oil."

For the Odones the discovery of Lorenzo's Oil was both a triumph and a tragedy. That they succeeded where medical science failed is potent testimony to the power of parental love. But it took them nearly three years of painstaking research and by the time the oil was available it was too late to save Lorenzo from being ravaged by the disease.

There was considerable controversy, too, about whether Lorenzo's Oil really worked. The medical establishment - accused by the Odones of being hidebound and aloof - reacted with predictable outrage and ridiculed the notion of a "miracle cure". Actually, the Odones never claimed that Lorenzo's Oil could cure ALD, only that it might slow the progress of the disease. That their son was still alive, although grievously handicapped, was surely proof.

I liked the Odones very much when I first met them in Washington and greatly admired their refusal to give up on their adored son. What they had achieved was extraordinary, a triumph of the human spirit, but I could also see the strain both of them were under. We were having dinner together one night in a restaurant in Georgetown, a posh enclave of Washington, when Augusto and Michaela suddenly began to argue - some silly domestic issue - and Michaela stalked out. Augusto was obviously embarrassed - as was I. "I'm sorry," he said. "We are so focussed on Lorenzo that we sometimes forget our manners."

On the day after my feature appeared in the Magazine I received a telephone call, out of the blue, from Sydney, Australia. On the line was George Miller (no relation), an Australian film director best known for the *Mad Max* films and *Witches of Eastwick*. He said he had just read my feature about Lorenzo's Oil and was very moved by the plight of the Odones and that he thought their story would make a wonderfully inspiring film.

I asked him how, in Australia, he had managed to see a copy of yesterday's *Sunday Times Magazine* and he explained that a friend in London had sent him a copy by fax, then comparatively new technology. He wanted to know how long I had spent with the Odones and when I told him three days he seemed very surprised - and obviously unfamiliar with the time constraints of journalism. "I'm amazed you were able to grasp such a complex story in such a short time," he said. It is quite possible he was just trying to butter me up, but if he was, it worked.

I said I would need to ask the Odones' permission before I could pass on any contact details, or any of my research, to which he agreed. E-mails were still a few years away, so I telephoned Augusto later that day. He had never heard of George Miller and was sceptical about a movie, but said he would be willing to talk to him and gave me the OK to take it forward.

It was at this crucial point that I missed a trick. If I had been sufficiently quick thinking - and I clearly wasn't - I could have tried to make a deal with George. I obviously knew a great deal about the story - in return for handing over all my interview transcripts and contacts, why not let me have first crack at drafting a script? I would not have placed him under any obligation to accept my treatment and so, theoretically, there was no reason for him to refuse.

Nothing would have given me greater pleasure than to be involved, as a writer, in the making of a movie. I had zero experience as a scriptwriter, but that did not mean I could not learn - fast. In the end, I said nothing. I did not even ask, if a movie materialised, if the magazine could be given credit for its inspiration, which would certainly not be unreasonable. What I got was nothing, because I asked for nothing.

I knew, of course, that many scripts are written and few movies are made and it may be I thought this project would fall into that category, but it did not. I soon heard that Susan Sarandon and Nick Nolte had been cast to play Augusto and Michaela and that Peter Ustinov was to play the professor whose help the Odones enlisted. The script was being written by George Miller and his Australian playwright friend, Nick Enright.

Lorenzo's Oil was released nationwide in January 1993 and was well received by the critics, but bombed at the box office, grossing only $7.2 million against its $30 million budget. It received two nominations at the 65th Academy Awards that year: Best Actress in a Leading Role for Susan Sarandon and Best Original Screenplay for Miller and Enright.

Roger Ebert of the *Chicago Sun Times* gave the film four out of four stars and called it an "immensely moving and challenging movie" but ultimately the subject matter was too challenging for popular appeal. Had Lorenzo been cured and seen at the end of the movie resuming a normal life it would have been more palatable, but that was not the case. While the oil had delayed progress of disease, the neurological damage that Lorenzo had sustained could not be reversed and he remained needing 24-hour nursing care, although Michaela devised a system through which he could communicate by blinking or wiggling his fingers.

Shortly before the movie was released I wrote a follow-up feature for the Magazine. The Odones were by then heavily involved in the next phase of their research. ALD attacks and destroys the body's myelin, a fatty substance that sheathes the nerve fibres. If a way could be found to restore or replace the myelin in Lorenzo's body there was a possibility that he could be unshackled from the disease.

It did not much matter to the Odones that *Lorenzo's Oil*, the movie, was not a box office success. What it did, very successfully, was to raise awareness of ALD and bolster support for the Myelin Project, a non-profit organisation set up by the Odones to further research into the disease. Susan Sarandon became its official spokesperson.

Sadly the Myelin Project did not restore Lorenzo's health. He died on May 30, 2008, the day after his 30th birthday, having survived more than two decades longer than predicted by doctors.

* * * * *

Travel was one of the great and enduring joys of my job. I never stepped off a plane without a frisson of excitement about what challenges might, or might not, lie ahead. I recently discovered that British Airways tracked and collated the travels of its Executive Club members. This shows that since 1990, when I became a member, I have flown 648,510 miles and spent 1,297 hours in the air on BA flights - and BA was by no means the only airline I used.

The United States was my primary beat. I always covered some element of the US Presidential elections - usually either a profile of a candidate or reporting from the stump. Travelling in the Press plane that followed the candidate's was an interesting experience: no one bothered with the usual restrictions of flight - like wearing a seatbelt, or not using a mobile phone - and the flight attendants made no attempt to impose them. As we were taking off on my first trip in the Press plane there were raucous whoops as two photographers, taking advantage of the step ascent, shot down the aisle riding on tin trays like sledges.

Because of the increasing demand for celebrity profiles, I got to know Los Angeles as well as I knew London and I was so often in the city that the doormen at the Century Plaza Tower - my preferred lodgings - used to greet me by name: "Hey Russ, welcome back!" (These worthies, black to a man, were obliged to wear ludicrous uniforms strongly reminiscent of those worn by Beefeaters in the Tower of London, even though the Century Plaza Tower - a gleaming skyscraper - bore no resemblance to its London namesake.)

1992 was a pretty typical year. I made five trips to Los Angeles, one to interview Arnold Schwarzenegger, another to interview the adorable Geena Davis, and a third and fourth to talk to the film directors Oliver Stone and Tim Burton. The fifth was to report on a delicious Hollywood saga of how two hustlers - a hotshot lawyer by the name of Peter Gruber and his friend Jon Peters, Barbara Streisand's former hairdresser, contrived to take over Columbia Pictures; I wrote it as a spoof screenplay.

In New York I interviewed Graydon Carter, who was stepping into Tina Brown's shoes as editor of *Vanity Fair*. On an assignment to write about increasing gun violence in US schools, I was at Thomas Jefferson High School in Brooklyn on the very day a student pulled out a gun and shot two other boys dead.

In the Ozark mountains in Arkansas, in a wood cabin built with his own hands, I interviewed Thomas Robb, an ordained minister in the Baptist church who also happened to be the "Grand Wizard" of the Ku Klux Klan, then enjoying a resurgence in the deep South. An accomplished and charismatic speaker, Robb was viewed by civil rights experts as the most dangerous of the new breed of white supremacists because of his communication skills, political ambitions and an impressive ability to cloak the underlying message of hatred and intolerance in an avuncular garb of reason and logic.

He invited myself and photographer Philip Jones Griffiths to attend a cross-burning ceremony the following weekend: "On a dark, moonless night in rural Alabama, 30 white-robed and hooded figures move like ghosts across a rough stubble field, occasionally tripping and muttering curses under their breath. Each selects a wooden stake fashioned as a crude torch and dunks the end in a bucket of kerosene before forming a circle around a cross 40 feet high and just visible in silhouette against the deep purple sky. One torch is lit and the flame is passed from stake to stake until each figure, eyes glittering in the sockets of their pointed hoods, is holding aloft a bright burning flare. In silent salutation to the cross, the torches are waved up and down in unison, then from side to side. Finally one is applied to the base of the cross and fire licks quickly up the kerosene soaked burlap wrapped around the timber. Suddenly it bursts into flames, casting a flickering light over the ground and illuminating a weird and sinister tableau. The robed figures march forward, cast their torches into the blaze, then take several steps backwards before saluting fascist-style, right arms and fingertips outstretched, some shouting "White power!" In an America riven once more by racial tension, the Ku Klux Klan , after years of decline, is back in business…"

In Boston I interviewed high-profile lawyer Alan Dershowitz recently hired to try and clear the name of boxer Mike Tyson, currently in prison for the rape of 18-year-old Desiree Washington in a hotel room in Indianapolis. He claimed on appeal that new evidence would prove that his client, who he described as a "sweet young man", was innocent. He failed.

In Washington DC I wrote a feature about the Secret Service: "When Bill Clinton became president-elect of the United States last month, his life changed forever and his right to privacy was effectively abolished. For he and his wife, Hillary, will now be protected by the Secret Service for the rest of their lives…

"The Clintons will have plenty of opportunity, during the next four years, to become accustomed to the Kafka-esque reality of living cheek by jowl with changing rotas of dour men wearing grey suits and carrying guns, for the president of the

United States and the first lady are the most rigorously, expensively and publicly protected couple in the world...."

While I was frequently criss-crossing the Atlantic, I also managed to get around other, more obscure, parts of the world. In Taiwan, an island off the mainland of China where the republican forces of Chiang Kai-Shek retreated after their defeat by the Communists in 1949, I was obliged to wear a badge identifying me as a "Visiting Journalist" at all times. I quickly discovered that a little ritual is involved when meeting a Chinese official: he will bow and present you with his visiting card, then wait for you to give him your card. The problem was that as a freelance I had never bothered with business cards. So after I had received a card the official I was meeting would stand and wait expectantly, looking increasingly discombobulated when no reciprocal card was forthcoming. I tried to persuade my pretty young interpreter to explain my situation but it was inconceivable to her that I would travel without a stack of business cards.

I was in Taiwan to report on a new mood of realism that was emerging with talk of independence. Taiwan's insistence that it was the legitimate government of the whole of China and that it would one day "recover" the mainland from the Communists had led to its isolation and continuing tension with the People's Republic of China, but the official line remained focussed on the chimera of reunification. Taipei, the capital, once a sprawl of wooden shacks, had developed into one of the fastest growing cities in the world: my hotel, the Lai Lai Sheraton, boasted a Gucci boutique and the women shoppers, with their mini skirts and bolstered shoulders, could have been browsing in Bond Street or on Fifth Avenue. But the city also had a noxious underbelly. In a night market known as Snake Alley, live snakes were slit open and drained of blood and bile, which was then sold in small glasses as a tonic for increasing male virility. I declined to sample a glass.

Behind Snake Alley was a warren of narrow passages lined with wood-shack brothels. I was told that of the 1,000 prostitutes working there, more than a third were children, many as young as ten or eleven. I left the area profoundly depressed.

I had wanted for some time to write about the scandal of child labour in India and the first World Summit for Children, meeting in New York, gave me the necessary "peg". India had the largest child labour force in the world and it was growing, despite increasing international concern, internal pressure for reform and a statute book bulging with laws forbidding the employment and exploitation of children.

Just ten miles outside of Delhi, I found children breaking rocks for road building:

"The heat and the dust are almost unbearable, but at least predictable, accustomed. It is the noise, the relentless clickety-clack so redolent of penal colonies, that is truly terrible.

It is not a loud noise, but it is almost painful in its chinking pitilessness. It speaks of back-breaking toil, of aching muscles, of despair. It is the sound of many sledgehammers striking, and splitting, blocks of granite.

In this rubble-strewn field the child labourers bend and twist and swing their hammers like automatons. Sometimes the hammer bounces off the rock, sending shudders up their arms and down their spines. Sometimes the rock splinters and shards of granite fly through the air. Many of the workers are cut about their legs and arms; all of them are scarred. The great boulders they are breaking are hewn from nearby quarries and brought here by tipper trucks.

In the fiercest summer months the noonday temperature soars to 45°C. The rocks become too hot to touch and the reflected heat turns the site into a shimmering furnace. But the work never stops and the rates of pay never change - 75 rupees (£2.25) for breaking a three-ton truckload of granite into small pieces. On every pile of rocks you can see scrawny figures bending and straightening. And the hellish clattering of their hammers is a sound I will take, guiltily to my grave, for many of these slave labourers are younger than my 11-year-old son, whose idea of arduous physical labour is emptying the dishwasher.

Ganesh Sayanna is only eight years old. He works here nine hours a day, seven days a week, and the palms of his small hands are already thick with callouses. He cannot yet lift a full-sized sledgehammer so, like his 10-year-old sister Malati, he uses a smaller hammer, although it is still heavy enough to split chunks of granite. Ganesh has already learned the technique: one foot on the stone to steady it, lift, swing and smash. Lift, swing and smash. Lift, swing and smash. With every broken rock, the memory of his brief childhood recedes. At the age of eight, Ganesh has begun a lifetime sentence of hard labour for the crime of poverty…"

I am afraid I lost my temper when, after this piece was published, a reader wrote in to point out that most of the children in the photographs seemed to be smiling and perfectly happy. I wrote a very rude reply and he complained to the editor, Andrew Neil, as a result of which I received a formal reprimand. I knew Andrew sympathised with my views but at the same time he pointed out that it was not a good idea to call a loyal reader an "asinine moron".

In the Ukraine, with photographer Harry Benson, we encountered, once again, the obstructive bureaucracy that makes working in Russia so frustrating for journalists. I had worked with Harry on several previous assignments. A wonderfully dour Scot who had been resident in New York for many years, he had made his name as the official photographer travelling with the Beatles on their inaugural tour of the US in 1964. A few years older than I, he had been "around the block" quite a few times and was cheerfully undaunted by official obstruction.

Our assignment was to see what had happened to the thousands of people who had been evacuated after the Chernobyl disaster. The explosion of the nuclear power station at Chernobyl in April 1986 was the worst nuclear accident in history. A plume of radioactive material - 30 to 40 times bigger than the fallout from the bombs at Hiroshima and Nagasaki - spread across large parts of the globe. More than 336,000 people were displaced from their homes, virtually overnight.

We were to visit a collective farm at the small town of Makarov, where 600 evacuees from near Chernobyl had been rehoused. It was something of a miracle that we got official permission to visit the area at all, but from the start we were hamstrung by our "guide", a stolid, humourless apparatchik by the name of Anatoly whose orders, it soon became clear, were to make it as difficult as possible for us.

The settlement comprised three parallel streets of prefabricated houses on a bleak treeless plain about 30 miles from Chernobyl. All the residents came from the same village and had been obliged to leave behind all their worldly possessions; they were evacuated with nothing but the clothes they stood up in. I was assured that they would all be happy to talk to me, except all the interviews were conducted in the presence of Anatoly and Nadezhda Ukrainetz, the chairperson of Makarov's Soviet of Workers' Deputies, a large woman with a shining pink face, hair drawn tightly back in a no-nonsense bun and a disconcerting mouthful of silver fillings.

It was, then, hardly a surprise that everyone we talked to professed to be happy, grateful to the government for being resettled and for the compensation they had received for the loss of their homes. No one expressed any desire to return to their old village, but it was quite obvious, from their nervous glances at Anatoly and Ms Ukrainetz, that they had been coached what to say. While our escorts were busy supervising a picture Harry was taking, an elderly man pushed a note into my hand and put a finger to his lips. I was able to put the note in my pocket without being observed and got it translated later that night. It said, in Cyrillic: "Everyone wants to go back, but we are not allowed."

At four o'clock in the afternoon Anatoly announced it was time to leave. We had not nearly finished what we wanted to do, but he assured us we could return the following day. "He's lying," Harry whispered to me. "He won't let us come back. We need to stay." He pretended he had not heard and carried on shooting pictures. We were able to string out the visit for about another 30 minutes but were then more or less frogmarched back to our official car.

Harry was absolutely right. We were sitting in the lobby of our hotel in Kiev the following morning, waiting for Anatoly, when he emerged through the swing doors looking remarkably cheerful. We stood and started to pick up our bags when he held out a hand and said: "So sorry. Visit not possible. No transport."

"What do you mean?" I asked rather stupidly.

"Sorry, no transport." he repeated, without any further explanation.

Harry looked at me as if to say I told you so. Trying to contain my anger I said" "OK, that's no problem. We'll rent a car." Followed by Anatoly, I walked across the lobby to the car rental counter, pulled out a credit card and my driving licence and asked to rent a car. I could see the clerk looking over my shoulder at Anatoly. "I'm sorry sir," he said. "We have no cars available." Harry told me later that Anatoly was slowly shaking his head as a warning to the clerk.

"OK," I said, increasingly desperate, "we'll take a taxi."

"Not possible," Anatoly said. "Makarov is in prohibited zone, no taxis allowed."

I knew that in Kiev drivers of private cars often made pocket money by acting as unofficial taxis and picking up people in the street. "Anatoly," I said, "if you can't supply transport I'm going to find my own. I'm going to go out into the street and wave a fistful of roubles until I find a driver willing to take us to Makarov."

Anatoly stopped smiling. "You may do that if you wish, Mr Miller," he said evenly. "But if you are successful I can assure you the driver will be arrested and he will not see his family for a very long time."

We never did get back to Makarov.

The next time I saw Harry Benson was at Hewanorra International Airport in St Lucia. He had flown in from New York and I had flown in from London. We were on our way to Mustique, a 25-minute flight in ten-seater twin-prop aircraft operated by Mustique Airways.

"Is this job supposed to be payback for that fuck-up in Chernobyl?" Harry demanded as he shouldered his camera bag.

A week in Mustique - there was only one flight a week - might have seemed more like a holiday than an assignment, but I didn't like the place at all. The island itself was beautiful, a Caribbean nirvana, but the residents were loathsome - narcissistic, unashamed snobs, exceptionally pleased with themselves. I couldn't wait to get away.

While I never tired of foreign assignments, I have to admit I was frequently lonely, particularly when I was not working with a photographer. Inevitably there were longish periods of inactivity when I had done all the research, looked at everything I needed to look at and was just waiting for the next interview. Even if I was in some glamorous location I never bothered to go sight-seeing by myself (I could never see the point), but I enjoyed taking long walks and sometimes went shopping for the family. Otherwise I tended to hang out in my hotel room transcribing notes, reading or watching television.

If there were no friends around with whom I could spend the evenings I usually opted for room service rather than going out to eat alone. When I did venture out, my hopes to be inconspicuous were often dashed. In New Orleans I booked a table for one at Antoine's, a posh restaurant in the French Quarter and the setting for a murder mystery novel by Frances Parkinson Keyes, *Dinner at Antoine's*. Established in 1840, Antoine's was the oldest family-run restaurant in the United States and was the birthplace of French Creole cuisine. It was regularly patronised by celebrities, although rarely by English journalists eating alone.

No eyebrows were raised when I arrived to claim my reservation and the *maître d'* showed me to a table set for one at the back of the mirrored - and crowded - main dining room. It was impossible not to observe that all the other tables were occupied by two or more people; indeed there were several large and noisy parties going on. I had considered taking a book with me, but decided to steel myself to present an image to the world (or at least the restaurant) of a man who *enjoyed* eating alone.

The waiter brought a menu and I ordered a large glass of merlot. As soon as he had set it in front of me I realised I had dropped my napkin and as I leaned down to retrieve it I knocked over the wine, which spread like a bloodstain over the crisp white tablecloth. I sat there mute with embarrassment while the waiters, assuring me that I was not to be concerned, made a great fuss of changing all the table linen. By then everyone in the restaurant was aware that someone was eating alone in Antoine's.

Something similar happened in San Francisco. There was a popular fish restaurant on Fisherman's Wharf that I wanted to try. It was very informal and I imagined that a single diner would not attract any attention. It was full when I arrived and people were milling around outside, but I was in no hurry and gave my name to the table captain and waited my turn. What I did not realise was that as tables became available names were called out over a rasping loudspeaker: "Chuck, party of eight", "Chelsea party of four", "Grant, party of six" …and then, the ultimate dining humiliation, "Russell, party of one."

But the worst, the very worst, night was in Telluride, a very fancy skiing resort in Colorado. How it happened I do not know, but I arrived in Telluride on a fourth Thursday in November - Thanksgiving, the most important holiday of the year in the United States, a time when family and friends move heaven and earth to get together. When I arrived at my hotel - I had been travelling all day and was starving - I discovered that it had neither a restaurant, nor room service. However, the very helpful receptionist said there was an excellent restaurant next door where I might be able to get a table.

It was, of course, full. (On Thanksgiving, every restaurant is full.) I was about to leave when the *maître d'* , who had obviously taken pity on me, suggested setting up a table, just for me, in what was more or less the entrance lobby, next to a big wood stove. It would be no trouble, he said, he could get the waiters to do it in a few minutes. I would much rather have been put in a dark corner, but I thought it would be churlish to refuse his offer and I badly wanted to eat.

So it was I could be found sitting alone in the lobby of a restaurant in a Colorado skiing resort on Thanksgiving, munching through turkey (the traditional dinner was all that was on the menu), at a table passed by all the other arriving diners - it was almost as if I was on display - not one of whom failed to stare and presumably wonder what was so wrong with that man that he had no friends and family on Thanksgiving.

CHAPTER 18: ACID RAINE

One of the many enjoyable aspects of working for the *Sunday Times Magazine* was that the editors were always open to new ideas and were not strangled by convention. When I was asked to write a profile of Raine Spencer, the daughter of the novelist Dame Barbara Cartland and the reviled stepmother of Princess Diana, she refused to be interviewed, but I began to wonder if it might be possible to write the whole piece as a parody of one of her mother's ghastly novels. I had to read quite a few to get the tone right, which was, unquestionably, an ordeal.

This was the result:

"Rain spattered on the windows of her charming bijou house in Mayfair as Raine, Dowager Countess Spencer, worked her way through the morning mail. Slipped in among the gilt-edged and embossed invitations - how was one expected to attend so many functions? - was a letter from someone called Russell Miller. He said he wanted to interview her for The Sunday Times Magazine about her extraordinary life. He quite understood, he wrote, that there would be certain matters she would not wish to talk about and he wanted to assure her that he would not expect her to discuss the royal family. Oh dear, had she not heard that before?

He sounded rather nice, but no, she was not to be tempted. On a coffee table was a recent issue of *Hello!* magazine in which she featured prominently attending a charity gala at the home of Baron and Baroness de Rothschild in the company of Princess Barbara of Yugoslavia, Princess Beatrice de Bourbon-Siciles, Prince Michel de France, Duchess Sophie of Württemberg, Prince Edward of Lobkowicz and Princess Hermine de Clement-Tonnerre. But *Hello!* was one thing. The *Sunday Times* was quite another.

She took out a vanilla-coloured notelet, bordered and printed with her address in vermillion, and began to write in her strong, confident hand: "Dear Mr Miller, Thank you for such a kind and considerate letter. I wish I could help, but I am at present totally against the whole idea of any publicity, or dredging up the past, however tastefully done. Please understand. I have had to create a new life without John [*her husband, Earl Spencer, had died the previous year*] and I miss him enormously. Sixteen years of happiness and stability are difficult to replace. Thank you. Raine Spencer."

As she popped the notelet into a matching envelope lined with crimson tissue she glanced up and noticed it had stopped raining. The windows were now speckled with raindrops which glistened like a thousand diamonds. Just like the diamonds she wore when Johnnie was alive. Mr Miller was right to describe her life as 'extraordinary'. She might almost, and she smiled at the thought, have stepped out of one of Mummy's novels. Except perhaps not even the famous Barbara Cartland could have written such a romantic story, such a saga of swirling passions…

* * * * *

It was 1948, not long after the dark days of the war, and the finest champagne was once again flowing freely at coming-out dances all over London. Raine McCorquodale was just 18 years old and the Deb of the Year. With her irrepressible gaiety, her pale golden hair, her perfect oval face, small pointed chin and large eyes, blue and clear as a summer sky, it was no wonder she was pursued by suitors wherever she went.

But she left, perforce, a trail of broken hearts, for how were those gay young swains, those spirited stallions, to know that she had fallen madly in love with the Honourable Gerald Legge, dashingly handsome heir to the earldom of Dartmouth?

They met, of all places, on the top of a mountain in Switzerland. She would never forget his first kiss. Gerald was clearly entranced by her beauty. When he looked down at her, her eyes were held by his, and very slowly and gently, as if it was something ordained since the beginning of time, his lips found hers. It was as if the vibrations from them both were linked together and his heart touched her heart, his soul hers. For a long moment their kiss was sacred and almost inhuman…

They married at St Margaret's, Westminster, that very year. Sixteen bridesmaids in crinolines (twice as many as the wedding of Princess Elizabeth to Philip Mountbatten) attended the lovely Raine as she plighted her troth and became, in the fashion of the time, Mrs Gerald Legge. Four fine children blessed their union and Mrs Legge sailed forth on a dazzling career in local government and the selfless doing of good works, while being at the same time a leading Mayfair hostess.

Despite her tender years and genteel upbringing, she was a forceful personality and at 23 was elected the youngest member of Westminster City Council, designing her own delightful little tricorn hat to wear with her council robes. Not long afterwards, when on her way too Paris with the Viscomtesse de Ribes, she discovered a "disgraceful mess" - dirty teacups and overflowing ashtrays - in the departure lounge at London Airport and caused such a rumpus that she became something of an overnight celebrity, the heroine of newspaper cartoons and music-hall jokes. The gentlemen of the press appeared to find her quite as fascinating as her fascinating mother, who was often interviewed on matters of the heart and the benefits of royal jelly. In 1959 Raine confessed she had 19 enormous books of press cuttings.

As a child, when people asked her what she wanted to be when she grew up, she replied: "I want to be a lady." Lo and behold, when Mr Legge succeeded to the title of Viscount Lewisham, Mrs Gerald Legge became Lady Lewisham and, by happy circumstance, the member for Lewisham West on London County Council. In 1962 Viscount Lewisham inherited the earldom off Dartmouth, created in 1711, and Lady Lewisham became Countess of Dartmouth. Her husband, she told the Daily Mail, was "divine", her "rock of Gibraltar."

She would receive, in an average week, at least 50 invitations to functions of one kind or another; indeed she spent so much time gadding about town that her husband, left behind at home, was known as "Left Legge". People marvelled at how she was able to fit so much into her busy day.

Her career in local government spanned 17 years. Mummy taught her that when one was blessed with so many good things in life, one must always give something back. Raine gave back by working tirelessly in the fields of town planning, architectural heritage and the environment, never frightened to speak out, always insistent on getting things done.

In appearance and demeanour the Countess of Dartmouth rather resembled the dynamic new secretary of state for education, one Margaret Hilda Thatcher. She had the same iron self-discipline, same determination, same dauntless energy, same blithe disregard for opposing views. But behind the facade of cool efficiency there beat the heart of a truly passionate woman, a woman who was to find herself at the mercy of uncontrollable Rapture.

Raine had been happily married for 28 years when she scandalised society by falling in love with craggily handsome Johnnie Spencer, who had recently inherited an earldom and a stately home, Althorp, following the death of his father, the seventh Earl Spencer. They met on a heritage committee. She did not know how it happened, but suddenly there was nothing in the whole world but the sunshine and him.

It was, she confessed to Mummy, "just like one of your books. I'm wildly in love and there's nothing anyone can do about it." Mummy was completely understanding, as well she might have been - had she not divorced Daddy and caused a terrible fuss, when Raine was only three, back in 1933, and promptly remarried another McCorquodale, Daddy's cousin?

Mummy had described the passions burning within her so well in *The Explosion of Love*. "She could not explain it even to herself, but it was a Rapture and a Glory that was like sunshine…. She felt it was a melody which was in the air and in her heart and was not only physical but a Glory that she knew existed somewhere outside herself, yet it was part of her mind and her imagination."

Countess Dartmouth and Earl Spencer married in 1976, just two months after she was divorced by the obliging Earl of Dartmouth on the grounds of adultery.

Earl Spencer's four children took it badly. Johnnie and his first wife, Frances, the ravishing daughter of the fourth Baron Fermoy, had separated in 1967 after she ran off with wallpaper heir Peter Shand Kydd. Their two eldest daughters, Sarah and Jane, were away at boarding school; Diana was six and Charlie four. Johnnie had won an acrimonious court battle for custody of the children and so for nearly 10 years they had enjoyed their father's devoted and undiluted attention. Was it any wonder they resented the appearance of a rival for their father's affections?

So it was the cruellest fate, but perhaps inevitable, that the new Countess Spencer, formerly Countess of Dartmouth, formerly Lady Lewisham, formerly Mrs Gerald Legge, formerly Miss Raine McCorquodale, would be cast in the role of wicked stepmother. And as her youngest stepdaughter would soon become the wife of the future king of Britain, it was equally inevitable that she would become the most famous wicked stepmother in the land.

* * * * *

Every time Countess Spencer arrived at the great iron gates of Althorp in Northamptonshire her heart gave a little lurch. Althorp, with its mellow red brick and tall chimneys and what seemed like a thousand windows gleaming like diamonds in the afternoon sun across a wide expanse of green lawn, had been the home of the Spencers since 1508; now it was her home. But how she wished, with all her heart, that it could have been a happier home.

Was it her fault that she had, at the age of 46, fallen madly in love with Johnnie Spencer? Was it her fault that his children were so disagreeable to her? Sarah was constantly giving orders to the staff over her head; Jane simply didn't speak to her, even if they passed in a corridor; the other two, little mice, kept out of the way.

It was so tiresome, yet her love for Johnnie remained strong and true. It was so perfect, so wonderful, so rapturous, she felt almost as if there were flames within her, setting her on fire. Once, when they were out on a drive in the country with friends, they stopped for petrol and Johnnie booked a room in an adjoining motel for a cuddle, leaving their friends twiddling their thumbs in the back seat of the car.

Only two years after their marriage the dark shadow of tragedy loomed across Althorp. Johnnie suffered a severe stroke which nearly killed him. Raine nursed him back to health, sitting by his bed hour after hour, day after day, positively *willing* him to live, while he lay in a coma. He eventually recovered, totally convinced he had been saved by Raine's devotion. Thereafter in his eyes, understandably, she could do no wrong. This was not a view shared by his graceless children, who had taken to entertaining themselves with amusing versions of the nursery rhyme "Rain, rain, go away…"

Raine was hurt, desperately hurt, but unbowed. She was a woman used to having her own way; not for nothing was it said, when she was Mrs Legge, that she wore the trousers. She was certainly not the kind of person to shirk what she saw as her responsibilities as the new Countess Spencer.

First item on the agenda was doing something about Althorp, which had been allowed to fall into shocking disrepair. Johnnie was a charmer, of that there was no doubt, but he was not good with money. With the estate he had also inherited debts of around £3.5 million, but he still opened a bottle of champagne promptly at 11 o'clock every morning and liked to potter round Harrods spending freely on trinkets he did not need. It fell to Raine to look for ways to pay the bills. Althorp possessed a magnificent collection of pictures, furniture and china, built up by the Spencer family over generations. What would it matter if a few bits and pieces were sold, even if the children did carp behind her back about selling the "family silver"?

Althorp was opened to the public every day and after the announcement of the engagement of Lady Diana Spencer to the Prince of Wales visitor numbers increased dramatically. The amiable earl could sometimes be found taking money at the door, while Raine served behind the counter in the gift shop. Sometimes they would catch each other's eye and smile and the movement of her heart became a wave that swept warm and wonderful through her body. This was love. This was what she sought with a man. This was why she had known she could not marry without love, for love was life itself.

The royal wedding was not the happiest of occasions for Raine. First, Mummy was pointedly not invited. Then no seat could be found for her, the bride's stepmother, in any of the official carriages to and from St Paul's Cathedral. Finally she was excluded from the family photograph and had to endure watching her husband's former wife, the glamorous Mrs Shand Kydd, take the place at his side. Honestly!

All this humiliation, and more, Raine bore with fortitude. But worse was to come when disaffected staff began to sell their stories of life at Althorp to the gutter press. The so-called butler - actually he was just a boy who worked in the pantry - told The Sun that Princess Diana disliked her stepmother so much that she refused to visit Althorp and her brother had threatened to evict his stepmother the moment he inherited the estate. Then the chef resigned and rushed off to the Sunday Mirror with a lot of nonsense about how Raine ruled the staff with a rod of iron, frequently swore at them and was nicknamed "Acid Raine". Raine was not, she had to admit, displeased to learn that the selfsame chef had ended up in a backstreet cafe in Wakefield cooking scampi-in-a-basket, whatever that might be.

Even so-called respectable newspapers seemed to take a delight in attacking Raine and Mummy. Some horrible person called Clive James, or something like that, wrote in *The Observer* that Mummy's face looked like a chalk cliff into which two crows had flown and become stuck. Really! So hurtful. And she had just been honoured with the title Dame of the British Empire. Did no one know the meaning of the word "respect"?

Then there was all the fuss about Althorp, with the children whining that family heirlooms were being sold secretly and too cheaply.And some frightfully common people even suggested that the redecoration was making the house look like a bordello, for heaven's sake, or an "Arab's gin palace", or, even worse, "suburban". Did they not realise that gold and vermillion were the original interior colours of such houses?

Sometimes it seemed there would be no end to the children's cavilling. They objected when Raine bought two new houses in Bognor, even though she explained they were for seaside holidays for Johnnie's grandchildren. They objected when a large portrait of Raine appeared among their ancestors at the top of the stairs at Althorp. They said it was garish, just because it was bright and cheerful and colourful, rather like the cover of one of Mummy's books. The picture showed Raine in a low-cut mauve dress against an electric blue sky. Some unkind person said it looked like the top of a chocolate box.

Mummy, as always, was very supportive, loved what Raine had done to Althorp, loved to visit. She always used to say that she could just see one of her heroines tripping down the library steps and falling into the hero's arms.

So many scenes from Mummy's books could have taken place at Althorp, like the ball in *Never Forget Love*: "The men looked resplendent, wearing their decorations on their evening coats or uniforms, but the prince stood out, wearing the ribbon of St Michael across his chest and innumerable diamond decorations on his evening coat. He put his arm around her as the orchestra struck up a waltz by Strauss and they swept over the polished floor, moving so smoothly it was as if they were gliding over ice. He felt the contessa move a little closer to him and he knew that her eyes seeking his held an unmistakeable invitation in them…"

Johnny absolutely adored Mummy and always used to get out the pink champagne whenever she came. Thankfully, Raine was able to shield him from most of the upsets. He was a darling man and so brave; one of his little jokes was to say, with a faint smile playing on his lips, that the doctors had given him "another 20 years".

It was not to be. On a cold, grey day in March last year, Earl Spencer died suddenly after a massive heart attack.

Raine knew, of course, that she would be expected to leave Althorp, her home for the past 16 years, with all its memories; but she was unprepared for how quickly her departure was to be arranged. Tousle-haired Charlie Spencer, the new earl, told his stepmother that she would be allowed to remove only her own personal possessions. When they were packed, Charlie and Diana inspected each suitcase at the door. Diana noticed that two of the suitcases were engraved with an S and belonged to her father; she ordered the contents to be tipped into black plastic bin liners and the cases to be left behind. Without being asked, Raine removed the "chocolate box" painting of herself.

At the memorial service a month later the whole family put on a show of unity, with Princess Diana and Raine publicly embracing on the steps of St Margaret's Church, Westminster, in the very shadow of Westminster Abbey, where Earl Spencer married the princess's mother 38 years before. Raine told waiting reporters that it was a "very jolly" service, not too long, and her late husband would have loved it.

* * * * *

With typical fortitude, the Dowager Countess Spencer wasted no time in making a new life for herself. She refused to cry. As Johnnie used to say, "I like people who are cheerful. I don't like people who are gloomy." She moved into the small house in Farm Street, Mayfair, and a few weeks later was featured in *Hello!* on a visit to Rome to see her daughter and son-in-law, the Duc Don Alexander Castello di Caraci.

It was not long before she began to be seen out and about and tongues started wagging that she was a rather merry widow on the lookout for a new husband. One week she would be in Monte Carlo, the next in Paris, the next in Bermuda. When she arrived to stay with friends in Palm Beach, Florida, the *Palm Beach Daily News* announced her arrival with a story beginning, "Practise those curtsies and dust off your tiaras…"

She was spotted, carrying a white parasol, on the arm of 76-year-old Francis Kellogg, the cereal magnate, whose wife Mercedes had run away with a Texas billionaire. She had already been seen "canoodling" in a Manhattan nightclub with Mr Kellog, and gossip said that he was "besotted" with her. There was also talk that an unidentified member of the House of Lords was "smitten".

Well, maybe so. As Mummy always says, in almost all her books, Love is eternal. One of Raine's favourites was *Miracle for a Madonna* in which Lord Mere rescues the lovely Florencia from the clutches of the perfectly dreadful Prince Vincente di Gorizia. The story ends well, with the lovers in each other's arms. "Then he was kissing her again, kissing her until the fire blazed in them both. He could feel her heart beating beneath his and knew that she wanted him as he wanted her and they were neither of them complete without the other. Then as the flames within them swept up into the sky they became one with the burning sun, while the stars twinkled around them. This was Love in all its Glory, the Love that is eternal and which is life itself…"

Raine was suddenly disturbed from her reveries. Perhaps a window rattled. She looked up and out through the window of her bijou house in Mayfair. It had started to rain again. The raindrops that were jewels had become tears streaking down the glass, like the tears in her heart…"

[The Sunday Times cheekily included this feature in a portfolio of my work submitted for the 1992 British Press Awards. I was never consulted about which features would be submitted and I don't think I would have chosen this one, since it was not really journalism. I was surprised to learn that I had been named once again as Magazine Writer of the Year.

Many years earlier I had interviewed Raine's mother, Dame Barbara Cartland, at her home, Camfield Place in Hertfordshire, for a feature in the Radio Times. She explained in great detail how she worked - lying on a chaise longue with a glass of champagne and dictating her books to a secretary sitting behind the chair. She strongly recommended that I should adopt the same technique. In vain did I attempt to explain that journalism was rather different from writing romantic novels.]

CHAPTER 19: THE CRAFTY ART OF THE INTERVIEW

Hollywood publicists, a loathsome crowd by and large, grew in power year by year in the Nineties; the bigger the star they represented, the more difficult and demanding they (the publicist) could be, imposing conditions about the kind of questions that could be asked or demanding the cover as the price of an interview. When a movie was being promoted, publicists would often install the star into a hotel suite and then allow journalists 15-minute time slots for interviews throughout the day on a rota basis. As far as I was concerned, this was a complete waste of time. Fifteen minutes in a hotel room did not begin to provide what was needed for a profile.

One of the problems with interviewing actors was that because they were often asked the same questions they often gave the same answers. I interviewed David Duchovny, who played FBI agent Fox Mulder in the television series *The X-files*, in his silver Airstream trailer on the set in Vancouver, where the series was being filmed.

In 1995 *The X-files*, which was predicated on the US Government covering up evidence of terrifying supernatural events, was well on the way to being one of the most successful televisions series ever made. It was being shown in more than

60 different countries and had turned Duchovny into one of the best-known actors in the world.

I asked him if he could explain its success and this was his reply: "It is obviously tapping into *something* people want. I think it has to do with religious stirrings, a sort of new-age yearning for an alternative reality and the search for some kind of extrasensory good. Couple that with a cynical, jaded, dispossessed feeling of having been lied to by the government and you've got a pretty powerful combination for a TV show."

It was a quote that should have rung bells, because Duchovny had given the same reply, word for word, to another journalist in an interview published a few months earlier. That journalist, not unreasonably, assumed I had lifted the quote from his piece and alerted *Private Eye*, which duly pilloried me as a plagiarist. I did not bother to defend myself and in any case I felt a bit guilty - I must have read the other interview when I was researching Duchovny, before I left for Vancouver, and I should have remembered it.

Duchovny was a nice man, highly intelligent, but clearly bored with talking about *The X-files* and who could blame him? I did not tell him I wasn't a fan and had only watched a couple of episodes because I was due to interview him. Neither did I tell Anne Rice, the American author of very successful gothic fiction and vampire novels, that I only read a couple because I had to. I was not looking forward to interviewing her. Her books - florid moustache-twirling prose about bloodsucking vampires, ghosts, ghouls and witches - were just not my thing. But in the event, bless her, she gifted me a dream opening for my feature, better than anything I could have ever imagined:

"Dark clouds are gathering over the elegant Garden District in New Orleans this Thursday afternoon. It is horribly humid, somewhere in the high 90s, and it is evident from the lowering sky and hot wind tugging at the flowering myrtle trees that there is going to be a storm. Somewhere not far distant there is a low rumble of thunder. In an upstairs room of a fine antebellum mansion on First Street, Anne Rice, creator of vampires, is stepping into a long black velvet gown of the kind favoured by ladies in mourning during the Civil War. She is dressing in preparation for entering her coffin.

"Your unsuspecting reporter is parking his rental car and looking up at the impressive Greek Revival façade, with its Doric columns and thick ivy creeping over the wrought-iron balustrade of the first-floor balcony. Coach lights are flickering each side of the massive front door, which is opened by one of Rice's four secretaries, a thin young woman with a chalk-white face and vermilion lips. She is dressed entirely in black.

"Mrs Rice hopes you won't mind," she says without a trace of a smirk, "if she sits in a coffin during the interview."

[Will I *mind*? No, I'd be absolutely bloody *delighted*.]

"I am shown into a large room with enormously high ceilings and apricot walls. Heavy drapes border tall, lace-curtained windows. Incense burns from a holder on top of a grand piano in one corner. A black stuffed cockerel glares at me from the marbled mantlepiece; a wooden skeleton lounges in a damask chair; an ornate carved cupboard houses a collection of curiously sinister china-faced dolls. On the Persian carpet in the centre of the room is a shiny black coffin with the lid open, revealing an interior lined with cream ruched satin.

"Can I get you something to drink?" asks the figure in black. It is only with the greatest of restraint that I am able to resist asking for a glass of blood. I settle, instead for a cup of coffee.

"She leaves me sitting in an upright chair facing the coffin and wondering what to make of all this malarkey, particularly Anne Rice's often-quoted desire to be taken as a serious writer.

It seems the room is unusually chilly, or is it just my imagination?

"After a few minutes, Rice herself appears, the drama of the moment perhaps rather spoiled by the fact that she is short and plump and wears spectacles and is accompanied by yet another secretary whose function appears to be to manoeuvre her into the coffin. It soon becomes clear that this is not as easy as it might first appear.

"Now, how am I going to do this?"

"Get your legs round this way."

"Like this?"

"That's it, there you go."

"Great, now I'm comfortable."

"Do you want some cushions behind you?"

""Get some of the pillows from upstairs, that will be fine."

Rice is at last sitting in the coffin, a cold drink in a can on the floor beside her, claiming to be relaxed and comfortable although, in truth, it is hard to see how a coffin can be more comfortable than one of the sofas or easy chairs in the room…"

Sometimes a request for an interview is submitted more in faint hope than expectation of success. Sometimes you get a surprise. In 1994 President Alberto Fujimori of Peru was beset by allegations of corruption and was involved in a very messy and acrimonious divorce from his wife, who had accused him of being a "tyrant" and was planning to set up her own political party in an attempt to kick him out of office. Under these circumstances, I was more than a little surprised to find myself on a flight to Lima to interview him.

Fujimori was a Peruvian citizen born of Japanese immigrants (although there was a serious question mark over whether he had really been born in Peru and thus eligible to be president). He had a successful career as an academic and was a dark horse candidate when he won the presidential election in

1990, beating the writer Mario Vargas Llosa in a surprising upset. It was the first time in history that somebody of Japanese ancestry had become the head off state of a country outside Japan.

In his first term in office he enacted widespread neo-liberal reforms, restored Peru's economic stability and defeated the *Sendero Luminoso* (the Shining Path), a very nasty Maoist guerrilla movement that had terrorised Peru for years. In his second term he easily won re-election with two-thirds of the vote, but then everything started to go wrong, with myriad accusations of criminality and human rights abuses, not helped by a messy and very public divorce. When Fujimori separated from his wife, Susana Higuchi, he formally stripped her of her title as First Lady and replaced her with their eldest daughter. Higuchi went on the warpath, denouncing his administration as thoroughly corrupt.

I was amazed when Fujimori agreed to an interview, no more so than the editor at the Magazine who had set it up. My instructions were to report to the national air base outside Lima at four o'clock in the afternoon and await his arrival. I was then to accompany him on a tour of areas of the country recently liberated from the *Sendero Luminoso* insurgency. I arrived half an hour early and was told that the President was engaged on urgent parliamentary business and would be a little late.

I waited one hour, then two, then three. At eight o'clock I was offered dinner - actually Fujimori's dinner - on the presidential jet, which was parked on the tarmac next to the VIP suite where I was waiting. His aides were beside themselves with embarrassment and kept apologising, but I wasn't in the least bothered. I knew the longer he kept me waiting, the more obligated he would feel to give me plenty of time later.

And so it proved. At half past eleven - eight hours after I had arrived at the airfield - there was a sudden flurry of activity and a motorcade with police outriders and wailing sirens swept into the air base. Fujimori jumped out of a limousine, ignored the line of officials waiting to greet him, strode over to where I was standing, pumped my hand and apologised profusely for keeping me waiting. Within minutes we were airborne in the presidential jet; I was sitting next to the president with a glass of champagne in my hand.

For the next four days I was close by his side as he toured the country to a mainly rapturous reception from the crowds. I was even obliged, at his insistence, to take a seat on the platform with local dignitaries every time he gave a speech. He must have told me a dozen times that we were in territory which, just a few years ago, was entirely under the control of the *Sendero Luminoso*.

Back in Lima I tackled the difficult part of the assignment. I wanted to talk to Susana Higuchi, his estranged wife, but I did not want him to know about it. Despite his popularity, Fujimori ran Peru virtually as a police state and his intelligence department, the *Servicio Inteligencia Nacional* (SIN), led by a particularly nasty individual by the name of Vladimiro Montesinos, was greatly feared. I suspected that the telephone in my hotel room was tapped and that I was being followed while I was in Lima, both of which turned out to be correct.

I was able to warn the Magazine to be discreet when they called me by telephoning Renate at home and telling her that I was fine and everything was going well and that I had noticed the "dogs in Lima had extraordinarily large ears." She got the message and passed it on to the editor. I just hoped that the *SIN* agent listening in to my telephone was not familiar with Cockney rhyming slang: "dog" = "dog and bone" = phone.

It took quite a little while to arrange an interview with Higuchi and involved a number of meetings in bars and cafes with intermediaries. Eventually late one night I was driven to a shop somewhere in the back streets of Lima, hustled up a grubby flight of stairs lit by a single bulb and ushered into a room where Higuchi was waiting. She talked - ranted would probably be a better description - for about two hours, alleged she had been tortured and that her husband was planning to have her killed. I did not know how much to believe, but I did notice as I was leaving that there was a Chevrolet with darkened windows, the vehicle of choice of the SIN, parked on the opposite side of the street. I could just discern the shapes of two men sitting inside and the red glow from the tips of their cigarettes.

Fujimori's presidency collapsed in 2000 and he fled to Japan amid a major scandal involving corruption and human rights violations. He maintained a self-imposed exile until he was arrested while visiting Chile in 2005 and was eventually sent to prison after being found guilty of a multitude of human rights abuses, including murder, kidnapping and crimes against humanity. I actually quite liked him.

When mini cassette portable tape recorders with built-in microphones first came on the market it became pretty much routine for journalists to record their interviews. The advantages were huge. Even if you had immaculate shorthand (and I did not) having a precise record of not just what was said but how it was said was invaluable; an interviewee's choice of words could sometimes, in and of itself, be revealing. I always asked permission to use a tape recorder before I set it up and I tried to place it somewhere unobtrusive so that the interviewee would soon forget it was there.

Interviewees who were reluctant to be recorded tended to be nervous about what was going on and worried about what they might say. Having to use a notebook generated its own problems. If the interviewer suddenly started scribbling furiously, the interviewee often faltered, wondering what it was he or she had said that prompted such a reaction. I developed a subterfuge - "rat-like cunning" - to get around this difficulty. If the interviewee said something really interesting, or apposite, or controversial, I lodged it in my mind, asked an innocuous question and while that was being answered jotted down the previous answer.

When Mary Archer told me, over Sunday lunch at the Old Vicarage, Grantchester, that her husband, Jeffrey, had "a gift for inaccurate precis" I had to keep repeating it over and over in my head all through lunch to remember the exact words. What she was saying, in her elegant and academic way, was that her husband, rather like President Trump, was an inveterate liar. After I had said goodbye and got into my car to drive home, I stopped at the first lay-by to write it down. It was a marvellous quote that would repeatedly be attached to anything written about Jeffrey in the future, but only *Granta* magazine ever credited me as the source.

Of all the people I interviewed over the years, only two became friends. One was Adam Faith, as I mentioned earlier, the other was Anita Roddick, the founder of The Body Shop. I was introduced to Anita by a mutual friend when she was looking for a writer to ghost her autobiography. I had never really seen myself as a ghost writer, but we hit it off immediately. Anita was funny, direct and shrewd, unabashed by a propensity to pepper her conversation with hilarious malapropisms. She had started The Body Shop with a single rented outlet in Brighton and turned it into one of the world's leading ethical corporations, promoting fair trade and the responsibility of business to the community - issues about which she was positively messianic. I could recognise that the message she was promoting was entirely worthwhile and by the end of our first meeting I had agreed I would write her book. I did not think it would be difficult - she loved to talk and was very open and honest about her life and times.

I suggested that my agent, Michael Sissons, should set up a publishing deal and a couple of weeks later Michael and I travelled down to The Body Shop headquarters at Littlehampton to sign a contract. Unbeknown to us, when we arrived in Littlehampton, some major problem had arisen with the European Union and Anita kept us waiting for more than an hour. Michael got very, very tetchy. Unlike me, he was unaccustomed to being kept waiting and was on the point of walking out when a secretary came down and said that at last Anita was ready to see us.

He stalked into her office, red-faced and angry, but Anita disarmed him immediately. She apologised, briefly explained the problem and then demanded: "Are you a nice person?" Michael opened and closed his mouth without a word coming out. I could see he had no idea how to reply and I had to turn away to hide my smile. We agreed that Michael would auction a proposal for the book and that Anita and I would split the proceeds 50-50. She planned to donate her share to charity.

Michael was confident that an Anita Roddick autobiography would generate intense interest and he was right. The auction was won by Random House with an offer of an advance of £200,000. My share would be more, much more, than I had earned from any of my previous books and it also rather seemed as if it would be a lot less work. All I had to do, I told myself, was conduct a series of extended and very detailed interviews with Anita.

And that was the problem. Getting Anita to sit down for five minutes, let alone two or three hours, was virtually impossible (she did not even have a chair in her office at The

Body Shop headquarters). She was too busy trying to save the world as a human rights activist and environmental campaigner, too distracted by a million other projects, too involved in spreading her business philosophy of community engagement and social change. Full of energy and ideas, she lived her life at a hectic pace, rushing hither and thither, moving from one project to another like a gadfly. She could no more sit down with me to talk about her life than she could write her own autobiography.

In the end the interviews took place in the only environment where Anita was absolutely forced to sit still - on an aeroplane. At the time she was frequently commuting across the Atlantic, mainly to New York, so we agreed that I would travel with her. She was amazing - she could talk for the entire seven hours it took to fly from London to New York and continue talking in the limousine taking us into Manhattan. She would repeat the performance on the return journey. I can't remember how many trips we took together, but it was a lot.

Her book, *Body & Soul*, was a big success and deserved to be. It won a number of awards and was included in an anthology of the year's best non-fiction. My name appeared nowhere, which was how I wanted it to be, but a little while later she was interviewed by *The Guardian* and asked to name her favourite journalist. It was me.

I was greatly saddened when Anita died suddenly and unexpectedly of a brain haemorrhage in September 2007, aged only 64. She had always told me that she had no intention of leaving anything to her family - she had two grown-up daughters - and she did not. Her entire estate, some £50 million plus, went to charities.

CHAPTER 20: THE ATTEMPTED ASSASSINATION OF PRINCE CHARLES

As a general rule I always believed that the more time you can spend with the subject of a profile the better. The one possible exception to this rule was Mrs Imelda Marcos, the former First Lady of the Philippines. After six uninterrupted hours in Imelda's company in Manila, during which she talked non-stop and barely paused for breath, I was ready to open my veins rather than endure a seventh.

Her late husband. Ferdinand Marcos, was president of the Philippines for 21 years during which time his regime became infamous for corruption, extravagance and brutality; it was alleged he and his avaricious wife plundered up to $10 billion from the poverty-stricken Filipino people. Imelda became a byword for conspicuous consumption; "imeldific" means shameless and vulgar extravagance. When the Marcos' were removed from power in 1986 and forced to flee the country, the doors of the presidential palace were flung open to reveal her personal wardrobe included 3,000 pairs of shoes, 2,000 ball gowns, 35 racks of furs and five shelves of unused Gucci handbags.

After Ferdinand's death in 1989 Imelda was surprisingly allowed to return to Manila from exile in Hawaii. She was immediately indicted on corruption charges and was still fighting the case when she agreed to an interview for the *Sunday Times Magazine.* She was also appealing a US Federal Court award of $1.2 billion in damages for the 10,000 people tortured during her husband's regime and a further 298 charges were pending.

I foolishly arranged to meet her on the day after I arrived in Manila after a 13-hour flight from London. The Philippines is seven hours ahead of the United Kingdom, so it was three o'clock in the morning (my time) and I had had very little sleep when I arrived at her luxury apartment on the 34th floor of a prestigious block in the centre of Manila. A maid showed me into a large room furnished in a gaudy rococo style. I only waited a few minutes before Madame Marcos (her preferred form of address) swept in, smiling broadly. Immaculately turned out, she was wearing a simple black tunic top, black ski pants and stiletto-heeled mules, with full make-up and not a hair of her strange, instantly recognisable, beehive, out of place

It soon became clear that 64-year-old Madame Marcos enjoyed being interviewed and welcomed the opportunity to present herself as the misunderstood, innocent victim and martyred widow. While I sat on a sofa facing her, struggling to concentrate and stay awake, she perched on the edge of a gilt armchair and talked and talked and talked and talked…

Sometimes she adopted a syrupy little-girl voice, sometimes she declaimed as if addressing a political rally, sometimes she was indignant, sometimes sorrowful at the folly of her enemies. One minute she was tub-thumping about the need for a new world order, the next she was a poor oppressed widow, the next a defiant crusader for justice, the next the loving mother of the nation. She wept, she giggled, she fluttered her thick eyelashes. It was, unquestionably, a bravura performance.

Utterly unrepentant and apparently unconcerned by the array of charges against her, she denied everything. Not only had she not stolen any money from the people, but her husband, a very rich man, had used his personal fortune to finance many community and civic projects. Yes, it was true she owned many pairs of shoes, but only because she had been asked to perform the opening ceremony at hundreds of shoe factories in the country and had accepted shoes as a gift. Ninety-nine per cent of her shoes she had never worn.

Was she upset, I asked her when I could get a word in, by being described in court as a world-class shopper. "Shopping?" she said in a slightly puzzled voice as if she was unfamiliar with the term. She stared out of the window at the grey blanket of pollution hanging over Manila and eventually continued "Yes, it is true I was a shopper, but I was shopping for the hospitals, the museums, the housing projects. Because I could afford it I bought beautiful things - paintings, Matisse, Monet, works of art for my country, to fill museums and cultural centres. I wanted the best for my people. But for me, personally, nothing. *Nothing.*"

She claimed that government had stolen everything from her and that she now owned nothing. But what about the $356 million the government was currently trying to extricate from a secret Swiss bank account? Had she not offered to release the money in exchange for a complete exoneration from all the charges against her?

She sighed heavily. "What you have to understand, Mr Miller," she said, her eyes misting over, "is that money is not as important as justice. They can take my money, but not my good name, my dignity and my sacred honour. In all of this I have been strong and it is the strength of someone who is at peace with the truth. I have a very childlike attitude to life. My only mistake was to look on everyone as good."

At lunchtime a maid brought in a tray of cold drinks and sandwiches and I thought we might be able to take a break, but Madame Marcos declined to eat anything, perhaps because she did not want to talk with her mouth full and so she kept talking. When at last it seemed this interminable interview was finally drawing to a close, the maid was summoned to bring in an easel. I wondered what on earth was going on as she disappeared and then reappeared carrying a block of paper which she propped up on the easel.

Madame Marcos stood, walked across to the easel, picked up a felt tip pen and launched into a lengthy exposition - a very lengthy exposition, complete with complicated flow charts drawn with coloured felt tip pens - about her plans to save the world with a new world order based on love and respect. It was all bonkers, of course, but it occupied at least another hour.

My smile by then was a rictus, I ached in every bone in my body, my eyelids felt as if they were made of lead and I was certain there were small braziers burning behind each of my retinas. After six hours I could stand it no longer. When she paused for a brief and blessed moment, I looked at my watch and said, as if startled, "Good heavens! I hadn't realised I had taken up so much of your time" and switched off my tape recorder to signal the interview was at an end. She looked for a moment as she might object, but then changed her mind. I clambered wearily to my feet, thanked her profusely and apologised again for taking up so much of her time. She pouted, a mite sulkily, but shook my outstretched hand. Before she called the maid to show me to the door, she presented me with a sheaf of flow-charts and suggested I should study them later.

I staggered out into the street, eyeballs swivelling, and hailed a taxi. Back in my room at the Manila Intercontinental I junked the flow-charts into a waste bin, threw myself onto the bed and slept for ten straight hours.

* * * * *

I returned home to Buckinghamshire on, I think, a Tuesday. On Wednesday morning I got a call from the editor of the Review section of the newspaper. (Although I always regarded my contract was with the Magazine, it was in fact with the *Sunday Times* as a whole and I had occasionally written pieces for the newspaper.) He asked me if I would be free to fly to Sydney that night to cover Prince Charles' tour of Australia.

"Blimey," I said, "twenty four hours ago I was in the Philippines, two thirds of the way there. Why didn't you ask me before I left?"

He apologised and said a decision to cover the tour had only been made at the editorial conference that morning. It was the fact that the tour was taking place against a background of rising republican sentiment in Australia that made it more interesting. I could have refused to go, but I had already turned down a couple of assignments for the Review section and I did not want to get a reputation for being "difficult" or, even worse, a prima donna, so I agreed to do it. Renate thought I was mad, and I probably was.

It was my first royal tour and, I hoped, my last. I was far from a monarchist; in my view the only justification for the monarchy was its value as a tourist attraction and covering Charles' visit to Australia did nothing to change my mind. It was billed as an opportunity for the future King of England to get to know Australia and the Australians, but in reality it was nothing more than an endless round of tedious photo opportunities.

At the time of the tour, January 1994, Charles' reputation at home was at an all-time low. He had been widely blamed for the break-up of his marriage to the (then) saintly Diana and mercilessly ridiculed when the "Camillagate" tapes were leaked. In a late-night telephone conversation with his married lover, Mrs Camilla Parker Bowles, the heir to the throne could be heard talking about his desire to be inside her person, possibly as a tampon.

It was generally agreed that Charles needed the tour to be a success to add a little lustre to his tarnished public image, but the prognosis, long before he arrived, was that it would be a flop, first because he no longer had the glamorous Princess Diana at his side and second because of increasing support for the creation of an Australian republic.

The prince's last visit to Australia, for the bicentennial in 1988, was judged a big success, largely because of the ecstatic crowds that turned out to get a glimpse of his wife. But that was then. A lonely, unpopular prince with cranky views and his private life in a turmoil could hardly be described as an irresistible attraction six years later.

There was surprise, too, that prime minister Paul Keating, a republic supporter, had invited the prince. But Keating was a wily political street fighter who was widely suspected of manipulating the republican game plan in the hope of carving himself a place in history by becoming the first president of Australia. If his judgement was that the prince's visit would be largely ignored, then that very fact would likely spike the monarchists' guns and further underline the case for a republic.

When I arrived in Sydney a few days before the prince, I discovered that the royal rat pack which always accompanied tours had been stiffened by the presence of correspondents, like me. Jennie Bond, the BBC's court correspondent, interviewed by *The Australian* newspaper, explained a lot of the media contingent were in Australia solely because of the potentially embarrassing republican issue. "We want to see," she added cheerfully, "what kind of a fist he makes of it."

It was already obvious that there was deep public apathy towards the visit. There was virtually no pre-publicity and few Australians knew, or perhaps even cared, that the visit was taking place. As the host of a local phone-in radio show quipped: "Indifference is rising to fever pitch."

The darkest fears of the prince's entourage must have been confirmed when they looked out from the first-class cabin of their Quantas 747 as it taxied to gate 45 at Sydney airport on Saturday evening. Waiting on the tarmac to welcome the heir to the throne to Australia was a forlorn little gathering of rather fewer than 200 people, mostly middle-aged women, waving Union flags. A single protester carrying a placard "Go home Charles, we prefer our head of state and our tampons to be made in Australia" had earlier been removed by the police.

When the prince emerged he was greeted by the governor-general ("Gee-Gee" to Australians) and a posse of various dignitaries and was required to inspect an obligatory guard of honour. Afterwards he walked across to talk briefly with the "crowd" and was then driven swiftly off to Admiralty House, the governor-general's residence overlooking Sydney harbour and the opera house, where he was to stay.

Next morning a similar crowd (in fact it might have been the *same* crowd) waited to wave at him when he arrived at the old parliament building for the opening session of the Prince of Wales Business Forum, an international charity he founded to promote "corporate citizenship" via good business practice and sustainable development.

One might have thought that as this was a cause close to his heart he would have stayed to listen to the debate, but no, a photo opportunity beckoned and he was whisked away to meet a handful of churlish youngsters at the Sydney City Mission, which cared for the homeless and disadvantaged. Then it was back to the business leaders' forum to deliver the closing address, an appeal for corporate environmental responsibility.

Despite years of practice and presumably expert coaching, the prince was not a gifted, or particularly charismatic, speaker. I could see that his speech had been written out for him, complete with ponderous jokes, with the words to be emphasised underlined. But he chose to emphasise words at random, with little regard for the construction of the sentence. Perhaps he made up in anguished sincerity what he lacked in verbal dexterity, for members of the forum applauded as if they had just been treated to a great peroration.

Travelling at close quarters on a royal tour with the prince I came to the conclusion that he was a decent bloke carrying out a job that was almost surreal its pointless absurdity. I was also increasingly struck by the strain he was under, living life in a fish bowl. While he sat at the top table listening to various speeches, perhaps 20 photographers were ranged along a gallery overlooking the chamber. Every time the prince raised an eyebrow or made the slightest facial expression, you could hear the massed clicking of camera shutters. It would not have been surprising if he had nodded off so soon after a long flight from London, but he must have known better than anyone that the consequences hardly bore thinking about.

What was also blindingly obvious was that the stated aims of the tour were a delusion. The prince, we were told, did not want to be seen as a remote figure waving from the back of a car or arriving and leaving private receptions for VIPs and establishment figures. No, that was the old-style royal tour; he wanted to get out and meet the *people*, get a feel for what was going on, find out what ordinary people were thinking.

As far as I could observe, none of that happened. The prince travelled everywhere by motorcade that swept through the streets with police outriders, causing endless irritation and inconvenience to drivers stuck in the resulting traffic jams. When the motorcade stopped, he got out of his car, smiled and waved, shook a few outstretched hands and perhaps indulged in a little light banter with the crowd. Then he was introduced to the people who were waiting to meet him.

The minutes ticked away and soon it was time for him to move on. He walked back towards the waiting convoy, shaking a few more hands. Then, after a final smile and wave, the motorcade was off with the royal standard flying from the bonnet of his car and blue lights flashing on the bikes of the outriders. This was a performance repeated over and over again. He was, no question, always charming and diligent, but he was not even getting close to what people thought. What insights could he possibly have gleaned about Australia from meetings with total strangers measured in minutes?

Then there were the ritual exchanges of presents. At one point he could be found standing in his socks on a red cushion in the middle of a Buddhist temple while saffron-robed monks all around him prayed in Vietnamese. When the prayers had finished, the Buddhist patriarch presented him with an enormous framed colour photograph of a Buddha and he reciprocated by giving the monk a copy of his book, *Highgrove - Portrait of a Garden*. It was a scene strangely reminiscent of an Evelyn Waugh novel.

Australia Day, Wednesday, 26 January, promised to be another tedious round of photo opportunities, the kind of non-events that formed the bulk of the tour programme. For the accompanying media, the only spark of interest was a rumour that he intended to make a mention of the country's republican aspirations in a speech he was to deliver that evening at Darling Harbour convention centre.

But first he was due to present prizes to schoolchildren at an Australia Day party in Tumbalong Park...

It was a glorious afternoon, hot, sunny, a clear blue sky. I was standing alone in the shade of a palm tree, watching what was going on without much interest. All the other reporters had gone to collect advance copies of the speech the prince was due to deliver later. I didn't bother to join them - if he said anything of interest it would be in tomorrow's daily papers and of no interest by Sunday.

Charles was sitting with other dignitaries on an open air stage while a military band played. The audience, mainly children, were sitting cross-legged on the grass. As the band finished up and Charles got to his feet to approach a bank of microphones, I noticed out of the corner of my eye that someone in the audience had stood up. It was a young man and he was running through the crowd towards the stage and in his right hand I could clearly see he held a gun. A shot rang out as he leapt the fence in front of the stage. People began screaming and then there was another shot as the shooter tripped on a microphone cable and fell flat on his face.

For a moment I was too shocked to move. By the time I ran forward to try and see what was happening, everyone was on their feet amid rising panic. All I could see on the stage was a struggling mêlée of men in suits and a pair of feet belonging to a body on the ground. For one terrible moment it looked as if a tragedy had occurred. Christ, I thought, the heir to the throne has been assassinated! But then I saw the Prince of Wales standing behind his bodyguard, fidgeting furiously with his cuffs and looking over his bodyguard's shoulder to see what was going on.

In less than a minute the shooter had been dragged away and a woman's voice was appealing for calm over the sound system. There was nothing to worry about, she said, no one had been hurt and everyone should return to their seats. It took some time for calm to be restored, but when it was the prince returned to the microphone, admirably cool, and began his speech in typical fashion as if nothing had happened. "It is, if I may say so, an enormous pleasure to be here…"

At a press conference shortly after the incident it was hard not to be impressed by the prince's composure. He thanked various members of his security detail who had apprehended the assailant and assured everyone he was fine and the tour would continue as planned. By then it had been revealed that the man was firing blanks from a starting pistol, but no one knew that at the time. What I witnessed was a man with a gun aiming directly at the prince at close range.

(Later that day we learned that the shooter was a student protesting about Australia's treatment of Cambodian asylum seekers. He was charged with threatening unlawful violence and sentenced to 500 hours community service.)

Ironically, being shot at was probably the best thing that could have happened to the prince. The tour that had been dismissed as an irrelevant image-building exercise was suddenly front page news around the world and the prince even figured among the various heroes the incident threw up, drawing deserved praise for his commendable sang-froid. "Plucky Prince Makes the Poms Proud," read the headline in the *Sydney Morning Herald*.

Next day, amid noticeably tighter security (there were fears of copy-cat attacks) it was back to dreary business as usual. In central western New South Wales, in the old gold mining town of Parkes, and in searing heat, the prince could be found doing his princely duty, planting a tree….

CHAPTER 21: DID OJ DO IT? YES!

I think I was driving through High Wycombe on some domestic errand not far from my home on a hot summer day in June 1994 when I heard on the car radio that an American football player suspected of murdering his estranged wife had failed to surrender bail and had fled in a white Ford Bronco which was being pursued along the San Diego Freeway by a phalanx of police cruisers. Their quarry was said to be armed and suicidal. His name was O.J.Simpson.

It was the first act of a drama that would become one of the most widely publicised events in American history. I was not in the least surprised to receive a telephone call the following day from the Magazine asking me to get over to Los Angeles as soon as I could. When I arrived at the Century Plaza Tower the black doorman immediately guessed why I was in town. "Hi Russ," he said. "Are you here for OJ? He didn't do it, man. He's totally innocent. Tell everyone."

This was the view of the majority of the black community in the US and it endured throughout the long trial that followed. Simpson was a genuine American sporting hero, too famous, too popular and too *nice* to be guilty of murder.

I begged to differ. It seemed to me inconceivable that Simpson was innocent - all the evidence pointed to his guilt.

His former wife, Nicole Brown Simpson and a male friend, Ron Goodman, were found stabbed to death on the path leading to Nicole's house on South Bundy Drive, Brentwood, shortly after midnight on Monday, June 13. A few minutes earlier Simpson had checked in at LAX for an overnight flight to Chicago where he was due to make an appearance at a function sponsored by Hertz, the car rental company, with whom he had a promotion contract. Fellow passengers in the first-class cabin would later contradict each other about his demeanour - some said he was nervous and agitated, others that he seemed perfectly normal.

At 8 o'clock on Monday morning, Los Angeles police contacted Simpson at the O"Hare Plaza Hotel near Chicago airport, told him what had happened and asked him to return immediately to Los Angeles. He got back to find his house in Rockingham Avenue, not far from Nicole's, besieged by reporters and television crews. Clearly visible in the drive were pieces of cardboard said to cover spatters of blood.

Simpson was taken into custody, questioned for three hours and then released and allowed to return home. Through Tuesday and Wednesday, while the police investigation continued, Simpson's celebrity friends stepped forward to assert his innocence and his gentle nature. This sat rather uncomfortably with official files which revealed that police had been called nine times to Rockingham Avenue while Simpson and Nicole were married to investigate claims of domestic violence. On one occasion Nicole had been so badly beaten up she had to be hospitalised.

On Friday the police warned Simpson's lawyer, Robert Shapiro, that his client was about to be charged with murder. Shapiro agreed to surrender Simpson to police headquarters but then had to admit that he had disappeared and left three notes, one to his children, one to his mother and a third to the public.

There was little doubt, by their self-pitying tone, that Simpson was suicidal and that while he denied any involvement in Nicole's murder he nevertheless intended to take his own life. "Don't feel sorry for me," one note concluded. "I've had a great life, great friends. Please think of the real OJ and not this lost person…"

At 5.56 pm the California Highway Patrol reported that a white Ford Bronco being driven by a friend of Simpson's had refused orders to pull over. It was revealed that Simpson was sitting in the back holding a gun to his head. The CHP was following and other patrol cars joined in, not so much in pursuit as in procession. Seven media helicopters were in the air relaying live pictures. By the time the Bronco reached the outskirts of LA, America had virtually come to a halt. Across the nation people were transfixed, glued to their television sets. When the Bronco finally pulled into the driveway of Simpson's house the worldwide television audience was estimated at 95 million. It took trained negotiators more than an hour to persuade Simpson to step out of the car and leave his gun behind. He was allowed to enter his house briefly before being driven off to police headquarters and charged with double homicide.

The massive media focus on the story - it was estimated that around 1,000 reporters and photographers had assembled to witness Simpson's arrest - meant that there was little I could do other than pull all the strands together. There were many of them - a celebrity facing the death sentence for a brutal double murder, the damning fact that he had tried to run away, his soon to be revealed history of domestic violence and underlying it all the troubling issue of race. I visited the scene of the crime, tracked what had happened hour by hour and talked to anyone and everyone with some knowledge of what had happened.

My piece ran in the July 31, 1994, magazine and filled seven pages under the headline "OJ Simpson, America's favourite sporting son, stands accused of murder. So how did such a mighty hero fall from grace, and could his country ever let him go to the gas chamber? Russell Miller reports."

I returned to LA in April 1995 to cover the start of Simpson's trial, which was being televised every day and which was being turned into a media circus. Directly opposite the Criminal Courts Building, where the trial was being held, a higgledy-piggledy settlement known as "Camp OJ" had been set up in the forecourt of the old Hall of Justice. Eight hundred telephone lines and 50 miles of broadcast cable had been installed, along with satellite trucks, catering wagons, mobile offices, tented pavilions and spindly towers of scaffolding rising higher and higher towards the rear so that each overlooked those in front.

At the top of each tower, covered by corrugated sheeting, was a mini television studio complete with cameras and lights. From these towers reporters covering the trial could go live on-air with the Criminal Courts Building in the background. At prime time, with the lights on top of every tower blazing, Camp OJ looked like a grounded space station.

On the other side of the street, outside the court building itself, there was a daily gathering of rubberneckers, crackpots, sleazebags and zealots waving banners offering biblical quotations and warnings about the need to repent, or partisan messages of support like "We Love Ya OJ" and "Loose the Juice." ("The Juice" was OJ's street name.) At one corner a young black man hustled an astonishing variety of OJ lapel buttons and at the other was a stall selling OJ T-shirts. One bore the slogan "OJ: Guilty or not, he's my hero" and was voted by *Los Angeles* magazine as the "T-shirt most likely to be worn by a moron."

Every day the court was in session an untidy gauntlet of television cameramen, sound recordists, reporters and photographers was stationed between the door used by lawyers and the sidewalk, ready to waylay anyone who would talk. They made themselves comfortable in a way that only journalists on long and tedious assignments knew how, with folding tables and chairs, plenty of books and newspapers, televisions, telephones, an *al fresco* poker school and runners to bring a constant supply of snacks and sodas. This duty was considered only slightly preferable to the "jail watch" - those luckless individuals required to kick their heels behind the building to film Simpson's arrival in a van from the county jail in the morning and his departure at the end of the day.

Inside the court building a chaotic media centre had been set up on the 12th floor, where an "overflow room" with a video feed accommodated all those reporters not able to get seats in the courtroom itself, or obliged to share seats on a rotation basis with other media organisations. The allocation of the 27 media seats in the courtroom was the cause of considerable strife, with black reporters bitterly complaining of discrimination by being relegated to the back rows.

Particular umbrage was taken when it was realised that two writers working on books, Dominick Dunne and Joe McGinnis, had each been given permanent seats in the front row. Dunne, a fine writer who was covering the trial for *Vanity Fair* magazine, was probably better qualified than any other reporter in America to have a front seat at the trial: his actress daughter, Dominique, was herself murdered in the early 1980s. Her killer served only two and a half years for voluntary manslaughter and Dunne was harshly critical of the judge after the trial for refusing to allow the jury to hear evidence of his history of violence against women, an eerie replay of pre-trial arguments in the Simpson case.

I liked Nick Dunne a lot and sat next to him in the court on the day I had been allocated a seat. We had dinner together that night at Spago's in Beverly Hills and I remember his prophesy that although he was convinced of Simpson's guilt he was equally convinced that the jury would never, never convict.

* * * * *

This is what I believe happened on that night in June, 1994. Contrary to his convivial public image, Simpson was a violent, unstable and controlling man. He was obsessed with his former wife, occasionally stalked her and could not bear the thought of her with another man. Nicole told two friends only a few weeks before her death that Simpson had warned her he would kill her if he ever found her with another man.

Nicole was an 18-year-old waitress when she met Simpson at a private club where she was working in Beverly Hills. They married in 1985 and had two children, a girl, Sydney and a boy, Justin. Simpson was investigated multiple times for domestic abuse during the marriage. On at least one occasion Nicole thought her life was in danger at the hands of her then husband. At 3 am on New Year's Day, 1989, when police arrived at Simpson's house in response to an emergency call, Nicole ran out screaming "He's going to kill me, he's going to kill me." They divorced in 1992.

On the day of the murders, Nicole took her parents, two of her sisters and her six-year-old son to watch her daughter, Sydney, in a dance performance at the Paul Revere Middle School in Brentwood, an upscale neighbourhood west of the city centre.

She seemed surprised when her former husband showed up at the school. He was obviously irritated that no seat had been saved for him, but nevertheless they sat together, perhaps for the sake of the children . After the performance Simpson asked to talk to Nicole in private, but she told him that anything he wanted to say would have to be said in front of her family. Simpson stalked off.

After the performance Nicole and her family went to a favourite restaurant, the Mezzaluna on San Vincente Boulevard, not far from her home, for dinner. Nicole often ate there and was friendly with one of the waiters, a personable young man by the name of Ron Goodman. He was on duty that night, but did not serve their table.

At 25, Goodman was ten years younger than Nicole and while he was a man who unashamedly enjoyed the company of beautiful women, he and Nicole were not lovers. She had met him at a gym near the Mezzaluna. He was good looking - he had once modelled for an Armani advertisement - fun to be with and nice to her kids. They occasionally hung out together at the Renaissance, a popular club in Santa Monica, and The Gate, a dance joint in West Hollywood.

The dinner party at the Mezzaluna broke up at about 8.30 pm. At 9.15 pm Nicole telephoned the restaurant to say her mother had left her glasses there. Goodman offered to drop them off at her house when he finished his shift.

Simpson was probably sitting in his white Bronco outside his former wife's house when Goodman arrived at about ten clock. Why he was there we can only speculate; but he was certainly carrying a knife. When Nicole opened the door to her friend, Simpson jumped out of his car, ran up the path and stabbed her. In the fight that followed both victims tried to defend themselves as evidenced by multiple wounds on their arms. Nicole was found lying in a foetal position, her throat slashed, at the bottom of the stairs leading to the front door. Goodman was lying against a tree covered in blood with wounds to his head, back, neck, hands and thigh. Close to his right foot was a white envelope containing a pair of glasses.

In his haste to leave the scene, Simpson dropped a leather glove soaked in blood. He drove off in the Bronco at high speed, narrowly missing crashing into another car at the junction of Bundy and San Vicente. A limousine driver arrived at his house on Rockingham Avenue (five minutes' drive from Bundy) at 10.25 pm to take Simpson to the airport. Simpson did not emerge from the house until 10.54 pm and explained to the driver that he had fallen asleep. In reality, he was almost certainly cleaning up - he would have been covered in blood from the attack.

No bloodied clothes or murder weapon were ever found but a video exists of Simpson's close friend, Robert Kardashian, leaving the Rockingham house carried a large sports bag and it is my belief that both were in that bag. (At the time Kardashian was a little-known lawyer. Whatever secrets he had he took to the grave with him in 2003, some years before his prodigiously endowed daughters became stars in the dire American reality television show, *Keeping Up With The Kardashians*.)

At two o'clock in the morning, after the discovery of the bodies on Bundy Drive, an LAPD detective climbed over the wall around Simpson's house without a search warrant and unlocked the gate to allow other detectives to enter. They found a bloodied glove in the grounds matching that picked up at the murder scene. DNA later confirmed that the blood came from both victims. Simpson's high-profile defence team would later successfully argue that DNA - then a science in its comparative infancy and not widely understood - was unreliable and that the glove had been planted by a corrupt detective.

Further DNA evidence of specks of Nicole's blood found on a pair of Simpson's socks in his bedroom was discounted when the defence claimed that samples had been hopelessly contaminated.

Under normal circumstances Simpson's "suicide" notes and the Bronco chase would be strong evidence of his guilt. *Why would an innocent man consider suicide?* It is possible Simpson had a Plan B and that he was planning to disappear if he failed to kill himself. A false goatee beard and moustache were found in the Bronco, along with $8,000 in cash. *Why would an innocent man want to disappear?*

Bloody shoe prints found at the crime scene were identified as having been made by extremely expensive size 12 Bruno Magli shoes. Simpson took size 12 but denied ever owning such a pair of shoes until a freelance photographer produced a picture of Simpson taken at a public event in 1993 wearing them.

Two witnesses - one who claimed she saw the Bronco speeding away from Nicole's address and the other a cutlery salesman who claimed to have sold Simpson a stiletto knife exactly like that used in the murders - were disbarred from giving evidence because they had sold their stories to the media.

Simpson's expensive cadre of defence lawyers was nicknamed "the dream team". I always thought of them as the "nightmare team" - unscrupulous men who were prepared to go to any lengths to obtain freedom for a man who was so evidently guilty but was happy to pay their outrageous fees. Their strategy was to constantly muddy the water with alternative hypotheses, allegations of racism in the LAPD, of evidence being planted, of hit men hired by drug cartels, of dubious science - anything, anything at all, that might assist their client.

My friend Dominick Dunne was absolutely right. After a trial lasting eleven months, the jury deliberated for just four hours before finding Simpson not guilty on both charges. When I watched the verdict being delivered on television the camera swivelled to record the reaction of people in the courtroom and I saw Nick's jaw drop in astonishment. "As you know," he told me later, "it was what I expected, but I thought the jury would at least have the decency go through the *motion* of deliberating the evidence. To come up with a verdict in just four hours… it was obvious they had all made up their minds even before they had been sent out. The whole trial was a travesty."

CHAPTER 22: MAGNUM FORCE

In the "good old days", the golden days of magazine journalism before editorial budgets began to be squeezed, it was routine for writers and photographers to work together as a team, to meet up before an assignment, travel together and stay on the job together. As long as each supported the other and recognised and respected that each had differing needs and requirements, it was an arrangement that usually worked pretty well.

I was always happy to help carry equipment, help re-arrange furniture in a room if that was what the photographer wanted (he/she usually did), hold reflecting sheets or lights and generally act as a dogsbody while pictures were being taken. In return, I expected the photographer to allow me the time to get on with my work and not to interrupt when I was conducting an interview. I never interfered when the photographer was working, and I did not expect the photographer to interfere when I was.

I can only remember one occasion when it went seriously wrong, although the details are hazy. I was in the middle of what I recall was a rather tricky interview when, to my dismay and fury, the photographer suddenly intervened, took exception to something the interviewee had just said and basically called him a liar. Within minutes a full-scale argument had developed between the interviewee and the photographer while I was trying to placate the interviewee and get the photographer to shut up. The interview was ruined and I never worked with that photographer again.

Many of the photographers with whom I worked at the *Sunday Times* were members of Magnum, the pre-eminent photographic agency founded after the Second World War by four giants of photo-journalism, Robert Capa, Henri Cartier-Bresson, David Seymour and George Rodger. They were the unlikeliest band of brothers imaginable. The inspiration and driving force was Capa, a swarthy Hungarian adventurer, notorious womaniser and incorrigible gambler who became known as the world's greatest war photographer. Cartier-Bresson was a radical left-wing French intellectual who liked to insist, a mite tetchily, that his main interest was painting but who nevertheless went on to inspire generations of photo-journalists. David Seymour, known to everyone as Chim, was a plump, owl-like Polish Jew, a shy, gentle polyglot and epicurean who, unusually for a photographer, invariably wore a suit and collar and tie. (Seymour's real name was Szymin, pronounced "Shimmin", hence Chim.) Finally there was Rodger, the quiet, urbane Englishman and former public schoolboy, a dreamer who only drifted into photography as a means of seeing the world.

I greatly admired Magnum photographers, and a number of them were friends. I once sat in a brothel in Ciudad Juarez, Mexico, for two days with Susan Meiselas from Magnum's New York office. We were working on a story about *feminicidio* - the violent unexplained deaths of hundreds of young women and girls whose bodies were regularly dumped in the nearby desert. We had called at the brothel to talk to the girls about what was happening. Susan was fascinated by them

- one was a boy wearing a very pretty and oddly demure summer dress - and insisted we stayed and return the following day, although it had little to do with the assignment. She wanted to stay long enough so that our presence was unobtrusive and she could take natural pictures.

It had not occurred to me that the agency might be a promising subject for a book until it was suggested to me by my close friend Professor Graeme Salaman, the sociologist and bibliophile. Graeme gave me a copy of a biography of Capa by Richard Whelan, which he had picked up in a second-hand bookshop, and mentioned that he would like to read more about Magnum but had found very little available. Would it not, he asked, be a good subject for you?

After I had read Whelan's book I certainly thought there was an excellent book to be written about Magnum, particularly as the agency would soon be celebrating its 50th anniversary. It had been conceived over a convivial lunch at the Museum of Modern Art in New York in the spring of 1947 and over the years had accumulated in its archive some of the most memorable still images ever captured - Capa's death of a soldier in the Spanisb Civil War, Cartier-Bresson's lyrical family picnic on the banks of the river Marne, Dennis Stock's picture of James Dean in Times Square, René Burri's iconic portrait of a cigar-chewing Che Guevara and many more.

I imagined, naively, that as I was known to many of the members that securing the agency's co-operation would be a formality. I could not have been more wrong.

What I had failed to understand was that Magnum, a co-operative owned by its members, was in reality a large, unruly, dysfunctional family comprised of fractious and temperamental mavericks with huge egos and short fuses, riddled with jealousy and intrigue. On top of this, there was also continuous internecine feuding between the offices. Magnum maintained offices in London, Paris and New York and there was little love lost between them. It took almost a year of patient negotiation before enough members decided that (a) a book was a good idea and (b) that I would be allowed to write it. This was not, by any means, an unanimous decision. None of the French photographers in the Paris office wanted an Englishman to write the book - they wanted a French writer who would protect and promote their interests, not a *rosbif* who would clearly be biased towards the British members.

Then there were some members who insisted that Magnum should have the right to approve the final manuscript. I thought this was an absurd proposition from people who had built their careers on the principle of editorial freedom and I managed to get a majority to agree that I should be free to write whatever I wanted.

To start my research I was invited to attend, as an observer, Magnum's annual general meeting which was being held that year (1996) in Paris. Only members who are sulking, or who are on unavoidable assignments, miss the AGM, even though it often means travelling half way around the world. Part business meeting, part social gathering, part therapy session, part family reunion and part tedious debating chamber, the Magnum AGM was notorious for its bad behaviour, heated passions, vituperation and hurled insults. Rare was the meeting not marked by tantrums, slammed doors, someone flouncing out or taking offence at a slight, real or imagined. Paris did not disappoint.

The traditional opening event was a slide show during which members had the opportunity to show what they had been working on during the previous twelve months."Please make it very tight," the agenda pleaded, "around 30 slides per presentation, as there are a lot of people."

For the next hour or so those present were whisked around the world as a carousel clicked and black and white images were projected onto a white wall. Bleak pictures of the homeless and urban dispossessed in London; the destruction of the rain forest in Sarawak; the Mafia in Russia; the funeral of François Mitterrand; the work of *Médecins sans Frontières* in the mountains of Guatemala; a Mennonite community in Mexico; children in Nepal considered to be reincarnations of deceased lamas; invalids clinging to faith and hope on a pilgrimage to Lourdes…

As a demonstration of a truly international organisation it was impressive in every way, not least in the backgrounds of the presenters, who were: an Englishman born in Burma; a German living in America; a Frenchman; a Greek; a Belgian; an Iranian living in France; a Canadian; an American born in Paris to Russian immigrants; a Welshman born in England; a Belgian raised in America and married to a Frenchman; an American and an Italian.

At four o'clock it was time for the first business meeting. The news that president Chris Steele-Perkins had to impart to his colleagues was uniformly bad. Magnum, he said, was facing the worst crisis in its history. It was different from the crises that were always raised at every annual meeting: this one was life threatening. Unless urgent action was taken, Magnum would collapse. The figures continued to go down relentlessly. Assignments, both editorial and commercial, were decreasing every year. The archive, the so-called "gold mine" that everyone said Magnum was sitting on, was not being sufficiently exploited, particularly in America, which was the biggest market in the world. The debts incurred by the New York office were now no longer sustainable, but none of the offices was working properly. A new, radical business strategy had to be devised and additional funding identified, if Magnum was to stand any chance of surviving…

The members received all this with remarkable equanimity. It was immediately clear that Magnum business meetings were unlike any corporate meeting anywhere in the world. While Steele-Perkins was talking, people wandered in and out, whispered among themselves, read newspapers, took photographs and occasionally nodded off to sleep. My friend Philip Jones Griffiths, whose courageous coverage of the Vietnam war opened the eyes of the American public to what was happening to the benighted Vietnamese people, remained engrossed in *Private Eye* more or less throughout.

"When I looked at the consolidated figures," Steele-Perkins continued, "I find it very depressing that a lot of the new members are only earning peanuts, making $9,000 a year or even less…"

Jones Griffiths looked up from his magazine for a moment to offer the following: "Everything that has happened in the world of photography we did first and here we are bankrupt and divided and on our knees and our competitors are millionaires. Why? Everyone think on that before they go to sleep tonight."

We must have a business plan, someone said. Every year we make plans, said another, and every year they are forgotten as soon as we walk out of the door. The reason the New York office is such a disaster, a third said, was that the photographers won't work together because they all hate each other.

"We've never been businessmen," Leonard Freed put in. "If we're a business, let's hire businessmen to run it." Freed, who made his name documenting the civil rights movement in America, was wearing a T-shirt which resonated curiously with the despairing nature of the debate. Written across his chest was "What does it all mean? What is the purpose of it all?"

"Options," said Steele-Perkins, summing up, "will be put on the table and you will have to decide. It's your company."

With these words, the meeting adjourned for the day, leaving everyone with just about enough time to prepare for the party which was always held on the first evening. No stranger attending the crowded event on the roof of the Paris office that night would ever have guessed that Magnum had a care in the world. It was a wonderfully warm evening with the last rays of the sun bathing the surrounding rooftops in a pink glow. Taittinger champagne flowed, appropriately by the magnum, the buffet was magnificent and spirits were high to judge by the animated conversation and laughter. Only later did the Paris bureau chief admit that Taittinger had donated the champagne in return for a Magnum member photographing the bottle for an advertisement.

Friday was the big day for the presentation and assessment of portfolios from photographers aspiring to join Magnum. It was sometimes claimed, not entirely facetiously, that at any one moment in time there were 500 photographers around the world yearning to get into Magnum and fifty (in other words the entire membership) yearning to get out. To join Magnum at the lowest level a photographer must submit a portfolio to the scrutiny of all the existing members at the annual meeting. If a majority approved, the applicant was invited to become a nominee, entitled to present himself/herself as a Magnum photographer but with no voting rights. After a minimum of two years the nominee can apply to become an associate, still with no rights. A further portfolio had to be submitted and approved before full membership was granted.

At the Paris meeting a young French photographer, Luc Delahaye, was admitted as an associate. Thirty-three-year-old Delahaye was a popular figure in the Paris office and was a being talked about as a worthy successor to Robert Capa. By the time he joined Magnum in 1994 he was already a veteran of conflicts in Beirut, Bosnia, Afghanistan and Rwanda, where he shot horrific pictures of bodies being tipped into a mass grave by bulldozer. Only a few months after being elected as a nominee he was arrested by the Serbs in Bosnia and held blindfold for three days, during which time he was tortured and frequently told he was going to be taken outside and executed as a spy. He was only released after Magnum put pressure on the French foreign ministry to take action.

If there were any reservations about Delahaye's work it was only that it conformed too closely to Magnum's bulging archive of war pictures. "I've seen so many photographs in war situations," sighed one member, "that I'm starting to think I have seen them all before."

American James Nachtwey, Magnum's best-known and most experienced war photographer, argued persuasively that while the world suffered from war it had to be covered. He was supported by Stuart Franklin, the British photographer who took the famous picture of the student standing in front of a tank in Tiananmen Square during the uprising in Beijing in 1989.

In the afternoon it was time to consider the portfolios submitted by would-be nominees. They were spread around on tables in the studio and were mercilessly scrutinised. None provoked much enthusiasm and most were dismissed as not worthy of serious consideration. Only one submission generated any heat - a portfolio by a woman photographer of Russian working class families, photographed in colour at home staring solemnly at the camera. They were curiously compelling, but had nothing to do with photo-journalism and thus immediately aroused the animosity of the photo-journalists, while the "art photographers" waxed enthusiastic.

In the acrimonious debate that followed, it became clear that those who considered themselves to be serious photojournalists, engaged in the important task of documenting history and trying to help people understand an increasingly confusing world, had little time for their fellow members involved in the struggle to produce art. The "art photographers", in turn could barely disguise their contempt for the grubby business of servicing popular magazines.

When everyone started talking at once, their voices rising to make themselves heard, Philip Jones Griffiths boomed "WE ARE NOT ARTISTS!" and pandemonium ensued, with many members on their feet shouting, some quivering with rage.

(As mentioned earlier, I worked with Philip on the Ku Klux Klan story in Alabama. When the cross was set ablaze, I could see, in the light of the leaping flames, that he seemed to be having problems with his camera. He was fiddling with the controls instead of taking pictures. It transpired that all Magnum members had recently been given the latest Nikons and Philip, naturally, had not bothered to read the instruction book. Fortunately, he managed to sort it out before the flames died and took some great pictures.)

Saturday was devoted to the thorny question of how Magnum could survive and a discussion on a rescue package put forward by the London and Paris bureau chiefs. It was interrupted when Patrick Zachmann, a French photographer who had been sitting on the floor on one side of the room, suddenly stood up, shaking his head and muttering something in French, threw his bag over his shoulder and stalked out, his dark eyes flashing furiously. It took half a dozen other members half an hour to persuade him to return, but he would only stand at the back, glowering.

Zachmann was an "art photographer" who only took pictures, he explained to me later, to "express himself". It did not stop his being shot. He happened to be in South Africa working on a personal project when Nelson Mandela was released from prison. Because he was a Magnum photographer and because he thought he might make a little money, he thought he ought to try and record the situation. He was waiting with two other photographers for the great man to arrive at City Hall in Cape Town when they heard shooting. They ran to where the noise was coming from, straight into a confrontation between nervous white policemen and a crowd looting shops. As Zachmann turned a corner the police fired and he took a full blast of buckshot in the chest, legs and arms. He clearly remembered falling and thinking he was going to die and being angry at the injustice of being shot when he wasn't even a journalist. He was also rather irritated that one of his companions, who clearly was a journalist, took a picture of him being dragged into shelter.

During the lunch break Philip Jones Griffiths repeated a wonderfully malicious, and probably apocryphal, story about the bitter rivalry between the New York and the Paris offices. American photographers infuriated their French colleagues when they organised a project illustrating a day in the life of the French capital. When the project was selected for inclusion in an exhibition in a Paris gallery it was the last straw. On the day before the exhibition was due to open Henri Cartier-Bresson organised a van to be loaded with pictures taken by French photographers. The van was driven to the gallery in the dead of night, all the American pictures were removed and replaced by French works.

"Totally untrue," Cartier-Bresson told me later. "Absolute rubbish." In 1996 Cartier-Bresson was 88 years old and the only founding member of Magnum still alive. Although he had not been working as a photographer for more than 20 years and his main interest was painting, he was happy to talk to me about Magnum at his apartment on the rue de Rivoli, overlooking the Tuileries. He recalled with delight that the year he was chairman of the board the minutes of the annual meeting recorded that "the chairman was kindly requested to avoid doing water colours during the meeting."

"Magnum," he said, "is a community of thought, a shared human quality, a curiosity about what is going on in the world, a respect for what is going on and a desire to transcribe it visually. That is why the group has survived. That's what holds it together."

All but two of the 40 members of Magnum agreed to be interviewed for the book. As a courtesy I consented to their reading what I had written about them, on the clear understanding that I would be unwilling to make any changes, except for errors of fact. It soon became clear that many of them were using me, and the book, to pay off old scores and to shed the worst possible light on those members they perceived as enemies or rivals. I was astonished by the loathing some demonstrated towards so-called colleagues; I tiptoed through this tumult of emotions as best I could.

I had more or less finished my manuscript and was on assignment in New York when I got a call from Gilles Peress, one of those who had refused to be interviewed. Not only did he not want to talk about his years at Magnum for reasons he kept to himself, but furthermore he did not want anyone else at Magnum to talk about *him*, which naturally prompted me to ask *everyone* about him. A picture emerged of a difficult, temperamental prima donna, whose arrogant behaviour made him very unpopular in the New York office.

Peress, a Frenchman based in New York, asked if we could meet urgently for breakfast the following morning at my hotel. I was surprised to hear from him, but of course I agreed. He turned up with Jim Nachtwey, presumably for moral support.

After the usual formalities and after we had all ordered our food, Peress fixed me with a baleful stare and said: "Russell, if your book is published as it is, I will never be able to work again." To say I was startled would be an understatement.

Everything everyone had said about him, he went on to claim, were lies. He never shouted at the staff (everyone said he did), he never threw tantrums (he was notorious for it), he was always reasonable (no, he was always *unreasonable*) and so it went on.

I listened to his litany of complaints with increasing irritation. You would never allow your work to be censored, I told him, why do you think you have the right to censor mine? Why would anyone lie about his behaviour in the office? Multiple sources confirmed everything I had written. We argued for most of the morning (Nachtwey said nothing throughout) and I agreed to make a few very minor changes, but Peress remained very unhappy and left threatening legal action. I never heard another word from him.

Magnum, Fifty Years at the Front Line of History was published in the spring of 1997, was very well received, both in Britain and the United States and was translated into several foreign languages. In a review for the *Daily Telegraph* John Simpson, the world affairs editor of the BBC, described it as "the best account of the reality of photo-journalism I have ever read… a sheer delight."

As far as I am aware, Gilles Peress continued to work after its publication.

CHAPTER 23: IMRAN, MORMONS AND A MOVIE PITCH

I never imagined I would leave the *Sunday Times*. It was the first of the colour magazines and in my view the best. I was proud to be a regular contributor and I felt appreciated; whenever the paper boasted about its team of writers I was usually mentioned. I occasionally had approaches to write for one or another of the other Sunday magazines, but I never considered them seriously. I could also have joined the staff at the *Sunday Times* but I was happy as a freelance, working from home as my own boss.

Things started to go a little bit sour for me when a new editor arrived at the magazine in 1995. I got off on the wrong foot with Robin Morgan almost from the start. His first issue was focussed on a single subject - sex. I thought it was dire and I told him so. Perhaps I had grown a little too big for my boots, but I became convinced he was intent on "dumbing down" the magazine and I was very unhappy about it. We had a long discussion about the future of the magazine in his office one afternoon which became quite acrimonious and ended with him warning me to "never underestimate" the strength of his relationship with John Witherow, the editor of the paper. I took that to be some kind of veiled threat.

Robin had suggested during our meeting that it would be a good idea if the magazine's writers got together every now and then. I agreed. The writers rarely met each other except at parties - usually once a year at Christmas - and so I organised a lunch in a private room at the Groucho Club in Soho and invited all the regular contributors to the magazine. (Some who had not been invited, heard about it and invited themselves.)

The Groucho, named after Groucho Marx's famous declaration that he would not want to be a member of any club that would have him as a member, had been opened about ten years at that time and was the premier watering hole in London for media folk.

We had a very convivial lunch with many bottles of wine and Robin's name was bandied about a good bit. Everyone seemed to have an outrageous story to tell about him as an editor, but it was all very good natured. I described how Robin had tried to persuade me to interview Pamela Anderson, the pneumatic star of *Bay Watch*, and when I demurred, he had said "Think of it as a dream date." I was 58 years old at the time, twice married and the father of four children. I was well beyond "dream dating" a television star half my age, that was for sure.

Unfortunately someone leaked news of the lunch to *Private Eye* and added a sinister insinuation that the writers were so disaffected by Robin's editorship that they had met to plot ways to oust him.

Nothing could have been further from the truth, but Robin refused to believe my protestation that Private Eye had got it wrong, that the lunch was an entirely social occasion and that there was no plotting, not even any talk of plotting. I pointed out that it was his idea for the writers to get together now and then, but he became quite paranoid about it, seemed convinced that the writers were gunning for him and that I was the leader of the so-called plotters, perhaps not unreasonably, as I had arranged the lunch. I think he would have liked to have got rid of me, but by then I was too well established as one of the magazine's regular contributors.

It was against this background that I got a call, out of the blue, from Simon Kelner, the newly appointed editor of *Night & Day*, the magazine of the *Mail on Sunday*, inviting me for a drink to discuss a proposition he wanted to put to me. It did not require a genius to guess that he was going to offer me a job. Under normal circumstances, I would never have even considered working for Associated Newspapers, the owner of the *Daily Mail* and the *Mail on Sunday*, because of the rabid right-wing views that tainted both newspapers, but I was thoroughly disenchanted with Robin and so I agreed to meet Simon.

(Many years earlier, I had had a run-in with John Lees, the editor of the original *Mail on Sunday* magazine. He had tried to tempt me to leave the *Sunday Times* and because I was flattered I pretended I was interested, but at the last minute I bowed out, saying I had decided I would not be comfortable working for such a right-wing newspaper. Lees was obviously furious and wrote me a peremptory and intemperate note sarcastically thanking me for wasting his time and adding that he was "glad" I was not going to work for him. I thought it was a ridiculous over-reaction and I replied the following day: "Dear John, Thank you for your letter confirming the wisdom of my decision not to work for you.")

Simon and I met in the cocktail bar of the Hilton in west London. He laid out his stall without preamble. He had been given a brief, and a budget, to make *Night & Day* a magazine that would feature the very best photo-journalism in Britain, covering major international stories. He told me that he and the editor-in-chief of Associated Newspapers, David English, had each independently made a wish-list of British writers they would like to recruit. My name was at the top of both lists. What would it take, Simon asked, for me to join his team?

I did not know, but I told him I would think about it seriously. I was certainly attracted by the knowledge that *Night & Day* had a substantial editorial budget. Although the *Sunday Times* was hugely profitable, it was only one small part of Murdoch's media empire, much of which was sorely stretched by the massive cost of launching Sky Television in 1990 and the substantial losses incurred during its first years of operation. The result was a paring of editorial budgets in all Murdoch-owned newspapers, including the *Sunday Times*. Business travel was no longer allowed except in exceptional circumstances, expense sheets were more rigorously scrutinised and writers were encouraged to minimise the time spent on foreign assignments.

For someone who travelled as much as I did, these restrictions were particularly onerous and the prospect of shedding them was obviously attractive. I had two principal concerns about joining *Night & Day*. One was political. Although the *Mail on Sunday* was less rabid than its daily counterpart, it was still ferociously right-wing and I was worried that I would have to toe the party line in whatever I wrote. Kelner assured me that my fears were groundless: he had received solid guarantees of complete editorial freedom and would not have taken the job without them. The magazine would operate separately, and independently, from the newspaper; his priority would be seeking journalism of the highest quality, not journalism that supported the paper's political stance.

My other problem was that the *Sunday Times* was known and respected around the world. For nearly 30 years I had become accustomed to introducing myself as "Russell Miller of the *Sunday Times*" and even in the most remote backwoods no further explanation was generally required. How would I feel about becoming "Russell Miller of *Night & Day*"? I was not at all sure. I was even less enthusiastic about becoming "Russell Miller of the *Mail on Sunday*."

I had several more meetings with Kelner and one with David English, whom I liked a lot. (We had similar backgrounds - he and I went to the same grammar school, although at different times, and he started his career in journalism on a local newspaper at the age of 16.) We had not talked much about money, but it was understood they would have to offer me more than I was getting at the *Sunday Times* which, with syndication fees (I received 50% of all my stories sold to foreign outlets) was approaching £100,000 a year. In the end, after a great deal of agonising, I told Simon I was willing to join him for £110,000 a year guaranteed, regardless of how many stories I contributed, plus business class travel on all foreign assignments. He agreed immediately.

I would like to claim that I was motivated by high ideals - an opportunity to continue my career as a magazine writer untrammelled by editorial budget restrictions and thus have the ability to pursue stories beyond the reach of penny-pinching competitors - but it would not be true. It was a factor, of course, but I was at a stage in my life when a steady income and the ability to travel in relative comfort was increasingly attractive. Both were offered by *Night & Day*.

When the news broke that I was leaving the *Sunday Times* I was called by a reporter from the *UK Press Gazette*, the journalists' trade paper, who wanted to know why. I could have been mealy-mouthed and talked about needing a change or a new challenge or some other cliché. Instead I blamed Robin Morgan. I said I was having difficulties getting on with him and that I did not like the direction the magazine was taking, both of which were true, if extremely tactless. It was stupid of me and Robin was furious - when we met at an awards dinner a few months later he refused to shake my hand, although he eventually got over it.

Any doubts I had about the wisdom of what I was doing were initially dissipated by the welcome I received at *Night & Day*. I was designated "Chief Foreign Correspondent" - mainly so that I could have a visiting card that impressed functionaries in foreign parts (there were no other foreign correspondents) - and I was more or less told that any story I wanted to tackle, anywhere in the world, was mine.

The *Mail on Sunday* offices were far from Fleet Street or East London, to where many newspapers had migrated, and occupied a block in Derry Street, just off Kensington High Street. It was a highly fashionable area and had the great advantages of being close to many excellent restaurants, some of whom seemed to be almost entirely supported by Associated Newspapers employees lunching on expense accounts. After the austerity of the *Sunday Times*, the editorial budget at *Night & Day* seemed limitless. Simon Kelner had a chauffeur-driven Jaguar and an expense account that allowed him to host long lunches and outings where heavy drinking was *de rigueur*. I remember a party at the Groucho Club to celebrate the arrival of Bill Bryson, who was to write a column for the magazine. We were fourteen at dinner, much wine had been consumed, and as midnight approached there was no sign of the party winding down. I told Simon I had to leave as I would miss my last train to Buckinghamshire. "No, no," he said, "don't go. I'll get Geoff [his chauffeur] to take you home." So at two in the morning, poor Geoff was obliged to drive me home - an hour each way. He did not complain.

My first assignment, with photographer Don McCullin, was to spend two weeks in Pakistan on the stump with Imran Khan, the former Pakistan cricket captain, who was running for a seat in parliament. I did not fool myself that Simon Kelner would have commissioned a piece about Pakistan politics had the candidate not been the glamorous Imran Khan, but hiring a photographer of the stature of Don McCullin to accompany me was indicative he really was committed to making *Night & Day* a vehicle for serious photo journalism.

Don and I hooked up with Khan in Lahore, the capital of the Punjab and one of the most progressive and cosmopolitan cities in Pakistan. He was living alone in a comfortable apartment on the first floor of the family compound shared by his father and his married sisters and their families in Zaman Park, a posh residential district. His new wife, the socialite and heiress Jemima Goldsmith, whom he had married the previous year, was eight months' pregnant and had returned temporarily to the UK because of the heat. She had also, her husband explained, recently contracted amoebic dysentery - not, by any means, a difficult thing to do in Pakistan.

The following day, in a convoy of Toyota Land Cruisers and accompanied by armed guards, we set off on the campaign trail. Our first stop was the farming town of Sadiqabad, where Khan was to hold a rally for supporters of his newly formed political party, the Justice Movement. He was pretty much guaranteed to draw large crowds because he was a hero in Pakistan, having led his team to victory in the Cricket World Cup a few years earlier in 1992.

Three or four miles outside the town, we were met by a posse of youths on motorcycles waving red and blue Justice Movement flags who were to provide an escort for our procession into Sadiqabad. By the time we passed under a banner strung across the main street proclaiming Khan to be "The Voice of the People" there were enthusiastic crowds lining both sides of the street chanting "Imran Khan - Pakistan."

When Khan stood up through the open roof of the Land Cruiser, tank commander style, hundreds of people surged forward. Some clambered onto the vehicle to get closer to him. In the excitement we were shunted time and time again by the vehicle behind and all the time the mêlée around us became more and more frantic until it seemed certain that someone would fall under the wheels. It was an extraordinary scene, made all the more so by the fact that there was not a woman to be seen anywhere, neither in the crowd, nor on the street, nor in any of the open-front shops. "Very strict purdah here," our driver grunted by way of explanation.

Somehow we reached the centre of town, where a rostrum had been set up on two tractor trailers against a huge canvas backdrop which featured a lurid painting of someone with ruby lips and dark lustrous curls who could at first sight have been mistaken for Dorothy Lamour, but was probably Imran Khan. As soon as he stepped out of the vehicle he was mobbed, hung with garlands of jasmine and showered by rose petals. Miraculously he made it to the rostrum without his baggy white shalwar kameez being ripped from his body but then so many people tried to climb up after him that part of the stage collapsed, causing further pandemonium.

After a prayer intoned by an Imam and obligatory welcoming speeches from local bigwigs, Khan stepped up to the microphone to wild cheering and delivered his standard speech, in fluent Urdu, castigating the government of Benazir Bhutto, accusing all politicians of being corrupt and robbing the country blind, promising justice for the poor and calling for the overthrow of the existing political system. "For 50 years innocent people have been fooled," he thundered. "It's time to put an end to the looting and plundering."

The crowd, probably four or five thousand strong, predictably loved it. It looked to me, judging by the numbers he was attracting and the fervour with which he was greeted, that he was a shoo-in for a parliamentary seat and a stellar political career, but it was not to be: he fell far short of the number of votes needed when the election came around. It transpired that the crowds had gathered to see a sporting hero rather than an aspiring politician or a potential saviour of the country. His former reputation as a womanising playboy did not help, neither did his marriage to Jemima, a Jew, even though she had converted to Islam.

(Five years would pass before Khan was eventually elected to a seat in Parliament, but his personal reputation and stature as a politician slowly grew, as did the party he founded, and in 2018 he achieved his lifetime's ambition and was elected prime minister of Pakistan at the age of 66.)

When I got back from Pakistan I soon discovered that *Night & Day* was, understandably, determined to get its money's worth out of me. I went from one assignment to another, almost without a break, backwards and forwards to the United States, to Africa several times, to Montserrat to cover the volcano that had devastated half the island, to the Portuguese colony of Macau shortly before it was handed back to China, to Bhopal in India on the anniversary of the world's worst industrial disaster, when a gas leak from the Union Carbide factory killed at least 6,000 people.

In Zimbabwe I got roughed up by two of President Robert Mugabe's goons at a political rally outside Harare. I was in the country to report on the fallout of Mugabe's disastrous policy of so-called "land reform", which involved seizing white-owned farms, ostensibly to right the wrongs of colonialism. In theory the farms were to be handed over to black workers; in reality they were being given to Mugabe's cronies, to keep him in power. It was a policy that would lead to the ruination of the country, once the breadbasket of Africa and a beacon of hope in a continent wracked by corruption. Most of the farmers to whom I spoke were in despair - one had actually been visited by Mugabe's sister, who wanted to "look the place over" before moving in.

Mugabe loved to travel the country to bolster support at political rallies, often delivering speeches that lasted for several hours and basking in the apparent devotion of the crowd. (Actually those attending had usually been rounded up in surrounding towns and villages, handed T-shirts with Mugabe's picture on and then bussed in to the venue.) At the rally outside Harare it was depressing to see a small group of white farmers seated in the shade of a marquee and applauding Mugabe enthusiastically, perhaps in the hope that their farms would be spared if they showed sufficient adoration.

I did not want to sit with them and so I just wandered around, taking in the atmosphere. After a few minutes I found two heavies on each side of me, nudging me away from the platform and towards the edge of the crowd. I recognised them as members of Mugabe's bodyguard, who were reputed to be very nasty people. I began to worry I was going to get a beating and I reached into my back pocket, pulled out my press card and waved it at them. "I'm a journalist from London," I said. "I am here to report the President's speech and you are stopping me from doing my job."

Neither said a word; in fact they did not speak throughout the whole incident. I tried to wriggle away from them, but they stuck to me like limpets and kept me squeezed between them until we got to a field which was being used as a car park and where they gave me a shove which sent me sprawling into the dust. I picked myself up with as much dignity as I could muster. It was clear from their body language that I was not going to be allowed back into the rally and so I retreated to my rental car. The goons waited and watched until I had driven away.

Not long after that I was in Naples, working on a story about a spate of murders committed by the local mafia, the dreaded Comorra, when photographer Ian Berry and I were arrested. Ian was taking pictures of an armoured car which was patrolling the perimeter of Poggioreale prison when the prison gate suddenly opened and a posse of armed prison guards burst out, ran across the street, grabbed us and hustled us back into the prison, despite our vigorous protests that we were working journalists.

We were informed we were under arrest and in serious trouble as it was against the law to take photographs in the vicinity of the prison, where more than half the 2,000 inmates were members of the Comorra. After our passports and press credentials were examined, Ian was ordered to hand over the film in his camera. He refused. The prison superintendent was called and he, too, insisted that Ian hand over his film. Ian again refused. We were told we would be put in the cells until Ian agreed to release his film. He just shrugged.

I asked under whose authority we were being detained and the superintendent laughed. "Mine," he said. "I am the law here." I asked for the British consul in Naples to be informed of our arrest (I had interviewed him the previous day), but the superintendent just waved his hand in a dismissive gesture as if to say he would be making decisions about who to call, not me. After being held for two hours, and after innumerable excited telephone calls, it was finally agreed that we could leave as long as our credentials were copied to prove we were bona fide journalists on assignment.

The atmosphere suddenly relaxed and the superintendent insisted on shaking our hands before we departed. He was sorry for the inconvenience, he explained, but he had to protect his officers. His concern was that if Ian's pictures identified members of his staff and they were published in Italy, the Camorra would seek them out and kill them.

Outside the prison gates, Ian could not stop himself from laughing out loud. What was so funny, I asked him. He confessed he had managed to swap the film in his camera without anyone noticing as we were being hustled through the prison gates.

"Blimey, Ian," I said, "if it was a blank roll of film in your camera, why the hell didn't you just give it them? We could have got out of here hours ago."

"I couldn't have done that," he replied. "It was a matter of principle."

And then he started laughing again and punched me on the arm, the bastard.

* * * * *

In August, 1998 I was in Utah, one of my least favourite US states, to research a story about a courageous 16-year-old Mormon girl called Mary Ann Kingston, who had run away from a forced polygamous marriage and was preparing to give evidence in court against both her father and her uncle, her so-called "husband", on charges of incest, rape and child abuse.

Polygamy came to Utah in the 19th century with early Mormon pioneers who trekked across the Rockies to escape persecution and settled in Salt Lake City, now the spiritual home of the Church of Jesus Christ of Latter-day Saints, otherwise known as the Mormons. Joseph Smith, the church's founder, had 33 wives and called on his followers to embrace "The Principle" (polygamy) and "multiply themselves without end". Although polygamy was officially banned in 1890 (as the price of allowing Utah to join the Union) it is still widely practised in the state by breakaway fundamentalist sects.

The Kingston family belonged to such a sect, the Latter-day Church of Christ. Mary Ann's father, John Daniel Kingston, was said to have 20 wives. When Mary Ann was 13 she was informed by her father that she would soon have to leave school to get married. She was to become the 15th wife of her father's brother, her uncle, David Ortell Kingston.

Women in the Kingston clan were conditioned to be obedient, but Mary Ann was different. She told her father she did not want to get married, she wanted to stay at school and lead a normal life like other teenagers. Her father was furious and refused to listen and soon after her 16th birthday Mary Ann was married to her 32-year-old uncle in a secret ceremony in Salt Lake City. She cried throughout.

The first time she ran away from her new "husband", her father took her back. The second time she went home and pleaded with her mother to help her, but her mother simply telephoned her father and told him where she was. John Daniel Kingston arrived in a towering rage, dragged her into his truck and drove her to a barn on an isolated ranch owned by the family, 90 miles north of Salt Lake City. On the way he grabbed her by her hair, pulled her towards him and punched her twice in the face, cutting her lip.

Inside the barn, he ordered her to lower her trousers and lift up her shirt. Then he removed his leather belt and told her she that before the night was over she would think twice about running away again; he was going to give her "10 licks" for each of her sins. She lost count of how many times she was beaten before she passed out. When she came to, she was in a house occupied by another of her father's wives. Still determined to escape, she crept out in the night and limped seven miles along a dirt road before she saw the lights of a petrol station, where she knew there would be a telephone.

It was three o'clock in the morning when she dialled 911 and asked for help. When a patrol car arrived, a sheriff's deputy could see she had been badly beaten: her nose was swollen, her lips were cut, her arms and legs were purple with bruises. At first she refused to say what had happened to her. But slowly, over sodas and sympathy at the sheriff's office, she began to tell her appalling story.

Several weeks would pass before she would agree to testify against her father and her uncle, but once she had gathered her courage it did not fail her. Both men were sent to prison and Mary Ann Kingston managed to escape from the clutches of the Church of Latter-day Christ and make a new life for herself.

After my story was published in *Night & Day* I got a call from my friend Nicholas Claxton, a documentary film-maker. Nicholas had already piggy-backed on a couple of my stories for *Night & Day* - about police corruption in New Orleans and a serial killer in rural Texas - successfully turning them into documentaries for the A & E (Arts and Entertainment) Channel in the United States. I had written the scripts for both, a new experience for me, working in an editing suite and synching words to pictures. He was keen to do the same with the polygamy story.

Nicholas was a tall, good-looking guy with enormous personal charm, which I was sure contributed to his success. When he was starting out in his career as a documentary maker he blew a small inheritance from his grandfather on an ill-fated attempt to film the first interview with the Dalai Lama, then living in exile in Dharamshala, in northern India. With all the cheek and insouciance of youth, Nicholas had somehow made contact with His Holiness and persuaded him to agree to an interview. He flew to Delhi, hired a local film crew and a mini bus and drove nine hours to Dharamshala. He presented himself and his crew at the gates of the Dalai Lama's residence only to be told by a functionary that there had been a mistake: there would be no interview. By the time he got back to London his inheritance had been spent.

What Nicholas learned from that experience was never to be deterred by any setback and it was no surprise to me that he came back from Utah with amazing film of creepy Mormon families - men with upwards of 20 wives and innumerable children. Not only that, but after long negotiations with a lawyer representing Mary Ann, he had acquired exclusive rights to make a movie of her story. (He was hoping to move on from documentaries to feature films.)

It hadn't crossed my mind that he would try to clinch such a deal, but it certainly moved us into a new dimension: the possibility - remote, but real - that we might get a feature length-movie off the ground, either as a dramatisation of Mary Ann's story, or as a biopic, set against the weird background of polygamy and religious fundamentalism in Utah. I had never written a screenplay (I still regretted missing an opportunity with *Lorenzo's Oil*) and Nicholas had never directed a movie but, we told ourselves, there was always a first time.

I mentioned it to Peter Matson, my agent in New York, half expecting him to ridicule the idea, but he didn't. He said I should talk to Marti Blumenthal, his associate in Los Angeles, who had excellent contacts in Hollywood.

A couple of weeks later I was in Los Angeles and arranged to meet Marti for lunch at Musso and Frank Grill on Hollywood Boulevard. I was early and she was late but she apologised, instantly made me feel comfortable and said how much she liked my work. Peter had apparently sent her a copy of *Bunny* which she'd read in one sitting and thought was hysterical. She'd been to a party at the Playboy mansion once, she said, and had no plans to repeat the experience. Her main complaint seemed to be that no one made a pass at her.

"I think at 30 I was probably at least ten years too old," she said. Then she laughed and added "Maybe fifteen. All those dirty old men and Hefner in his ridiculous silk pyjamas… honestly. Anyway, we're not here to talk about Playboy. What have you got for me?"

I related Mary Ann's story, chronologically and without embellishment. She listened intently and did not interrupt, occasionally making a face as I described the many wives of Mary Ann's father and uncle and the lives they led.

When I had finished, she was silent for a moment and then she said "Wow! That is certainly some story." We talked some more about Utah and polygamy and the Mormons and then how to pitch the idea to studios. Many ideas were pitched and few movies were made, she said, but this story was certainly worth a shot. She would set up meetings with the studios who might be interested. "All you've got to do," she said, "is tell the story *exactly* the way you have told me. Keep it simple. Let them use their imaginations, if they have any."

A few minutes after two o'clock Marti looked at her watch, said she had to rush, got up from the table, kissed me on each cheek, said how much she enjoyed meeting me, thanked me for lunch and bustled out, waving at friends on other tables as she left.

I sat there for a few moments, deliciously speculating on what the immediate future might hold. Was it too soon to go house-hunting in Beverly Hills?

Two weeks later Nicholas and I arrived at LAX in high spirits. I had in my pocket a typed list of the appointments Marti had made for us - seven in all, including major studios - and the pitch, written and re-written, that I intended to deliver. I pretty much knew it off by heart as I wanted to make sure I did not miss out any significant twists and turns in the story.

We soon discovered that pitching a movie in Hollywood is one of the world's most humiliating, frustrating and embarrassing experiences. We showed up on time at every appointment and were never kept waiting less than half an hour - at one studio we waited two hours. This, I assume, was to ram home our supplicant status.

When, eventually, we got to see someone, they were always very junior executives - a couple looked like teenagers - and it seemed axiomatic that they should show no interest whatsoever in what we had to say and look bored throughout. Few of them asked any questions. One woman, I think at Sony, sat painting her fingernails. When I had finished she just said "Thank you. Do you know how to find your way out?" She was examining her fingernails with absorbed interest as we left.

After four depressing meetings I was ready to pack it in, but Nicholas insisted that we carry out the full schedule. The last pitch was to an Asian-American independent producer with offices on Sunset Boulevard. Just when we had given up hope that anyone would be interested in Mary Ann's story, this guy sat and listened intently, asked sensible and intelligent questions and showed every sign of being fascinated by the whole subject of polygamy. At the end he was unequivocally enthusiastic; he said it was a great subject and would make a great film. He was, he said, very, very interested and promised to get in touch with Marti shortly to discuss a possible deal.

Nicholas and I were cock-a-hoop as we left; we stood on the sidewalk outside his office and solemnly shook hands, convinced we had cracked it.

Marti never heard a word from him and neither did we.

CHAPTER 24: THE MISERY OF CHASING A PRESIDENTIAL CAMPAIGN

In May 1998 Simon Kelner was poached from *Night & Day* to take over as editor of *The Independent* and the following month David English, editor-in-chief of Associated Newspapers, died suddenly of a heart attack at the age of 67. *Night & Day* was very much English's pet project - he had guaranteed the magazine's budget to cover important international stories. His successor, the odious Paul Dacre, had very different ideas. He would move both newspapers very far to the right over the next few years, to the point where the titles almost became toxic and the *Daily Mail* became a byword for everything that was bad about tabloid journalism - racist, homophobic, xenophobic and fascistic.

More immediately important, at least from my point of view, was Dacre's decision to convert *Night & Day* into a celebrity/television listings magazine which would obviously not be interested in employing me - and I would, equally obviously, not be interested in working for it. However, he planned to introduce a pull-out Review section - inserted into the centre of the paper - which would cover serious international stories. I agreed to transfer to the new section.

Initially everything went well. One of my first assignments was to visit Srebenica, in Bosnia, on the fifth anniversary of the massacre of 8,000 men and boys by Serbian forces in 1995 - the worst mass murder in Europe since the end of the Second World War.

Srebrenica was one of six so-called "safe havens" negotiated by the UN at the height of the Bosnian war to provide refuge for civilians trapped in enemy territory. When the Bosnian Serb army, under the notorious General Ratko Mladic, laid siege to the enclave, it was inconceivable to the West that the Serbs would flout international law and mount an assault. Thus it was that when Serb tanks began shelling Srebrenica at the beginning of July 1995, the UN dithered and the 750 Dutch peacekeepers protecting the area were ordered not to do anything that would "provoke" the Serbs.

What followed was almost beyond belief. Serb forces occupied Srebrenica virtually without opposition and over five days began a systemic extermination of all the Muslim men and boys. While the women, children and the elderly were ordered to leave, the men were rounded up. With their hands bound behind their backs, they were loaded onto trucks and driven out to prepared execution sites, where they were machine-gunned and shovelled into mass graves by bulldozers.

Five years later, less than half of those who were killed had been found and, incredibly, only 76 had been identified. Their bodies were stored in a small white building in the centre of the town. Pasted on the doors was a small sign: ICMP (International Commission for Missing Persons) Identification Project. Nothing, but nothing, prepared me for the horrors within. As the doors were unlocked and thrown open, I was assaulted by a cloying and terrible odour: it filled my nose and mouth and seemed to coat the lining of my lungs.

It was the smell of decaying bones and it emanated from the remains of 3,968 Bosnian Muslims, literally bags of bones, stacked in tiers, three bags to a rack, in specially designed refrigeration units and still unidentified. Their meagre possessions, usually no more than a few ragged clothes, were stored in numbered cardboard boxes. None of them had any documentation on them and there was little hope they would ever be identified, or that their loved ones would ever be able to give them a proper burial.

I knew I would never forget that smell and I never have. Even as I write this, it comes back to me. I remember the countryside around Srebrenica was spectacular in the summer sunshine that year: the rolling hills carpeted in shades of green, the fruit trees heady with blossom, the locals selling wild strawberries in jars at the roadside... but most of all I remember that smell.

It is a commonplace in the newspaper business that executives who man desks often have little understanding of the realities - and logistical difficulties - of being on the road. The editor of the Review section therefore thought it was perfectly reasonable to telephone me at home on the afternoon of Tuesday, October 10, 2000, and ask me to fly to the United States as soon as possible to file a piece for that weekend on the US presidential election, then being contested by George W. Bush and Al Gore, the vice-president. He suggested I should join the Gore campaign, as at that stage it looked as if he would win (he didn't).

The only sensible way to cover a US presidential election is to apply in advance for accreditation and then pay for a seat on the Press plane, as I had done several times before. In this way you become part of the entourage, following the campaign from place to place in transport organised by the campaign and staying in hotels booked by a campaign aide. Nothing could be easier.

Without that it is a logistical nightmare, particularly if time is short. It was too late to catch a transatlantic flight that night and in any case *I had no idea where to go*. The itinerary of presidential candidates was not released in advance for security reasons: the following day's programme was usually announced at about three o'clock in the afternoon. Depending on which time zone Gore was in, I would not know his schedule until about eight o'clock that evening at the earliest.

Once I knew where he was and where he was going, I would then have to locate the nearest international airport, arrange to pick up a rental car, find the venue (this was in the days before GPS was widely available), find a place to park and talk my way past security (who were naturally suspicious that I was not with the press pack) to get access to the venue, always provided there were spare seats. When the following day's programme was released, I would have to decide where to stay the night, book an internal flight and then repeat the whole process.

None of this mattered to the commissioning editor at the Review; all he cared about was getting the copy in time to meet the deadline and get it into the paper on Sunday.

To add to the afore-mentioned difficulties, I was then living on the Isle of Wight, an hour's ferry ride from the mainland and a two hour drive to Heathrow. I decided I would book myself into a hotel at Heathrow for the night so that I was in place to catch the first available flight to wherever I needed to be.

Before I left the house I put in a call to my friend Dave Nyhan at the *Boston Globe*. I asked him if the *Globe* had a reporter with the Gore campaign. "Do bears shit in the woods?" he replied. When I explained my problem he had an immediate solution. As soon as Gore's schedule was released, he would ask the *Globe* man to fax him a copy and then he would forward it to me at my hotel in Heathrow. Simple. (Nyhan was good and close friend of mine for many years. I was devastated when, a few years later, he had a heart attack and died after shovelling snow outside his home in Brookline.)

The car ferry to Southampton was only a ten minute drive from my house and I was sitting on board a few minutes before it was due to leave when I suddenly realised I had not packed my laptop - a vital bit of equipment, not just to write my story but to file it to London. I ran down to the car deck and shouted at a couple of deck hands that I needed to get off with my car immediately. They must have thought I was some kind of madman. The sailing was held up for a short while cars were moved to enable me to reverse back down the ramp, off the ship and onto the quay.

By the time I had gone home, picked up my laptop, returned to catch the next ferry and driven to Heathrow I was exhausted. But waiting for me at the Sheraton was a fax from Nyhan with the details of Gore's schedule the following day. The candidate and his wife were due to leave Andrews Air Force Base in Maryland at 12 noon local time and fly to St Petersburg, Florida, where the candidate was due to address a rally at the Coliseum Ballroom at 4pm before flying on to Miami for a fund raiser at the Biltmore Hotel in Coral Gables.

This was not good news for me. Transatlantic flights from Heathrow don't really start before nine o'clock in the morning. It was a nine-hour flight to St Petersburg and there was no way I could get there before three o'clock local time. I decided it would be safer to head for Miami. There were many flights to Miami and I could get there in plenty of time to hire a car, wait for Gore's arrival then follow his motorcade to the Biltmore.

So it was that I could be found on Wednesday afternoon with a small group of reporters, photographers and newsreel cameramen corralled in a far corner of Miami airport waiting for the arrival of Air Force Two, the blue and white Boeing 757 vice-presidential jet. It landed precisely on time and taxied to a spot close to where we were standing. Steps were rolled up and a door opened and after a minute or two Gore and his wife, Tipper, emerged hand in hand. To my utter astonishment, they paused at the top of the steps, smiled and waved, turning this way and that, as if an enormous crowd was waiting to greet them.

"There's no one here," I said to a reporter standing next to me.

"No," he said. "Don't tell anyone. They're only doing it for the newsreel cameras." He inclined his head towards the three network cameramen. "If they weren't here, they wouldn't bother."

An armoured limousine pulled up at the bottom of the steps, followed by a motorcade of no less than 15 vehicles, not counting three buses for the media. In a flash they were gone.

I sprinted to my rental car and followed. I knew I had time as Gore was due to attend a private reception before the fund-raiser, so I was stationed in the ballroom at the Biltmore Hotel as the candidate appeared to chants of "Go, Al, go!" The crowd was mainly elderly and dressed in the pastel shades favoured by Florida residents; each of them had paid $1,000 for the privilege of attending.

The candidate was introduced by Tipper, who bounced up to the microphone and chirruped "Hi, everybody" as if she was greeting old friends. Her short speech was obviously tailored for the audience, since she claimed that "seniors" deserved more respect fo their contribution to society. "I would like to introduce a man who is a great champion of working people, a man who understand seniors deserve respect, my husband, and with your help, the next President of the United States.

The audience creaked to its feet as Gore stepped up to the rostrum. He began, as he always began, saying how proud he was to be sharing the stage with "the love of my life and the grandmother of my grandson." Gore liked to ram home the fact that he was a solid family man with a rock-steady marriage, unlikely to get up to no good with interns in the White House. (He once ludicrously suggested that he and Tipper were the inspiration for *Love Story*.)

Although many commentators claimed Gore was much improved as a public speaker, to me he seemed as wooden and robotic as ever. I had first heard him speak at a White House reception two years earlier and both people sitting on either side of me were asleep within five minutes. He delivered speeches in a monotone, could not seem to co-ordinate what he was saying with what his hands were doing and had no gift for timing. Instead of milking applause he droned relentlessly through it, allowing his words to be drowned out.

He always ended his speeches with a self-deprecating line that had proven popular at the Democratic convention. "I may not be the most exciting politician around, but if you entrust me with the Presidency, I will fight for you every day and I will fight for your families and your communities and I will never let you down."

(Both candidates had standard speeches they trotted out relentlessly on almost every occasion. On the Bush campaign, reporters were so familiar with the candidate's speech and intonations that they were able to silently mouth it, perfectly synchronised, along with him.)

At eight o'clock the following morning Air Force Two was in the air heading north for Ann Arbor, Michigan, where Gore was to take part in a forum. I was already on my way on an American Airlines flight that had left an hour earlier. Fortunately internal flights in the United States are frequent and reliable and so I was able to catch up with his schedule without too much difficulty.

The forum was to be taped for MTV - an important medium to reach out to America's disaffected young people, more than half of whom claimed they did not intend to vote. Gore strode onto the stage in a sage green open-necked shirt, but it did not make him look any more relaxed. The questions were polite and predictable and his answers were prepared and unsurprising.

Things livened up a bit when MTV screened an irreverent biography designed to give the candidate a little more street cred with American youth. Gore was shown as a long-haired teenager who "enjoyed rock music, rode a motor cycle and even smoked a herb". Over a shot of his prolonged kiss with Tipper at the Democratic convention the narrator explained he was "into PDA - public displays of affection" - and proceeded to lampoon the candidate as "President Clinton's straight man, the guy who has been standing motionless behind the President for the past eight years." In a clip of Gore and his daughter, Karenna, she asks him "Are all vice-president's that motionless?"

"No," he replied, "I did it real well."

The following day he was in Des Moines, Iowa, the third state he had visited in as many days, to deliver a speech on health care. It was not an event that generated much excitement among the accompanying media, but the day was saved by a feisty old lady named Winifred Skinner.

When Gore called for questions at the end of his speech, 79-year-old Winifred stood up and told him that her medical bills were so expensive that she went out every day, seven days a week, collecting aluminium cans on the streets of Des Moines for re-cycling.

"And how much do you make from that?" the candidate inquired.

"Why, you ain't gonna tell the Government, are yer?" Winifred cackled as the audience erupted in laughter and Gore himself cracked up. He threaded his way through the audience to give Winifred a hug for the benefit of the cameras, but not everybody got the shot so he repeated the performance at the end of the event.

At a Democratic National Committee dinner in Washington with his running mate, Joe Lieberman, the next day, all the reporters received a "care package" from Lieberman's 85-year-old mother. It contained a package of aspirin, lip balm, tissues, an apple, a packet of bagel chips, postcards for us to "write home to our mothers" and a handwritten note signed by "Marcia Lieberman (Joe's Mom!)" saying "Please be good to my son."

My piece was published in the Review section of the *Mail on Sunday* on October 15, 2000, under an unfortunate three-deck headline "HE'S CHEESY, BLAND AND HASN'T HAD A REAL JOB IN EIGHT YEARS - NO WONDER AL GORE IS POISED TO BE PRESIDENT…"

Three weeks later, George W. Bush was elected President of the United States.

* * * * *

The Isle of Wight was really not a sensible place for a journalist specialising in foreign assignments to live. It was made even less sensible by my imprudent propensity to check in at the last minute in airports. I had always held the view that airlines' insistence on checking in for a flight two or three hours in advance was a regulation introduced entirely for the convenience of the airlines and had nothing to do with the convenience of the passengers. I considered half an hour, particularly if you were not checking in any baggage, was usually plenty of time.

Sometimes, of course, things went wrong. Sometimes they went *spectacularly* wrong. When I had to interview Archbishop Desmond Tutu in Cape Town I decided to save time by catching an overnight flight which would arrive early on the morning the interview was scheduled. With a bit of luck I would be able to sleep on the newly introduced flat bed seats in Club Class and there is only a one-hour time difference between London and Cape Town, so I would not be troubled by jet lag.

My plan was to cross the Solent to the mainland on the Red Jet - a high-speed hydrofoil connecting Cowes, on the Isle of Wight, with Southampton. A courtesy bus at the Red Jet terminal in Southampton linked with the railway station. I would catch a train to Woking from where a coach would take me to Heathrow. It sounds complicated, but I had done it dozens of times before and it was usually quicker than a taxi.

The first problem was the weather. When I arrived at the Red Jet I discovered that fog was causing all the crossings to be delayed. As a result, I got to the railway station in Southampton just in time to see my train departing. I got the next train but the coach from Woking was held up in heavy traffic. Despite all this, I still arrived at Terminal 4 with an hour and a half in hand - unusual for me. It was 8.40 and my flight was due to leave at ten.

I was waiting patiently in the check-in queue when I became aware of a repeated tannoy call for the "last remaining passenger" on Virgin flight number whatever-it-was to Cape Town to "proceed immediately" to gate number whatever-it-was as the aircraft was "waiting to depart". I didn't take much notice as I was sure I was travelling on British Airways, but after the third or fourth announcement I took a discreet look at my travel documents and realised, to my horror, that the call was for me. I wasn't traveling BA on a flight that left at ten, I was travelling on Virgin at a flight that left at nine.

As soon as I identified myself I was whisked through check-in and security at top speed and then I ran to the departure gate. Extremely hot and bothered, I presented my passport at the desk where a male clerk began flicking through the pages as if looking for something. Finally, he looked up and said "I'm afraid I can't allow you to board."

I thought at first I had misheard but he went on to explain that South Africa had recently introduced new immigration restrictions requiring every traveller to have a blank page in his or her passport. It was the first I had heard of it. My poor battered passport was covered with visa stamps on every page; there was barely an inch of space, let alone an entirely blank page.

I tried to play the "important journalist" card: I was due to interview Archbishop Tutu in the morning; it was vitally important for me to be in Cape Town in time. Sorry, no deal. The South African authorities were being particularly pernickety, I was told, and were enforcing this new regulation very strictly; Virgin would be held responsible if I was allowed to board and would likely be fined. In desperation I looked through my passport. There was a blank page although it was marked "for official use only".

I showed it to the check-in clerk. "There," I said triumphantly, "there's a blank page. They can use that."

He shook his head and pointed to the "official use" restriction, but I talked and talked and argued and argued and eventually he let me on the plane with a surly warning that I would very likely be refused entry when I arrived at Cape Town airport.

He was very nearly right. The immigration people at the airport were all for sending me back once they had seen my passport but after a great deal of argument the magic name of Archbishop Tutu - and the fact that he was waiting to see me - persuaded them, very grudgingly, to let me through. It was the first time in my career that I had had to talk my way out of my own country and talk my way into another.

The Archbishop, by the way, was a delight.

CHAPTER 25: KABUL AND 9/11

Four weeks before 9/11 I was in Kabul, the only guest at the only hotel in the city still open - the 200-room Intercontinental. As far as I could tell, I was also the only foreign correspondent in the city.

Kabul in the summer of 2001, was not a welcoming city. While the Afghanistan capital was under the firm control of the Taliban, the forces of the rebel Northern Alliance were rocketing Kabul every night, greatly increasing the misery of the luckless inhabitants and destroying much of the city. On my first evening in Kabul I sat alone in the black night on the terrace of the Intercontinental watching what could have been a free fireworks show except it was a rocket barrage being fired from somewhere to the north by mujahideen loyal to a coalition of anti-Taliban militias.

The Taliban began in the 60's as a gathering of Sunni Islamic students from the Pashtun areas of eastern and southern Afghanistan who had been radicalised in the *madrasas* (religious schools) in Pakistan. Under the leadership of Mohammed Omar the movement spread rapidly throughout Afghanistan. When the Taliban seized power in 1996, decades of continuous warfare had devastated Afghanistan's infrastructure and economy. There was no running water, little electricity, few telephones, functioning roads or regular energy supplies. Basic necessities like water, food and housing were in desperately short supply. Afghanistan's infant mortality was the highest in the world.

If Afghans hoped their lives would be improved under the Taliban, they were soon disabused. Styling themselves the Islamic Emirates of Afghanistan, the Taliban harshly enforced their strict interpretation of Islamic Sharia law which resulted in the brutal mistreatment of thousands of citizens, especially women. Edicts were issued forbidding women to be educated or to leave the house without being accompanied by a male relative. They were all required to wear the *burqa* - traditional dress covering the entire body except for a small mesh screen over the face. Women who disobeyed the new laws were publicly flogged. Men were forbidden to shave their beards and alcohol, music, television and other forms of entertainment were banned as anti-Islamic.

Restrictions later became more severe: religious police forced all women off the streets and new regulations were issued ordering residents to blacken their windows so that women within could not be seen from the outside.

It was yet another bizarre Taliban regulation that brought me to Kabul. In the early summer of 2001 it was announced that non-Muslims in Afghanistan would be required to wear some kind of badge to identify them on the streets; some reports suggested - shades of the Holocaust - it would be a yellow star. Parallels were soon being drawn between the brutal totalitarianism of the Taliban and the Nazis, not all of them inaccurate, and I was dispatched to discover the truth.

Afghanistan at that time was isolated from the outside world by international abhorrence of the Taliban regime and its state-enforced Islamic orthodoxy. There were only two ways of entering the country - both of them difficult and one of them dangerous. It was possible to drive in and cross the border with Pakistan through the Khyber Pass - a wild area where banditry and tribal warfare were rife and where few ventured unarmed. The British fought several wars there in the days of the Raj and never completely subdued it. In the First Afghan war (1839-1842) it was said that a force of 16,000 soldiers and camp followers went into the Khyber Pass and *only one man came out alive.*

I did not consider the Khyber Pass option for too long. The only alternative was to go in by air. No commercial airlines serviced Afghanistan at that time but there was a weekly United Nations flight to Kabul carrying humanitarian relief from Islamabad. It was possible to hitch a ride on the UN flight, but you needed a visa issued by the Islamic Emirates of Afghanistan (IEA). In order to obtain a visa, you needed a reservation on the UN flight.

This classic Catch-22 problem was resolved by a local "fixer". It is my experience that there are "fixers" all over the world, particularly the undeveloped world, able to arrange anything for money. Through a friendly CNN female correspondent based in Pakistan I obtained the name and telephone number of her "fixer", a man called Khalil who lived in Kandahar, Afghanistan's second largest city, and who was always able to arrange visas for her whenever she needed to get into Afghanistan.

I never met Khalil and he remained a shadowy figure to me, although I talked to him numerous times on a crackling telephone line over the next few weeks. He always answered his telephone snapping, in English, "Yes?" as if he was irritated at being disturbed. He was very cagey when we first spoke - his English was perfect - and he seemed mystified that I thought he might be able to obtain a visa for me. Only after he had spoken to his CNN contact to establish my *bona fides* did he admit that yes, he might be able to help. It would take a little time, he said, but he could do it. The cost would be £200, transferred electronically in advance to his bank account in Pakistan.

His advice was to make my way to Islamabad, where the IEA had a consulate. He would not be able to tell me when my visa would be available; I should call at the consulate every day and one day it would be there waiting for me. Twenty four hours later I was checking into the Sheraton Hotel in Islamabad, a short walk from the IEA consulate.

I waited eleven frustrating days for my visa, calling at the consulate every day as Khalil suggested. The "consulate" was a shabby single-storey building in an even shabbier back street, usually surrounded by dozens of men, presumably also waiting for visas. It was rather shaming that the crowd always parted when I arrived, as if being a European I had some status. At first I tried to take my place in the queue but after two or three days I was so fed up that I took blatant advantage of being ushered to the head. Even so, I usually had to wait at least an hour before anyone was available to tell me whether or not my visa had arrived.

Islamabad is a modern city, designed and built in the 60s to replace the shambolic Karachi as the capital of Pakistan. Its wide, clean streets and modern buildings were pleasant enough, but there was little to see or do. Once I had visited the 15th century ruined Pharwala Fort beside the Swaan river, the restored village of Saidpur, the beautiful shrine of Meher Ali Shah, and the caves at Shah Allah Ditta, part of an ancient Buddha monastic community on the outskirts of the city, I had nothing to do but kick my heels and wait.

I spent most of the time reading in my hotel room or going for long walks. Unlike Karachi, Islamabad was one of the safest cities in Pakistan and I never felt threatened on the streets. (Everything changed when Pakistan joined the US-led "war on terror" after 9/11 and hotels became targets. During the next decade almost 100 people were killed in terrorist attacks on three hotels in Islamabad, including the Sheraton.)

The only excitement came when I returned to the hotel in a taxi from a shopping trip and was sitting in the front seat arguing with the driver, who was demanding an outrageous fare. The Sheraton commissionaire, a magnificent figure in a faux military uniform and carrying a heavy stick, opened the passenger door and asked me if there was a problem. I explained that the driver wanted me to pay 30 rupees for a very short trip. "Step out of the car, sir," he said, "and leave it to me." I did as I was told, whereupon the commissionaire walked round the taxi, wrenched open the driver's door and, without a word, began beating him across his head and shoulders with his stick. The driver finally managed to close his door and drove off.

"I didn't pay him anything," I said to the commissionaire.

"That's quite all right," said the commissionaire, smiling and wobbling his head. "The blackguard did not deserve a single rupee."

I kept pestering Khalil for news and he kept insisting that there was nothing he could do to hurry along the process. I was wondering how much longer I should wait and whether I should abandon the assignment (I had already racked up a hotel bill not far short of £3,000) when, on the eleventh day and my eleventh visit, a surly clerk at the consulate asked for my passport and stamped it with a visa allowing me to enter the Islamic Emirates of Afghanistan.

I was lucky: there was a UN flight the following day and I was able to get a seat on it. The plane was a De Havilland turbo prop with most of the seats removed to accommodate more freight and there were positively no frills, but the flight was only one hour and a half. My fellow passengers were all UN aid workers, most of them returning for a second or third stint. I was sitting next to a young Norwegian woman.

"What's it like in Kabul?" I asked her.

"Fucking awful," she replied. "The Taliban hate us and want to kill us because we are infidels, the people are too frightened to allow us to help them and city is being reduced to ruins by nightly rockets attacks. I'm sure you'll have fun."

As our flight banked before landing at Kabul International Airport I could see the airfield was still littered with Russian armour and equipment abandoned when the Taliban drove the Russians out of Afghanistan at the end of the Soviet-Afghan War. (The Russians foolishly invaded Afghanistan in 1979, overthrew the government and became embroiled in a nasty guerrilla war against various mujahideen groups which lasted for almost a decade before Mikhail Gorbachev ordered all Russian forces to withdraw - a humiliating defeat, the lesson of which was not learned, and has still not been learned, by Western attempts to drag Afghanistan into the 21st century.)

To my surprise, I was met at the airport by an unsmiling, bearded young man wearing traditional Afghan white cotton robes and a black turban, signifying membership of the Taliban. He introduced himself as Shahbaddin and explained he would be my guide. He would take me to my hotel, but first I had to report to the Ministry of Information for a briefing. He led the way to a battered Honda people-carrier parked outside the terminal.

We were very soon threading our way through crowded streets on the outskirts of Kabul. At first sight the city did not look very different from any other Asian city, except perhaps for the number of men carrying guns and the fact that the very,

very few women on the streets were all wearing dark blue *burqas* covering them from head to foot.

I pretended ignorance and asked Shahbaddin if the women were forced to wear *burqas*.

"It is required," he replied. It would be his stock answer to many questions over the next days.

At the Ministry of Information - a grim municipal building that had certainly seen better days - my "briefing" comprised a long list of "dos and don'ts", mainly "don'ts". I was being assigned a guide, Shahbaddin, an interpreter and a driver, all of whom would be with me for the duration of my stay and all of whom had to be paid for in advance. (The Taliban's notorious contempt for the West did not include contempt for US dollars.) A programme had been arranged for me. I was not to attempt to go anywhere alone, or speak to anyone, or leave my hotel without my escort. Should I attempt to do so, Shahbaddin would be severely punished. (This was a clever touch - making me responsible for whatever would happen to Shahbaddin if I broke the rules.) There was a dusk to dawn curfew in effect, which was strictly enforced. Night patrols had orders to shoot anyone on the streets during the curfew.

The man delivering the "briefing", dressed exactly the same as Shahbaddin but with a longer beard, spoke good English but in a monotone. When I entered his office he did not immediately look up from the papers on his desk, as if he was unaware of my presence. When he did condescend to look at me there was no smile, no welcome of any kind. He made it clear he had no interest in me, or in what I was doing; only that I should obey the rules.

On the way to the hotel I asked Shahbaddin what would happen to him if I did something wrong. He shook his head. "Tell me," I insisted. He shook his head again. "It is better," he said, "that you do as we ask. Better for me."

When the Kabul Intercontinental Hotel opened in 1969 it was the first luxury hotel in Afghanistan. Straddling a ridge west of the city, close to the abandoned royal palace, the Bagh-e Bala, built for the then Emir in 1893, it suffered extensive damage during a civil war before the Taliban seized power and by the time I arrived only 85 of the 200 rooms were inhabitable. I was, nevertheless, still surprised to find that I was the only guest.

It was just about functioning with a skeleton staff, but none of the facilities of a luxury hotel were available, partly due to the austere Taliban regime - all the televisions had been ripped out, no radios were allowed to be played, there was no entertainment of any kind and, of course, no alcohol.

The restaurant managed to produce basic meals and there was a servant to clean my room, but no other services - no telephones, no internet connection. It was a ghost hotel.

As I was checking in I heard shouting coming from the area of the outdoor swimming pool. The receptionist told me that as there was no one to use it, the hotel management had opened it to local youths - boys only, of course - one afternoon a week. I went outside to see what was going on and, true enough, the pool was full of young men, but they were not like young men in any other swimming pool in the world. Every one of them, in and out of the water, was wearing a long-sleeved T-shirt and curious three-quarter length cotton trousers - a requirement of the regime. It was, somehow, an infinitely sad sight.

On my first night I was eating dinner - cold chicken and rice - when the Northern Alliance began rocketing the city, as they did, I would learn, every night. Each rocket made a bang and whine and a flash, like lightning. I was assured by the waiter that the hotel was never hit, but it hardly made for a good night's sleep.

Over the next six days, despite the best efforts of my three "minders" to stop me seeing anything that might be considered remotely controversial, I got a very good idea of what life was like under the Taliban. It was impossible, for example, not to see the religious police who toured the city in black pick-up trucks, each of them carrying a stout stick to facilitate beating up citizens who strayed from the Taliban path of righteousness.

Any male Muslim on the street during daily prayers risked a beating, as did any unaccompanied woman, or any woman who allowed any part of her body to be visible. At one point, stuck in traffic, I watched three policemen leap from the back of a pick-up, grab a woman in a *burqa* and drag her behind a vegetable stall. I could not see what exactly they were doing to her, but I could see their sticks going up and down and I could hear her screaming.

"What had she done?" I asked Shahbaddin.

He shrugged. "Something wrong."

"Like what?" I persisted.

He shrugged again. "Maybe she was unescorted."

Meanwhile, a small crowd had gathered to watch the beating with apparent enjoyment. The sticks were still going up and down as the traffic cleared and we moved off. By then the screaming had turned into a dull moan.

It turned out, a little later, that my driver could obviously understand English and was something of a free spirit. I asked if I could be taken to see the sports stadium, where I knew that public executions were carried out very frequently. When we got there I asked Shahbaddin what went on in the stadium.

"Football," he said, suddenly surly.

"Anything else?" I asked.

"No, just football."

Behind his back I could see the driver grinning and drawing a finger across his throat.

Later, I interviewed Maulvi Qalamuddin, the "Minister for the Promotion of Virtue and Prevention of Vice" (an Orwellian title if ever there was one), who was responsible for enforcing strict religious codes through public beatings, imprisonment, torture and execution. He made no bones about the fact that the sports stadium was used for public executions - hanging for most offences and stoning to death for adultery or homosexuality. I asked if women were publicly executed by stoning.

"Of course," he said, as if it was a stupid question. "Why not?"

Qalamuddin claimed that the Taliban had banned farmers from growing opium poppies - their main source of income - but on a day trip out of Kabul I saw acres and acres of poppy fields. He also insisted that the practice of bacha baz - the sexual abuse of young boys forced to dress as girls to dance at men-only parties - had been eliminated despite a UN report that stated the practice was still widespread in rural areas and despite the fact that Mullah Omar, the Taliban's supreme leader, had ruled that sodomy was a capital crime.

In the surreal dystopia that was Afghanistan under the Taliban it was the plight of women and girls that most moved me. Basic human rights were denied to them as a matter of routine, or as if it had been decreed by the Koran. It was *The Handmaid's Tale* brought to life. Women were publicly beaten for showing their wrists, hands or ankles, or wearing socks that were not sufficiently opaque. Girls were not allowed to be educated, even in home-based schools.

On my last day in Kabul I invited Shahbaddin and his two compatriots to join me for lunch. To their disappointment (they would have preferred burgers) I wanted to go to a restaurant serving traditional Afghani food. We ended up at a place called Sufi, where the food was pretty awful and the service even worse. All three of them were awkward and, I think, embarrassed by my company. I suppose I should have expected them to be reluctant to talk about what was happening in their country and they were, so conversation was extremely stilted.

I asked them about their home lives. Shahbaddin said he was too young to be married, but he had a girl friend; both the interpreter and the driver were married. When I asked them if their partners were concerned about the restrictions on their lives, it was clear none of them wanted to answer, but they laughed when I explained that there was a widespread women's movement in the west pressing for equality with men. I think they thought I was joking.

It suddenly occurred to me that Shahbaddin was probably obliged to report my views to his superiors. I asked him if that was the case. He hesitated, then shook his head.

But behind him, the driver was nodding.

* * * * *

Back in Islamabad I filed two stories to the Review section: one on life in Afghanistan under the Taliban and the other about a major famine that was looming in the country after successive harvests had failed. Neither was published immediately but that did not especially bother me as neither was linked to a particular date.

Throughout this whole period, when I was not actively involved working for the Review I was researching a new book - *Behind The Lines*, an oral history of Special Operations in World War Two. (After the success of my D-Day book, I had found a little niche in military publishing.)

At the beginning of September I had arranged to fly to Washington DC to sift through the files at the National

Archives and conduct interviews with veterans of the OSS (the Office of Strategic Services) for my book. Renate and my daughter, Charlotte, came with me as we were staying with old friends, Lydia and Jim Hicks, in Alexandria, Virginia, just outside Washington, and they (Renate and Lottie) were going to use the trip as a holiday.

On September 9 I had arranged to interview a retired OSS officer in Arlington in the morning, while Renate, Lydia and Lottie were planning to drive into Washington DC and take a tour of the White House. As I was driving to Arlington, I heard on the car radio that an aircraft had hit one of the twin towers of the World Trade Centre in New York. I assumed that it was a light aircraft that had gone tragically astray and thought no more of it, but when I arrived in Arlington the man I was due to interview opened the door ashen-faced.

"You'd better come in," he said. "This is unbelievable." He led the way into his sitting room where the television was on and the screen was filled with images of both towers on fire. "It's a terrorist attack," he explained. "Two aircraft have been hi-jacked and flown into the towers."

I sat down with him and we watched, horror-struck, as people began hurling themselves from the upper floors and then, slowly and majestically, the South Tower collapsed. I could not believe what was happening or what I was watching on live television. At first I thought, absurdly, that just the top half of the tower had fallen; then I realised that it was the whole damn edifice, 110 floors full of people, had crashed to the ground on live television.

Reports starting coming in that a third hi-jacked aircraft had crashed into the Pentagon and that another was possibly on its way to the White House, where my wife and youngest child and my friend Lydia were headed. I was frantic with worry;

this was before everyone had mobile telephones and so there was no way I could warn them.

A few minutes later the North Tower collapsed and lower Manhattan was enveloped in that terrible, unforgettable, cloud of dust and debris and the New York skyline was changed forever. There was obviously no point in trying to carry out an interview while all this was going on and my interview subject obviously agreed, so I said goodbye and drove back to the Hicks' house in Alexandria through heavy traffic. My friend Jim was at home, watching the television of course, like the rest of the world. He had not heard from Lydia; there was nothing we could do but wait and worry.

Two hours later Lydia made contact from a payphone. They had very little idea about what was going on, although they had seen thick black smoke in the area of the Pentagon as they had driven in earlier that morning. When they got into downtown Washington they found a scene of utter chaos and panic, with sirens blaring everywhere and police blowing whistles and herding people about and shouting that the city had been locked down and everyone should leave on foot. Renate, Lydia and Lottie joined the crowds streaming across the Potomac bridges to get out of the city. All public transport had been suspended, so they started walking towards Alexandria until Lydia eventually found a working telephone and called Jim to come and collect them.

What became known simply as "9/11" - like Pearl Harbor, another "date which will live in infamy" - played a part in fracturing my relationship with the *Mail on Sunday*. As it soon became known that the terrorists involved had been recruited and trained by Al Qaeda in Afghanistan I assumed the paper would run my Taliban story since I was the last Western correspondent in the country and was in a unique position to report on what was going on there. The editor clearly did not agree. Neither of my Afghanistan stories ever appeared in the *Mail on Sunday* or, indeed, anywhere else, despite the fact that the assignment had cost thousands of pounds in expenses alone.

During the whole time I worked for the *Sunday Times Magazine* - some 40-odd years - I only ever had one story spiked. It was a profile of Beate Uhse, a German grandmother who ran a flourishing online porn business and it never ran because the photographs of her merchandise were just too explicit for a family newspaper. At the *Mail on Sunday* I was learning that it was not uncommon for commissioned features never to make it into the paper. The reason was that the newspaper was riven by rivalry and petty jealousies with commissioning editors fighting among themselves and maliciously rubbishing stories commissioned by rivals. Everyone who wrote for the paper had to accept that stories they might have slaved over could be casually discarded.

It was not a problem I had to put up with very much longer: about a year after 9/11 I parted company with the *Mail on Sunday*, or, more accurately, the *Mail on Sunday* parted company with me. I was fired in classic Fleet Street fashion. A senior editor took me out for a very expensive lunch, ordered a bottle of champagne, said how much he personally enjoyed my work and announced that my contract was not being renewed. I was not in the least surprised, or, indeed, disappointed. I was being paid a great deal of money and I was being used less and less. Weeks would pass without me being given a job; it was inevitable it would soon come to an end. I was also 63 years old and getting tired of running around the world chasing stories, particularly when the stories never got into print.

It was not quite the end of my journalistic career. Somewhat to my surprise, I was invited to write again, occasionally, for the *Sunday Times Magazine* - it seems I had been forgiven for shooting my mouth off when I left.

For me the *Sunday Times Magazine* was a still the cream of the crop; it still had the stature and authority of being not only the first colour magazine distributed with a Sunday newspaper, but the best. Many of my friends had turned against the *Sunday Times* after Times Newspapers had been added to Rupert Murdoch's burgeoning media empire. I understood their reservations, but insisted that at my very lowly level Murdoch's ownership had no impact on what I wrote.

If Murdoch had a malign influence on the *Sunday Times*, it was as nothing compared to the rabid right-wing ranting of the *Daily Mail* and, to a lesser extent, its sister paper, the paper for which I found myself working, the *Mail on Sunday*. I could protest until I was blue in the face that I was never required to slant anything I wrote for *Night & Day*, but the very fact that it was distributed with an extreme right-wing paper was enough to castigate me.

Despite Murdoch, I was not ashamed to admit that I was proud to work for the *Sunday Times Magazine*; I could not, if I was honest with myself, say the same about *Night & Day*, even though it operated quite separately from the newspaper.

And then there was the problem I had anticipated from the start. Since I was working almost exclusively on foreign assignments, I was usually obliged to go through the boring rigmarole of explaining that *Night & Day* was a magazine distributed with a newspaper called the *Mail on Sunday*. It was not in the least unusual for the person I was interviewing to be completely unaware of the existence of either. It made it difficult to be taken seriously and difficult to open doors. Why would anyone agree to be interviewed for a newspaper they had never heard of? It was a problem that never arose when I presented myself as "Russell Miller of the *Sunday Times*."

As far as I am aware, Murdoch only made one attempt to interfere with my work. Towards the end of my career, when I was back at the *Sunday Times Magazine*, I was commissioned to write a profile of Heather Mills, the pushy, self-promoting young woman whom Paul McCartney had been stupid enough to marry in 2002, four years after the death of his first wife, Linda.

Heather was a fantasist who had created for herself an exotic CV that positioned her, I wrote, "somewhere between Princess Di and Mother Teresa in the spectrum of angels." She claimed to have run away from home at the age of 13, joined a travelling circus but ended up homeless, sleeping in a cardboard box under the arches at Waterloo station. She became a top-flight catwalk model earning £200,000 a year, carried out charitable work under fire during the war in Bosnia, had been offered a peerage by the Labour government and was nominated for the Nobel prize.

It was all nonsense, of course, as was her claim to be a life-long vegan. Her former fiancé, who was unceremoniously dumped as soon as she met McCartney, told me her favourite dish was steak and kidney pudding.

I discovered, much later, that Heather had tried to get my feature stopped before it was published in November 2004. She must have realised that her fantasies were about to be exposed and so she prevailed on her husband to ask Murdoch to intervene. I was told that Murdoch called John Witherow, then the editor on the *Sunday Times*, and asked him to pull the feature. Witherow, to his great credit, refused.

I carried on working for a few more years, but it was clear the glory days were over. Editorial budgets were being relentlessly squeezed, business class travel was banned and there was no more swanning about America, doing as I pleased. Corners were being cut, assignment fees slashed; being a freelance journalist was a lot less fun.

But I had no regrets - and great memories.

EPILOGUE

It is July, 2019. A few days ago I celebrated my 81st birthday. I can scarcely believe it; only when I look in a mirror and see an old man, almost completely bald, staring back at me do I accept the reality. I am sitting at a computer in my book-lined study in our apartment overlooking the sea in Brighton. Everything around me is comfortingly familiar. We (Renate and I) have lived here for three years, in Brighton for about ten. It is unlikely we will move again.

Brighton, memorably described by my late friend Keith Waterhouse as "a town that always looks as if it is helping police with their inquiries" suits us well. There is always something going on here, it has a vibrant cultural life and very good restaurants. Our flat is on the Kemp Town Estate and so we have access to a large private communal garden, where we can sit in the sun with a coffee from Marmalade, our local cafe. Life is good.

I no longer write books, or features for magazines, but for the last two years I have been working intermittently on this memoir, an extraordinarily pleasurable and undeniably self-indulgent trip down memory lane. On a stool behind me in one corner of my study is a pile of tear sheets, mainly from the Sunday Times Magazine. It is more than a foot high; it is my life's work in journalism. On the bookshelf in the other corner are copies of my books. Renate has had the eleven original editions bound in leather, but there are also paperback versions and foreign translations and reprints filling other shelves.

Re-reading features I wrote decades ago brought memories flooding back, but it was also a chastening experience. I doubt if I could write now as reasonably well as I did then. (Today I have to search in a thesaurus for words which once came instantly to mind.) This is not to say that I ever considered myself as anything other than a workmanlike writer, rather than a gifted one, and so it was always a surprise and a delight when I started winning awards. I won five national press awards in a short space of time between the mid-80s and early 90s - the last in 1992. I sometimes wondered if I had a friend on the judging panel during that period, as I never won anything before 1985, or after 1992.

Stumbling into journalism at the age of 16 was, for me, the greatest good fortune imaginable. I could so easily have ended up in a boring office job, or stayed on as an officer in the army. Neither would have provided the excitement and stimulation of chasing stories around the world as a journalist, or the challenge of crafting several thousand words into a feature that would engage millions of readers. Neither would have provided me and my family with the comfortable lifestyle we were able to enjoy.

I have also been fortunate in my personal life, too. My first marriage ended in divorce, but not in acrimony. Stephenie was my second cousin - her maternal grandmother was my father's older sister. Our families lived near each other in Ilford and we began dating when she was 14 and I was four years older. All our friends assumed we would eventually get married and we did, in May, 1963. Our first child, Tamsin, was born on October 8, 1966 and Sasha, plump, rosy-cheeked and utterly adorable, followed on May 24, 1968.

We were by then living in a large rented apartment in Bayswater, a block from Hyde Park, and we had bought a cottage in rural Kent where we spent most weekends. I was doing well as a freelance, the children were happy and healthy, Steph was working intermittently as an assistant to Michael Boys, the *House Beautiful* photographer who had become a friend. Steph and I rarely argued and enjoyed each other's company; to the outside world we were one happy family.

What the outside world did not know was that we were both having affairs. As neither of us knew at the time what the other was getting up to, our marriage might have survived, except that I fell in love with Renate. She was married, as was I, and for both of us to leave our partners and move in with each other was the height of foolhardiness; we hardly knew each other. I think we both willing to take the very considerable risk that it might not work out, because we believed, rightly or wrongly, that if it did not we could probably return to our respective partners. As it turned out, we never had to test the theory.

Pain is the inevitable result of a marriage breaking up and I have no doubt I caused Steph a lot of pain, but she recovered rather more quickly than I did. I was almost overwhelmed by guilt about leaving my children, who were then eight and six; remnants of that guilt remain with me today. Steph and I both agreed that we should do everything in our power to minimise the damage to the children and so we remained loving friends, which, essentially, was what we were during our marriage. We never argued about my access to the children, or money matters, or indeed anything.

Steph's career really took off after we had separated. She gravitated from photographer's assistant, via styling television commercials, to the movies, where she became one of the best-regarded set decorators in the business. She won numerous awards - including an Oscar for *The English Patient* - and worked on all eight Harry Potter films. It was a matter of great personal sadness for me when she died from complications of ovarian cancer in August, 2013, at the age of 71. I was privileged to be the first speaker at her memorial service.

Renate and I have now been happily married for more than 40 years. By some miraculous quirk of serendipity the febrile passion of our initial affair metamorphosed into enduring love. We could easily have discovered things about each other which we did not like - we had only spent a very short time together before we decided to move in with each other - but we did not. In fact the reverse applied: the longer I was with her, the more I loved her. While I was travelling I resented every minute I had to spend away from her and would rush back from foreign assignments longing for the moment when I would catch the first heart-lurching glimpse of her waiting to meet me at Heathrow. Now we more or less live in each other's pockets, but there is no one in the world I would rather spend my time with.

Our two children, Barnaby and Charlotte, are married and have children of their own, as do Tamsin and Sasha. Although they are geographically far apart, they stay close through social media. Barnaby is a freelance designer and lives near us in Brighton; Charlotte (Lottie to the family) works as a fund raiser for a charity in the United States; Tamsin and her family live in Bristol; Sasha, to my great pleasure, successfully followed me in to journalism and now runs an online media company in Norfolk.

While I have been writing Rat-like Cunning, Brexit - the most divisive political crisis of my lifetime - has dominated headlines, poisoned discourse, wrecked friendships, greatly exacerbated the country's north/south split and paralysed government. At the time of the referendum we all thought it was inconceivable that there would be a majority to leave

Europe - why would any sensible person want to abandon a deal that had guaranteed peace and prosperity for so long? - and so the result was a profound shock.

What we had not anticipated was that the Leave campaign would swing the vote by telling blatant lies about the sunlit uplands that awaited us once we had extricated ourselves from the clutches of the evil bureaucrats in Brussels. Brexit was going to be quick, easy, painless and would mean that all the millions we currently paid to Brussels could be spent on ourselves: we'd be in clover. None of this, of course, was true.

Boris Johnson, Brexit's principal cheerleader and a man wholly without principles, is now in Downing Street, put there by 90,000 signed-up members of the Conservative party (this in a country that claims to be a democracy), despite his dodgy track record and his well-deserved reputation as a lazy opportunist and reckless buffoon with little regard for truth. There is only one politician I despise more than B. Johnson and that is the ignorant, twittering, narcissistic, racist jerk currently occupying the White House, Donald Trump.

I discovered, almost buried in my cuttings, that I interviewed Trump many years ago, in 1994, when he was a property developer and was locked in a bitter dispute with the flamboyant Leona Helmsley, the so-called "Queen of Mean" over the ownership of the Empire State Building in New York. Leona had recently been released from prison after being found guilty of avoiding tax. The two had fallen out to such an extent that when they both attended the same fancy parties Leona used to indicate her disaffection by giving Donald the finger from the other side of the room.

This is how I began my piece:

"Even for an incorrigible show-off like Donald Trump, it is a boast that takes the breath away. Here he is, sitting in his office in Trump Tower in New York, bragging about how he has just bought the Empire State Building - the world's most famous skyscraper - when everyone knows he didn't put up a brass farthing, not a dime, nothing.

'You know, Russell,' he says expansively, 'it's a great feeling to be the owner of the Empire State Building…'"

Yes, it probably was but he wasn't. Neither had he pulled off, as he claimed, "the world's biggest property deal" - a £2.5 billion development on the west side of New York. Neither were his casinos "breaking every record." His three casinos in Atlantic City ended up in bankruptcy.

The entertaining slanging match that developed between Trump and Mrs Helmsley delighted the media and much of New York. Leona variously described the future POTUS as a "son of a bitch" and a "skunk". She said, presciently, that she would not believe him even if "his tongue was notarised". Trump responded by calling her a "disgrace to humanity", a "vicious, horrible woman" and, mixing his metaphors somewhat, a "bitch on wheels." When, at a party, he told one of Leona's aides that he "looked forward to suing her ass off" the incident nearly developed into a fist fight.

When Trump announced, to general ridicule, that he was running for president I had completely forgotten I had interviewed him.

Looking back, I was fortunate to have joined the *Sunday Times Magazine* at a time when, pre-Murdoch, it was an exemplar of magazine journalism, respected around the world, as was the newspaper, then being edited by the dynamic Harry Evans, who masterminded the campaign to get justice for the victims off thalidomide, one of the longest and most successful newspaper investigations in history. After Murdoch's takeover, the chattering classes liked to dismiss the *Sunday Times* as hopelessly compromised, no more than a mouthpiece for its owner, and there is no doubt that its reputation suffered. But for me it remained the outlet in which I most wanted my work to appear.

Journalism is a very different game these days, of course. All newspapers are looking to increase their online presence and editorial staff, including freelances, have to adjust their working practices to feed the maw of the internet. Stories that once would not have been read before the first edition hit the streets are now published instantly on the internet, shifting the dynamic of the editorial process.

I still buy a printed newspaper every day - usually *The Times* and *The Sunday Times* (old loyalties die hard) - but to be honest I often choose to read the content on my tablet, since it is simply more convenient. I would not be surprised if, over the next few years, print newspapers slowly disappeared. I think most people of my generation would consider it to be a retrograde step and a great loss to society, but the truth is that the younger generation probably view the so-called "romance of print" - the hot metal, the type, the giant presses - as irrelevant.

Maybe, but it was great fun while it lasted.

Printed in Great Britain
by Amazon